toward a non-humanist humanism

toward a non-humanist humanism

THEORY AFTER 9/11

william v. spanos

SUNY PRESS

On the cover: A photograph by Geof Gould, "Native Child Behind a Barbed Wire Fence: Hoping for a Home." Courtesy of Geof Gould.

Published by State University of New York Press, Albany

Printed in the United States of America

For information, contact State University of New York Press, Albany, NY
www.sunypress.edu

Production, Dana Foote
Marketing, Fran Keneston

Library of Congress Cataloging-in-Publication Data

Names: Spanos, William V., author.
Title: Toward a non-humanist humanism : theory after 9/11 / by William V. Spanos.
Description: Albany : State University of New York Press, [2017] | Includes bibliographical references and index.
Identifiers: LCCN 2016039675 (print) | LCCN 2017010140 (ebook) | ISBN 9781438465975 (hardcover : alk. paper) | ISBN 9781438465968 (pbk. : alk. paper) | ISBN 9781438465982 (ebook)
Subjects: LCSH: Humanism—21st century. | Civilization, Modern—21st century.
Classification: LCC B821 .S73 2017 (print) | LCC B821 (ebook) | DDC 144—dc23
LC record available at https://lccn.loc.gov/2016039675

10 9 8 7 6 5 4 3 2 1

To all those uncountable humans who died during the Allied firebombing of Dresden in February 1945, which, for me, became a neighborhood of zero, in the hope that these untimely meditations might contribute to a coming non-humanist humanity.

Contents

Preface

The following meditation attempting to articulate a coming non-humanist humanism was completed shortly before the election of Donald Trump to the presidency of the United States. They thus might be read as academic exercises remote from the ominous realities of the present fraught political occasion. But on reading the final proofs during the election period in November 2016, I was struck by the uncanny anticipation of the disturbing advent of the Trump phenomenon—the latest and perhaps final—liminal—manifestation of the dehumanizing binary logic of the exceptionalist American nation-state—in each one of these chapters. Particularly pertinent in this respect are the pervasive themes, on the one hand, of American exceptionalism and the state of exception intrinsic to it, and, on the other, of the dehumanizing degradation of language—the "banality of evil" Hannah Arendt attributed to Adolph Eichmann at his trial in Jerusalem—and the intrinsically related theme, articulated by Giorgio Agamben, of "bare life," life that can be killed without the killing being called murder. Listening to Donald Trump's glib pronouncements during the Republican debates and his debates with Hillary Clinton, I was struck by the uncanny similarity between Trump's dehumanized and dehumanizing discourse and that ominous banality of modernity identified by my main intellectual witnesses—Edward Said, Hannah Arendt, Giorgio Agamben, Alain Badiou, Jacques Rancière, and Judith Butler, among others—as that which threatens the very humanity of human life in the post-9/11 era. I hope the reader will keep this implicit relationship between my diagnosis of the contemporary American political scene and the banality of Trump's vision, in the name of making "America great again," of the United States' future under his leadership in mind as he or she reads the following errant meditations on the interregnum in which we precariously dwell.

Acknowledgments

The difficult question of what it means to be human has been an urgent obsession of mine ever since my mind-shattering experience as a young prisoner of war in Dresden, Germany, in World War II, when, to appropriate an indispensable recent vocabulary, I lived five excruciatingly long and agonizing empty months of my adolescence in the limbo of bare life: life utterly bereft of the potential that makes human life worth living, and thus life that was disposable. At first, I was enabled by my American heritage to maintain that saving sense of human potential by attributing my dehumanized condition to the monstrous Nazi totalitarian aberration. But in the wake of the horrific Allied firebombing of Dresden in February 1945, which indiscriminately killed over a hundred thousand children, women, and men in one long night-and-day terrorist incendiary air raid, the Nazi prop failed as a sustaining rationale. From that epiphanic occasion, which bereaved me of any reason to be, to the very present moment of this writing, I have relentlessly and increasingly tried in my capacity as teacher, scholar, and editor to fathom what it is in the "benign" apparatuses of our (Western) civilization—so celebratory of its redemptive accomplishments in the name of humanity—that could reduce human life to bare life, and to rethink the question of the human in such a way as to avoid that relentlessly advancing dehumanizing banal fate. The following indissolubly related essays—I deliberately call them "variations on a theme" to contrast them with the now outmoded concept of the book—constitute the culmination of this long, sustained, and arduous untimely endeavor inaugurated in the abyssal midst of the smoldering ashes of the "Florence of the Elbe." In acknowledgment of their clamoring silent voices, I dedicate these meditations on the human to that multitude of human singularities who, having been reduced to ungrievable bare life in the name of the traditional humanism of the "free world," were killed with thoughtless impunity. For me, on that revelatory occasion of my youth, these dead and mutilated bodies became a "neighborhood of zero," that, in its unspeakable horror, called a future humanity—a non-human humanist humanity—to redeem their banalized wasted lives.

More immediately, I wish to acknowledge my debt to a number of friends and colleagues who, through the years of my abiding concern with the question of the human, engaged me in loving dialogical strife. These include the late Edward W. Said, whose criticism of my ontological focus enabled me to perceive the idea of the human as an indissoluble relationship between the ontological and the worldly or political sites on the continuum of being; and some members of the *boundary 2* editorial collective—Paul Bové, Ronald Judy, Aamir Mufti, Stathis Gourgouris, Marcia Landy, Michael Hays, and the late Kathryn Lindberg—whose resistance to the radically profane direction my critique of the traditional humanist ethos was taking always compelled me to rethink—but never to abandon—my perspective. Above all, I want to thank Daniel T. O'Hara and Donald E. Pease, who, despite their differing interpretation of the ineffable human condition, unfailingly, through the years, have encouraged my obsessive effort to think the humanness of the stinking bare life I threw into the horse-drawn wagons that blithely trotted their cargoes off to mass burial at the outskirts of the devastated city of Dresden.

I also wish to thank a number of my students both from the distant past—Aliki Bakopoulou Halls, R. Radhakrishnan, Jeanette McVicker, Giovanna Covi, Michael Clark, David Randall, Patrick McHugh, Philip Armstrong, Madeleine Sorapure, Deborah Reiter, and Robert Marzec—and the near present: Ayse Deniz, Christina Battista, Guy Risko, Jennifer Sweeney, Robert Wilson, Shawn Jasinski, Molly Goldblatt, Robert Ryan, James Fitzgerald, Marcus Heiligenthal, and, not least, my present research assistant, Mahmoud Zidan. All these, to me, young people have constituted contrapuntal voices that compelled my thinking to remain errantly open-ended in defiance of the cultural pressures that demand the acquiescence—the closure—of old age. The inquiring voices of these young students enabled me in my "old age" to write this testament of resistance in behalf of a coming non-humanist humanism. They, at least, will *hear* what I mean.

On a more personal register, I want to express my gratitude to my beloved brother, Charles, and sister-in-law, Joy, whose abiding love and wisdom—and their introduction to me of the "Martini moment" of the day—have sustained me, even at a distance, all through the late years of life; to my brilliant and caring former Greek student, Asimina Karavanta, for reasons having to do with *in illo tempore* that only she will understand, but I would be remiss not to mention; and to my former wife and present colleague, Susan Strehle, and our amazing son, Adam, without whose abiding support—both physical and intellectual, I want to emphasize—this errant project could not have been completed. Whatever is awry in the pages that follow is strictly the result of my doing in the caviling late style I so admired in Edward Said's late writing.

Chapter 1, "Posthumanism in the Age of Globalization: Rethinking *The End of Education*," was previously published in *Symplokē* (vol. 23, 1–2, 2015, 15–39). Chapter 2, "Speaking the Lie of the Truth to Power: A Meditation on the Truth of Modernity by an Incorrigible Caviler," was previously published in a special issue on truth and power in *Journal of Contemporary Thought*, vol. 38 (Summer 2014), 33–55. I am grateful to editors Jeffrey Di Leo and R. Radhakrishnan for permission to reprint these essays in somewhat altered forms.

1

Posthumanism in the Age of Globalization

Rethinking *The End of Education*

> To return to play its purely profane vocation is a political task.
>
> —Giorgio Agamben, "In Praise of Profanation"

I introduce this volume of essays on the urgent question of the human in the post-9/11 age by returning to my beginning over twenty years ago—in the aftermath of the Vietnam War—specifically, to my then controversial book *The End of Education: Toward Posthumanism* (1993)—from the liminal vantage point of the post-9/11 occasion, an expanse of volatile historical time that has borne witness to the implosion of the Soviet Union and the renewal of the United States' initiative (following its "kicking of the 'Vietnam syndrome'" at the time of the first Gulf War) to achieve global hegemony. I am referring to the American imperial initiative, precipitated, above all, by the *al Qaeda* bombing of the World Trade Center and the Pentagon, which, in providing the United States with a "new frontier" (enemy),[1] "justified" the George W. Bush administration's declaration of an unending global "War on Terror," which is to say, not only to undertake, in the name of "the clash of civilizations," unilateral "pre-emptive wars" against "rogues states" and the imposition of ventriloquized governments on them ("regime change"), but also, and equally, if not more important, particularly as it pertains to the issue of higher education (knowledge production) and the American polity, the announcement of the Homeland Security State, that is, the establishment of the state of exception as the universal norm. This return to the beginning of my engagement with the question of humanism and humanist education has not only offered me the pleasurable opportunity to reread for the first time what I wrote about higher education in the United States so long ago at such a volatile time but also, given the epochal transformations, both local and global, that have ensued in the interim, a certain anxiety about some of the recommendations concerning the university, humanist studies, and, not least, the "post-human" I proffered in the concluding chapter of that book. In the following remarks about *The End of Education*, written retrospectively from the vantage point of the fraught local and global post-9/11 occasion, I will first posit what I continue to think is not only valid about my initial understanding of the idea of humanism but, because it remains inadequately thought, in need of further elaboration: that humanism is not simply a worldly/historical, but also and at bottom an *ontological* phenomenon, that is, a way of representing (the truth of) being at large. Second, I will suggest that the modern University had its origins in the disciplining of being in the age of the Enlightenment. Third, I will show that the poststructuralists' de-centering of Man constituted a revolution—an event, in Alain Badiou's sense of the word—that was immediately betrayed by their failure to perceive the ontological de-centering of Man as a de-centering that also occurred at the more "worldly" sites on the continuum of being. Fourth, I will suggest that this betrayal, aided and abetted by the United States' globalization of the free market in the post–Cold War period and, after the bombings of the World Trade Center and the Pentagon by *al Qaeda* on September 11, 2001, its apotheosis of the "Homeland Security State" and the normalization of the state of exception, enabled an invasion of the University by neoliberal capitalism intended not only to recuperate but to aggrandize the control over knowledge production it lost during the turbulent Vietnam decade. I am referring to the corporate initiative tacitly (in the name of the failing economy) but massively committed to the obliteration of both the residual traditional function of the humanities (the production of good—nationalist—citizens of the nation-state) and, above all, the function of the humanities inaugurated by the protest movement in the 1960s and 1970s that would supersede the former—*the instigation of critical consciousness*—in favor of reducing them to *service* departments: instrumentalist apparatuses for providing students—native and foreign—with the skills (particularly "global English")[2] to operate the electronic tools of the neoliberal global free market. Fifth, and in keeping with the lesson of the betrayal, I will attempt to radicalize the concept of humanism (and of the secular with which humanism has been perennially associated) to more clearly distinguish it from the traditional Western understanding of the term, which identifies it with Western civilization. Sixth, I will return to the question of the post-human—and its implications for the University and the coming *polis*—as it has re-emerged in the context of the in-between time I have called an interregnum inaugurated by the self-de-struction of the American exceptionalist ethos with the United States' declaration of its unending war on terror. Taking my directives from the time of the now precipitated by this self-de-struction of the American calling, I will, finally, seventh, proffer a number of recommendations concerning higher education that the post-9/11 occasion has compelled into urgent visibility.

2

As I argued in *The End of Education* by way of an in-depth critical analysis of the influential discourses of exemplary modern post-theological, i.e., "secular," humanists—such as Matthew Arnold, Irving Babbitt, I. A. Richards[3]—and those modern university administrators (particularly at Harvard) who institutionalized their theoretical recommendations—humanism is not only a cultural (or worldly) but also an *ontological* category. Despite the obviousness of this point (as its apparent antithetical relation to theology testifies), traditional humanists, theorists and practitioners, from the Renaissance to the present, almost systematically failed to attend to the critical imperatives of this reality. They insistently represented God and Man, *Theologos* and *Anthropologos*, in binarist terms, but in failing to think (or in shrinking back from thinking) this opposition radically, they also failed to perceive that the new worldly (secular) dispensation demanded a radically different—anti-theological or de-*centered*—understanding of being, including human being. Unwilling in the last instance to abandon the ordering *Logos* (the Word), they posited a self-identical concept of Man that was the mirror image of the Self-identical God they were ostensibly rejecting. In the period of the Enlightenment (modernity), the The*logos* became the Anthropo*logos*. God as the measure of all things became Man the measure of all things. And the more complex secular world Man made was modeled on God's Creation. It became a natural supernaturalism in which the "Word" of Man—the *Anthropologos*—was determinative.

To put this historical continuity between medieval Theology and Renaissance Anthropology alternatively (in the Anthropological language culminating in Enlightenment modernity), the ontological interpretation of being in the "new" dispensation remained *metaphysical*. The be-*ing* of being—the transience of time, the radical temporality or *nothingness* that produces anxiety (that emotion that has no thing as its object)—was represented from a transcendental (other-worldly) perspective: *meta-ta-physica*, from above or beyond or after the (temporal) thing themselves. Thus, as in theology, this humanist ontology privileged the all-seeing eye as the agency of knowledge production at the expense of the other ("adulterating") senses. In so doing, this end-oriented or panoptic perspective *vis-á-vis* knowledge production also produced a binarist logic that unerringly privileged Identity over difference, Oneness over the transience of time, which is to say, endowed Man with a will to power over his differential others. As a result this metaphysical reduction, the be-*ing* of being underwent a momentous transformation. In *re-presenting* being from the fixed, Archimedean panoptic perspective, the "new" humanist/secular interpretation of being, like the old theological one, also reduced the anxiety-provoking temporality of the secular world to a reified Being or *Summum Ens*—or, in the language of poststructuralism, to a totalized (spatialized) *structure:* the all-encompassing centered circle. I quote Jacques Derrida's definitive, but still to be adequately registered, poststructuralist analysis of the function of the circle in the *Western* "logocentric" tradition at length not only to underscore the continuity in this tradition between the Sacred and the Secular, God and Man, Theology and Humanism, but also to retrieve the inaugural revolutionary impact of its de-centering of the Anthropological Center:

> It has always been thought that the center, which is by definition unique, constituted the very thing within structure which while governing the structure, escapes structurality. This is why classical thought concerning structure could say that the center is, paradoxically, *within* the structure and *outside it*. The center is the center of the totality, and yet, since the center does not belong to the totality (is not part of the totality), the totality *has its center elsewhere*. The center is not the center. The concept of centered structure—although it represents coherence itself, the condition of the epistémé as philosophy or science—is contradictorily coherent. And as always, coherence in contradiction always expresses the force of a desire. The concept of centered structure is in fact the concept of a play based on a fundamental ground, a play constituted on the basis of a fundamental immobility and a reassuring certitude, which

> itself is beyond the reach of free play. And on the basis of this certitude anxiety can be mastered, for anxiety is invariably the result of a certain mode of being implicated in the game, of being caught by the game, of being as it were at stake in the game from the outset. And again on the basis of what we call the center (and which, because it can be either inside or outside, can also indifferently be called the origin or end, *arché* or *telos*), repetitions, substitutions, transformations, and permutations are always *taken* from a history of meaning [*sens*]—that is, in a word, a history—whose origin may always be reawakened or whose end may always be anticipated in the form of presence. This is why one perhaps could say that the movement of any archeology, like that of any eschatology, is an accomplice of this reduction of the structurality of structure and always attempts to conceive of structure on the basis of a full presence which is beyond play. If this is so, the entire history of the concept of structure, before the rupture of which we are speaking, must be thought as a series of substitutions of center for center, as a linked chain of determinations of the center. Successively, and in a regulated fashion, the center receives different names. The history of metaphysics, like the history of the West, is the history of these metaphors and metonymies. Its matrix . . . is the determination of Being as *presence* in all sense of this word. It could be shown that all names related to fundamentals, to principles, or to the center have always designated an invariable presence—*eidos*, *arché*, *telos*, energeia, ousia (essence existence substance), aletheia, transcendentality, consciousness, God, man, and so forth.[4]

In positing humanism as an ontological category in *The End of Education*, however, I did not intend, as all too many "anti-humanist" poststructuralists, including Derrida, in effect, did, to restrict humanism—and the thinking of its operations—to the ontological register at the expense of the more "worldly" sites. On the contrary, I was attempting to retrieve the worldliness it lost in the wake of the modern Western humanists' division of being into disciplinary categories. More specifically, I was trying to show that being, far from being a worldless phenomenon, as it came to be understood under the aegis of post-Enlightenment humanism (then forgotten as a question, as Heidegger famously observed[5] in *Being and Time*), was, in fact, an indissolubly related dynamic continuum, however unevenly developed at any historical moment, ranging from being, the subject, and language (knowledge production), the ecos, to the alleged "more worldly" sites: culture, gender, race, economics, the social, the political, and the global. My purpose, in so doing, was to suggest that the very idea of the West, particularly as it emerged in the Renaissance (the rebirth of Roman civilization in the wake of the medieval "dark ages"), was grounded in a metaphysical interpretation of being that privileged a mode of knowledge production that was complicit with the will to power, and to suggest that a worldly critique of the Western nation-state and its imperialist politics that did not attend to the ontological site was inadequate, if not self-defeating, since these "more worldly" sites have their structural origins in the structure of the Western interpretation of being.

This complicity between ontology (metaphysics) and world, knowledge and power, informing the emergent Western humanist paradigm—this ultimately *dehumanizing* logic of Renaissance humanism—was the witness of Martin Heidegger in his famously provocative "Letter on Humanism," written in the immediate aftermath of World War II in response to Jean Beaufret's question, "*Comment redonner un sens au mot 'Humanisme'?*" (How can we restore meaning to the word "Humanism"?), where he traced the origins of modern Western humanism to Rome—its metaphysical reduction of the Greek understanding of truth, *a-letheia* (unconcealing), to *veritas* (the adequation of mind and things), that is, an originative thinking to a derivative or calculative apparatus of capture, and pointed to the complicity of Humanist ontology with worldly power: not only with education (disciplinary knowledge production) but also with Roman imperialism:

> *Humanitas*, explicitly so called, was first considered and striven for in the age of the Roman Republic. *Homo Humanus* was opposed to *homo barbarus*. *Homo humanus* here means the Romans, who exalted and honored Roman *virtus* through the "embodiment" of the *paideia* [education] taken over from the Greeks. These were the Greeks of the Hellenistic age, whose culture was acquired in the schools of philosophy. It was concerned with *eruditio et institutio in bonas artes* [scholarship and training in good conduct]. *Paideia* thus understood was translated as *humanitas*. This genuine *romanitas* of *homo romanus* consisted in such *humanitas*. We encounter the first humanism in Rome: it therefore remains in essence a specifically Roman phenomenon which emerged from the encounter of Roman civilization with the culture of late Greek civilization. The so-called Renaissance of the fourteenth and fifteenth centuries in Italy is a *renascentia romanitatis*. Because *romanitas is what matters*, it is concerned with *humanitas* and therefore with Greek *paideia*. But Greek civilization is always seen in its later form and this itself is seen from a Roman point of view. The *homo romanus* of the Renaissance also stands in opposition to *homo barbarus*. But now the in-humane is the supposed barbarism of gothic Scholasticism in the Middle Ages. Therefore a *studium humanitatis*, which in a certain way

> reaches back to the ancients and thus also becomes a revival of Greek civilization always adheres to historically understood humanism.[6]

But it is in the later uncannily proleptic essay "The Question of Technology," which addresses the developed modern (Enlightenment) version of Western humanism—its "Enframing" mode of revealing (*Ge-stell*)—that Heidegger articulates the full import of its dehumanizing logic:

> What kind of unconcealing is it, then, that is peculiar to that which results from the setting upon that challenges? Everywhere everything is ordered to stand by, to be immediately at hand, indeed, to stand there just so that it may be on call for a further ordering. Whatever is ordered about in this way has its own standing. We call it the standing-reserve [*Bestand*]. The word expresses here something more, and something more essential, than mere "stock." The word 'standing-reserve" assumes the rank of an inclusive rubric. It designates nothing less than the way in which everything presences that is wrought upon by the revealing that challenges. Whatever stands by in the sense of standing-reserve no longer stands over against us as object.[7]

In thus reducing being to standing-reserve, Man himself under the aegis of this Enframing of humanism, Heidegger goes on to say, becomes "standing-reserve"—or, as I prefer to translate *Bestand* for the sake of highlighting the proleptic implications of this extreme form of dehumanizing reduction to which I will return often in the chapters of this book, "disposable reserve":

> Yet when destining reigns in the name of Enframing, it is the supreme danger. This danger attests itself to us in two ways. As soon as what is unconcealed no longer concerns man even as object, but does so, rather, exclusively as standing-reserve, and man in the midst of objectlessness is nothing but the orderer of the standing-reserve, then he comes to the very brink of a precipitous fall; that is, he comes to the point where he himself will have to be taken as standing-reserve. Meanwhile man, precisely as the one so threatened, exalts himself to the posture of lord of the earth. In this way the impression comes to prevail that everything man encounters exists insofar as it is his construct. This illusion gives rise in turn to one final illusion. It seems as though man everywhere and always encounters only himself. . . . *In truth however, precisely nowhere does man today any longer encounter himself, i.e., his essence.* Man stands so decisively in attendance on the challenging-forth of Enframing that he does not grasp enframing as a claim, that he fails to see himself as the one spoken

> to, and hence also fails in every way to hear in what respect he ek-sists [is an ontic-ontological, outside-insider], from out of his essence, in the realm of an exhortation or address, and thus *can never* encounter only himself. (308; emphasis in original)

Seen in this light, Heidegger's genealogy of humanism is not only proleptic of the post-structuralist Michel Foucault, who, a generation later, pointed to the complicity of modern Western humanism with the reduction of politics to biopolitics, but also, as I will show at length in chapter 4, of those radical post-posthumanists—Giorgio Agamben, Alain Badiou, Slavoj Žižek, Jacques Rancière, Judith Butler, among others—whose theoretical discourses have, in one way or another, underscored "bare life," life that can be killed without its being called homicide, as the fulfillment of the logic of modern Western humanism.

3

To put the centered circle, the founding metaphysical humanist re-presentation (or cartography) of being in its productive modern (Enlightenment) historical/worldly form—the form, not incidentally, that became the model for the structure of the modern University—the humanist spatialization or structuralization of the secular world took the synecdochical form of the classificatory table inaugurated and developed by humanist biological scientists such as Buffon, Linnaeus, and Cuvier; humanist economists such as Adam Smith and Ricardo; military theorists such as J.A. de Guibert; architects such as Nicholas Ledoux; and political scientists such as Jeremy Bentham. This was the panoptic structure, enabled by thinking being *meta ta physica*, decisively analyzed by Michel Foucault. Deeply aware of its multiple applicability (and thus of the indissoluble relationality of the multiple sites of the continuum of being), Foucault was enabled by this genealogy of the "disciplinary society" to perceive the Panopticon as a polyvalent apparatus of capture, which, by way of reifying and individualizing the multiple and then assigning each to its proper place in the larger whole, enabled modern (Anthropological) Man to turn the anxiety-provoking (threatening) differences that time always already disseminates into "docile and useful" bodies:

> The first of the great operations of discipline is . . . the constitution of "*tableaux vivants*," which transforms the confused, useless or dangerous

> multitudes into ordered multiplicities. The drawing up of "tables" was one of the great problems of the scientific, political and economic technology of the eighteenth century: how one was to arrange botanical and zoological gardens, and construct at the same time rational classifications of living beings; how one is to observe, supervise, regularize the circulation of commodities and money and thus build up an economic table that might serve as the principle of the increase of wealth; how one was to inspect men, observe their presence and absence and constitute a general and permanent register of the armed forces; how one was to distribute patients, separate them from one another, divide up the hospital space and make a systematic classification of diseases: these were all twin operations in which the two elements—distribution and analysis, supervision and intelligibility—are inextricably bound up. In the eighteenth century the table was both a technique of power and a procedure of knowledge. It was a question of organizing the multiple, of providing oneself with an instrument to cover it and to master it; it was a question of imposing upon it an 'order.'"[8]

This anthropological/panoptic disciplinary table became the model of the structure of the modern/secular Western University, not only for its architecture (the administration building at the center of surrounding buildings of instruction, the classroom that structurally privileges the panoptic professor), but also for its departmental divisions. As I have noted, the panoptic Anthropological table (and its binarist logic) assumes the multitudinous to be both wasteful and threatening; it thus reifies/spatializes and individualizes its amorphous elements and then assigns them their proper place in the large Whole—that is, renders them docile and useful, or, in Heidegger's equally resonant term, "standing reserve" (i.e., disposable reserve). Similarly, the modern University assumed that being as an indissoluble continuum is wasteful and/or threatening in its amorphous primitive form and thus reified/spatialized "it" as a total structure and then compartmentalized its elements into individual disciplines—Sciences (geology, physics, chemistry, biology, and so on); Humanities (English, romance languages, classics, arts, history); Social Sciences (anthropology, sociology, geography, political science)—that took their dutiful/productive place in the larger whole.

Analogously, the student body, under this Anthropological paradigm, was assumed to be a primitive, amorphous, and errant multitude, and thus a waste and/or a threat to the community; but, like the multiple phenomena of being under the aegis of the classificatory table, it was an amorphous multitude informed by a principle of Presence (or

Center) that cultivation would bring to fruition. What "cultivation" meant, according to the dictates of this paradigm, was, as in the case of the multiple phenomena of the classificatory table, the reification and individualization of this student multitude not only for the purpose of defusing the threat of its volatility, but also, like the phenomena of the classificatory table, for the purpose of taking their productive place in the larger (national) whole. Accordingly, fruition meant not only the discovery of the student's latent Self but also of his/her mature vocation—servitude to the call of the secular nation. In Althusser's anti-humanist poststructuralist language, which remains resonant to a contemporary audience in its pointing to the complicity of the secular capitalist world with theology, cultivation/fruition means interpellation:

> The duplicate mirror-structure of ideology ensures simultaneously:
>
> 1. the interpellation of "individuals" as subjects;
> 2. their subjection to the Subject;
> 3. the mutual recognition of subjects and Subject, the subjects' recognition of each other, and finally the subject's recognition of himself;
> 4. the absolute guarantee that everything really is so, and that on condition that the subjects recognize what they are and behave accordingly, everything will be all right: "Amen—So be it."
>
> Result: caught in this quadruple system of interpellation as subjects, of subjection to the Subject, of universal recognition and of absolute guarantee, the subjects "work," they "work by themselves" in the majority of cases, with the exception of the "bad subjects" who on occasion provoke the intervention of one of the detachments of the (repressive) State Apparatuses. But the vast majority of (good) subjects work all right "all by themselves;" i.e. by ideology whose concrete forms are realized in the Ideological State Apparatuses. They are inserted into practices governed by the rituals of the ISAs [Ideological State Apparatuses]. They "recognize" the existing state of affairs . . . , that "it really is true that it is so and not otherwise," and they must be obedient to God, to their conscience, to the priest, to de Gaulle, to the boss, to the engineer, that thou shalt "love thy neighbor as thyself," etc. Their concrete, material behavior is simply the inscription in life of the admirable words of the prayer: "*Amen—So be it.*"[9]

4

The poststructuralist de-centering of the Western Center in the early 1970s, in the wake of the decolonization of the Western empires and particularly the Algerian and Vietnam Wars, constituted a global revolutionary initiative, indeed, an "event" in Alain Badiou's sense of the word, one that—if being is understood as an indissolubly related, however unevenly, developed continuum encompassing being as such, the subject, language, gender, race, economics, education (knowledge production), the ecos, the social domain, domestic politics, and the global order—not only threatened to subvert the globally hegemonic truth discourse of the West, but, in disclosing the nothing (*das Nichts*) that is ontologically prior to structure, also enabled the imagination of a new, commons-oriented community by way of thinking the positive possibilities of the multiple "differences" that the Western secular humanist tradition had relegated to non-being in the name of (Western) Man.

Though I did not emphasize the revolutionary implications of the "anti-humanist" poststructuralist initiative in *The End of Education*, it is this "evental" potentiality that I was intuiting in the immediate wake of the Vietnam War. But the revolutionary potential enabled by this event—this decisive theoretical de-centering of Man—was almost immediately betrayed in two related initiatives that emerged after the war, one at the site of "theory," and the other at the site of institutional pedagogy.

At the site of theory, the poststructuralists, blinded by their onto-textual insight, failed to extend or, rather, to underscore the indissoluble relationality between their ontological (Heidegger), psychological (Lacan), textual (Derrida) insight into the de-centering of the Western *Anthropologos* to the other more obvious "worldly" sites on the continuum of being. Despite the transdisciplinary imperatives of their de-centering of the anthropological center, they remained not only vestigially disciplinary but also, in focusing almost exclusively on the sites pertaining to textuality, nonpolitical. This poststructuralist tendency was rightly highlighted by Edward W. Said, who criticized the poststructuralists, particularly the deconstructionists, not simply for being "unworldly" in focusing almost exclusively on the textuality of texts, but also for denying human agency.[10] As I have argued elsewhere,[11] Said was not condemning the poststructuralist initiative as such, but rather its failure to extend its de-centering onto-psycho-textual insight into the repressive operations of the *Anthropologos* to the other more worldly sites on the continuum of being. Unfortunately, however, Said's followers—and the majority of academics in the humanities who were sympathetic with the students' clamor for a pedagogy of "relevance"—(mis)interpreted Said's critique of poststructuralism as a mandate to put the "unworldly" ontological/textual theoretical initiative into a binary opposition with the worldly initiative. The result of this unfortunate reductive bifurcation was the splintering of a potentially powerful, unified, multi-situated critical movement into warring factions.

This betrayal of the event by the practitioners of theory manifested itself at the institutional site of pedagogy in the 1980s and 1990s. Following the bifurcation of ontology and world, textual critique and political critique, at the site of theory, oppositional teachers in the humanities, particularly English departments, recuperated a form of disciplinarity that it had been one of the fundamental purposes of the original de-centering event to delegitimate. Despite their initial partial success in opening traditional male, white, and Anglo humanities departments to women, blacks, gays, and other minorities, and introducing a promising global perspective on English language literature by way of exposing the complicity of the canon (the "core curriculum") with racism, nationalism, and imperialism, these teachers, influenced by the argument of the "worldly" critics against "unworldly" poststructuralist "theory" (particularly deconstruction), perpetuated the division until it became a virtual given. The all-important ontological de-centering at the origins of the discursive revolution was forgotten, and the polyvalent (ontological, psychological, ecological, cultural, social, and political) revolutionary implications of the continuum of being it had disclosed were marginalized. Having blinded themselves to the polyvalent implications of the de-centering of the *Anthropologos*, "progressive" teachers of literature—many of them deriving from various minority backgrounds and beneficiaries of the de-centering—had no other option but to teach "their thing." As a result, this recuperated disciplinary orientation rendered impossible what, in *The End of Education*, I called, after Antonio Gramsci, the establishment of "historical blocs": the solidarity of different oppressed cultural identities—women, gays, blacks, working class, ethnic minorities, immigrants, and so on—in the struggle to revolutionize the humanist University and, more broadly, for emancipation from a system of cultural and political belonging that renders the constituencies they represent as useful and docile bodies, at best, and bare life at worst.

5

At the time I was writing *The End of Education*, the main object of my criticism was the post-Vietnam movement on the part of deputies of the government such as William Bennett and neoconservatives such as Allan Bloom and their University administrator allies to recuperate the "core curriculum" that was being eroded by the anti-war, civil rights, and feminist movements. I mean, more specifically, that humanist-based *studia humanitatis* that had emerged during the Enlightenment to produce good citizens of the nation-state (*eruditio et institutio in bonas artes*, to recall Heidegger's genealogy) in behalf of the United States' Cold War against Soviet communism. Since then, particularly after the implosion of the Soviet empire and the end of the Cold War and the United States' inauguration of its War on Terror in the wake of 9/11, the University has undergone something like a revolutionary transformation, a restructuring of its nation-state–oriented structure that was intended to serve the global reach of neoliberal capitalism. Simultaneous with the anti-canonical globalization of humanistic cultural studies in the University in the aftermath of the Cold War and the spectacular rise of the Internet as the essential means of planetary communication, that is, another, antithetical, form of globalization emerged in the West, under the aegis of the United States, to challenge the status quo of the nation-state: the expansion of the free market endemic to neoliberal capitalism. Given the essential importance of instrumental thinking and simultaneous communication to this free-market form of globalization, it is not surprising that the corporate capitalist apparatuses of capture—taking advantage of the dysfunctional state of the humanities and the predisposition of the new, globalized university administrators toward privatization, the sciences, particularly technology, and a quantified/consumerist concept of academic excellence[12]—would massively intervene to render the University an instrument of global capitalism. As Arif Dirlik writes in a deeply disturbing essay tracing the itinerary of this invasion:

> The shifting of capitalist competition to a transnational level demands a new kind of knowledge of sites of production, marketing, and consumption. Combined with technologies such as the internet, which has given substantial reality to globalization, the demand for "just-in-time" knowledge has invited the business invasion of higher education, in turn inducing or reinforcing the business turn in the organization and management of the

> university. In a global economy where knowledge itself has come to be regarded as "a force of production" (the so-called knowledge economy), universities are visibly pressured to assume greater strategic responsibilities by rescuing themselves from the ambivalent image of "ivory towers" into functional units of the global political economy. This also means there is pressure on knowledge production to produce the kind of knowledge that responds to the needs of the global economy.[13]

One of the most significant of the many changes that the University has undergone in the wake of the corporate intervention and the pressure it has mounted to "produce the kind of knowledge that responds to the needs of the global economy" has been the globalization of the student body. I refer to the massive initiative of American universities, private and public, to enroll foreign students, primarily from technologically and economically advanced, globally oriented countries such as China, South Korea, and India. Represented by American university administrators as "diversification" in the name of a democratic "multiculturalism," this globalizing initiative, however progressive it sounds, is, in fact, a masquerade. It produces the antithesis of the critical consciousness that is implied by "diversification." A university that is capable of achieving an authentic global multiculturalism would have to undertake structural changes that facilitate the dialogue (*Auseinandersetzung*) between American and foreign students that is its *sine qua non*: above all, the globalization not simply of the humanities but of the very idea of the human. The University, under the pressures of neoliberal capitalism, has not inaugurated such changes in the structure of the traditional nation-state–oriented university. On the contrary, the structural changes it has administered have been intended to facilitate and privilege a mode of knowledge production that reduces the student "diversity" to a de-differentiated student body of consumers, whose vocation is to serve the totalizing logic of neoliberal capitalism. This dehumanizing reduction is demonstrated by the University's extraordinary privileging and overdetermination of the theoretical sciences and the technology departments over the arts and the humanities in such a way as to appeal to foreign students, the vast majority of which come to major in these fields. Also, and more ominously, it is demonstrated by the radical downsizing of the humanities division (the cutting of faculty lines in these departments and the elimination of entire programs such as the classics and certain foreign language departments that are deemed to be no longer pertinent to the global market arena) and, above all, the initiative to reduce the English Department, the traditional center of the University and the nation-state it reflected, to a service department intended to serve the interests of neoliberal global capitalism. I am referring to the University administrators' initiative, motivated by the massive influx of foreign students deficient in English language skills, to pressure English departments into overdetermining "Global English," that purely instrumentalist (and dehumanized) apparatus of communication that has become the *lingua franca* of the global free market.[14]

Simultaneous with the dehumanizing effects on the student body resulting from the invasion of the University by global neoliberal free market capitalism are the dehumanizing effects at the site of higher education incumbent on the United States government's establishment of the Homeland Security State in the wake of the *al Qaeda* bombings of the World Trade Center and the Pentagon on September 11, 2001. This juxtaposition is essentially contradictory, since the former privileges the global order of the free market at the expense of the nation, and the latter privileges the nation at the expense of the global order of the free market. But in the case of the United States this contradiction is not, at least temporarily, a contradiction. And this is because, as a nation that has perennially represented itself as an exceptionalist nation, indeed, the chosen "redeemer nation" to all the others, and, since World War II, has possessed the military power and weapons of mass destruction to enforce this self-representation, the United States, in the context of the globalization of the free market, has been enabled to represent itself not only as the globalized nation *par excellence* but also as the primary sponsoring nation of the global free market, the nation that controls the logic of its global economy, and the nation that polices its operations to protect them from abuse.

In invoking the establishment of the Homeland Security State in the context of the post-9/11 University, I mean, above all, the establishment of the state of exception as the norm—*at all the sites of the continuum of being, not least, the site of knowledge production*—in which, as Giorgio Agamben has decisively shown by way of radicalizing Heidegger's disclosure of the reduction of ek-static/in-sistent man to disposable reserve (*Bestand*) under the aegis of technology and Foucault's disclosure of the biopoliticization of man under the aegis of the disciplinary society, the human (*bios politikos*) is reduced to *zoé*, "bare life" (*vida nuda*) that can be killed with impunity:

> We have already encountered a limit sphere of human action that is only ever maintained in a relation of exception. This sphere is that of the sovereign decision, which suspends law in the state of exception and

> thus implicates bare life within it. We must therefore ask ourselves if the structure of sovereignty and the structure of *sacratio* might be connected and if they might, from this perspective, be shown to illuminate each other. We may even then advance a hypothesis: once brought back to his proper place beyond both penal law and sacrifice, *homo sacer* presents the originary figure of life taken into the sovereign ban and preserves the memory of the originary exclusion through which the political dimension was first constituted. The political sphere of sovereignty was thus constituted through a double exclusion. An excrescence of the profane in the religious and of the religious in the profane, which takes the form of a zone of indistinction between sacrifice and homicide. The sovereign sphere is the sphere in which it is permitted to kill without committing homicide and without celebrating a sacrifice, and sacred life—that is, life that may be killed but not sacrificed—is the life that has been captured in this sphere.[15]

As in the case of knowledge production endemic to the neoliberal global free market, knowledge production under the aegis of the national security state, in which the state of exception has become the rule, becomes "banalized" (in Hannah Arendt's dehumanized sense of the word). As an instrument of banalization, which renders thinking "thoughtlessness,"[16] it lends itself to the reduction of the essential human capacity to *care* to indifference and thus, as I will show more fully in chapters 3 and 4, to the ominous modern momentum that is reducing human life to bare life—life that can be killed without the killing being considered murder.

6

The patent failure of oppositional intellectuals, both humanist and "antihumanist" poststructuralists, of the post-Vietnam era to resist the massive momentum toward the banalization of knowledge production and the dehumanization of humanity inaugurated by neoliberal corporate capitalism's and the American state's invasion of the University in the name of the global free market and homeland security, respectively, calls, as I have been suggesting, for a radical rethinking of the traditional idea of the human, humanism, the humanities (*studia humanitatis*), and the domain of the secular to which these are bound. I refer to a rethinking that underscores the existential resonance of humanity's "de-centering" or, more starkly, its ontologically exilic condition, that, in other words, eradicates the last vestiges of the transcendental homeland that have traditionally softened its "fall" into time—its "thrownness" (*Geworfenheit*), in Heidegger's chillingly provocative language, into the not-at-home (*die Unheimliche*), the irreparable transience of time or the nothingness of being. This world in which humanity at large finds itself thrown is not, as the Western humanist tradition has all too unthinkingly assumed, a realm of appearance that conceals a subsuming, higher *Telos*. Nor is the human being an essentially self-present subject whose earthly vocation is to cultivate that potential into fruition. That vocational interpretation, as we have seen by way of Louis Althusser's decisive critique of the traditional humanist subject, is the result of the interpellation of the human subject by a higher Subject: a call that renders the human subject a "subjected subject," the willing servant (under the guise of mastery) of a transcendental (unworldly) cause (the Law), who must, in the name of his or her vocational essence, postpone full existential engagement with the transient world of time (his or her "occasion"[17])—who, in short, must give up his or her radical freedom.

To radicalize the traditional idea of what it means to be human, then, we must entirely dissociate it from all forms (onto-theo-logical) of thinking *meta-ta-physica*. For such thinking—which puts the temporality humans think in a binary opposition with the identical *Logos*, thus allegedly elevating Man to the status of "master of all things"—renders him, in fact, as we have seen, the servant of a higher Caller, dehumanizing the living human. To break the insidiously tempting hold of this apparatus of capture, then, humans must acknowledge the radical transience of time—its profane essence, as it were. Or, to invoke the suggestive interpretations of Walter Benjamin's paradoxical materialist "messianic" understanding of time proffered by the post-poststructuralists Giorgio Agamben and Alain Badiou, to fulfill the worldly imperatives of the evental de-centering of humanist Man in their remarkable books on the apostle Paul, humans must acknowledge that they ek-sist/insist in the "the time of the now" (*ho nyn kairos)*, that *in-between* time that remains after the structured time of traditional humanism has been de-structured. For only such a radical, anti-vocational comportment toward being is capable of freeing humanity from servitude to the unworldly cause of Anthropology and its dehumanizing binary logic of belonging. As Agamben puts this paradoxical double emancipatory project:

> According to the apostle, this movement [of the calling—*kletos*, from *kaleo* (I call)] is, above all, a nullification: "Circumcision [the Law of the Jews] is nothing, and the foreskin [the law of the Greeks or Gentiles] is

> nothing." That which, according to the law, made one man a Jew and the other a *goy*, one a slave and another a free man, is now annulled by the vocation. Why remain in this nothing? Once again, *meneto* ("*remaining*") does not convey indifference. It signifies the immobile anaphoric gesture of the messianic calling, its being essentially and for most a *calling of the calling*. For this reason, it may apply to any condition; but for this same reason it *revokes* a condition and radically puts it into question in the very act of adhering to it.[18]

As I have elsewhere interpreted this resonant passage that, in Agamben's resonant word, renders the traditional understanding of calling/vocation as interpellation "inoperative":

> The Greco-Roman (Onto-logical), the Judeo-Christian (Theo-logical), and the Humanist (Anthropo-logical) vocation alienates human beings from the transient or finite time—the time of the now (*ho nyn kairos*), of being *inter esse* (in the midst of the inter-esting, of the occasion—coercively turns their minds' eye away from *this (unheimliche) world* to one (*heimliche*) beyond, to a future *Telos*. The evental "vocation," on the other hand, is, according to Agamben, "the revocation of every vocation." In the resonantly suggestive terms he borrows from Paul, it renders the Law, its binary logic, its dialectical promise-fulfillment structure, and its vocation to a higher cause "inoperative" (*katargein*). The law (and Works)—as opposed to faith (*pistis*)—its binary logic, its promise/fulfillment structure, its imperatives of belonging, and its vocation are not annulled; they remain, but they no longer work in the invisible polyvalent oppressive way they did, before the event, under the aegis of the Law.[19]

It is this "revocation of every vocation," this rendering of a system of naming and of belonging based on the metaphysical principle of Identity in the sense of self-presence (*nomos*, "the Law") and its binary logic of belonging *inoperative*, that comes readily to hand in the effort to radically rethink the Western idea of humanity, humanism, and the *studia humanitatis*. Following the directives of the time of the now that remains after the de-struction of the teleological time of metaphysics, we are enabled to say that the traditional (Anthropological) idea of humanity (and the secular world it has produced) is not a truth but a fabrication or fiction. That is, ontologically prior to this self-present humanist self is the nothing (*das Nichts*). Man, as Vico and Said have said, "makes his world." But what needs to be emphasized is that, in being an ek-sistent/

in-sistent (ontic/ontological) being—irreparably inside and outside the world—what he or she makes can be unmade when history discloses it to be inadequate to its dynamic imperatives.

Thanks to its consciousness, human life is in some sense privileged over the other phenomena of being. The Western humanist tradition, under the imperatives of the calling, interpreted this ontological difference as a justification for mastering all phenomena on the continuum of being—flora, fauna, and all humans who did not think, speak, and act like humans. It saw the Friend/foe binary as the principle mode of comportment toward the various phenomena of being. From the perspective of *ho nyn kairos* (and the potentiality *as such*—"means without end"[20]—it enables), however, this justification for mastery is rendered inoperative. The ontological privilege remains, but in the time of the now, the earlier priority of the Answer over the question becomes the priority of the question over the Answer, and the right of mastery becomes the humility of *care*, a profound and abiding responsibility, or, as this term implies, a "loving strife," an unending, mutually productive dialogic relationality.

Let me return at this juncture to an historical context, later than the one addressed in *The End of Education*, in which the debate over the viability of humanism (and the secular) in the globalized age of the waning nation-state re-emerged. I am referring above all to Edward W. Said's posthumously published *Humanism and Democratic Criticism*, in which he vigorously, if all too casually, defends humanism against the powerful systematic critique of the poststructuralists. Because it was written by and large as a response to its ("unworldly") textual-oriented poststructuralist critics, this text has all too often been read by "worldly" critics, particularly those who, following Said too literally, have represented poststructuralist textuality as unworldly, in such a way as to suggest that it constitutes a general defense of the Western secular humanist tradition. What this criticism has been blinded to by its worldly insight—its strange refusal to think humanism as a worldly ontological category—is a critical gesture, pervasive, if not adequately developed, in Said's text, that is uncannily similar to Agamben's gesture that renders the binary logic of the Law (Identity) inoperative (*non-piu-in-opera*: no-longer-at-work). I have analyzed Said's immensely suggestive gesture at some length elsewhere.[21] For the sake of economy, I will restrict my commentary here to a crucial but overlooked passage in Said's text—that, it should not be overlooked, builds on his determinative notion of the exilic (in-between) consciousness:

> The task of the humanist is not to occupy a position or place, nor simply to belong somewhere, but rather to be both insider and outsider to the circulating ideas and values that are at issue in our society or someone else's society or the society of the other. In this connection, it is invigorating to recall . . . Isaac Deutscher's insufficiently known book of essays, *The Non-Jewish Jew*, for an account of how great Jewish thinkers—Spinoza, chief among them, as well as Freud, Heine, Deutscher himself—were in, and at the same time renounced, their tradition, preserving their original tie by submitting it to the corrosive questioning that took them well beyond it, sometimes banishing them from the community in the process. Not many of us can or would want to aspire to such a dialectically fraught, so sensitively located class of individuals, but it is illuminating to see in such a destiny the crystallized role of the American humanist, *the non-humanist humanist as it were*.[22]

Just as Deutscher's corrosive questioning of the logic of belonging endemic to the Jewish people renders him a "non-Jewish Jew," so under the corrosive questioning of the humanist tradition Said becomes a "non-humanist humanist," an exilic figure. As such a paradoxical figure of in-betweenness, the identity intrinsic to traditional (Western) humanism and its logic of belonging are rendered inoperative. That is, they no longer demand, as they did under the traditional hegemonic version, a sense of vocation that pits the humanist against the non-humanist in a Friend/foe war to the end. The humanist remains a humanist, but his or her humanist identity is now understood as an historical construct. And the binary logic of belonging of Western humanism remains oppositional, but the violence of its traditional operations undergoes a metamorphosis: the war to the end becomes loving strife, in which strife enriches rather than degrades the antagonists.

7

Most readers of *The End of Education* have mistakenly taken its subtitle, *Toward Posthumanism*, to mean a rejection of the human in favor of a yet to be articulated non-human way of comportment toward being. This, no doubt, is partly because my critique of traditional humanism, mounted when the poststructuralists' massive attack on humanism was at its most intense, was read as another example of its anti-humanism. Above all, it was because, not having thought the human radically enough at that time, I was uncertain as to the meaning of the "post." In using the term "posthumanism," I was not, in fact, rejecting the human (nor, for that matter, I have claimed, were the poststructuralists[23]); I was, rather, attempting to go beyond its traditional Western meaning by returning to the point of its origins. This gesture of repetition (in Heidegger's sense of the word *Wiederholung*) was a promising start, but only that, a symptomatic insight, not a conscious one. I remained uncertain as to what "posthumanism" meant and a posthumanist praxis would entail. What I have become certain about, however, particularly in the wake of the globalization of the neoliberal free market and the United States' exceptionalist—and unilateral—declaration of its War on Terror after 9/11, is not only that the very humanity of human being is in crisis in a way that it has never been before, but also that this dehumanizing crisis has been the consequence of a practice undertaken in the name of humanity. I am, as I have been suggesting, referring to the United States' epochal establishment of the state of exception as the local and global norm and its support of corporate capitalism's neoliberal version of globalization: those initiatives of a democratic society, which allegedly espouses the humanity of all humanity as its *raison d'être*, that have contributed massively to the dehumanizing (Western) global momentum that is carelessly rendering the time of the now (the nonfoundational essence of human time) a vocational time; banalizing human language (in Hannah Arendt's sense of the term); reducing knowledge production understood as instigating critical consciousness to a "productive instrumentalism"; and, as the ultimate result of these systematic dehumanizing initiatives of this apparatus of capture, degrading human life to disposable life—bare life, in Agamben's term—life that can be killed with impunity.

Another way of putting what I have realized in rereading *The End of Education* from the perspective of the post-9/11 era, in which the Western logic of belonging has self-de-structed in fulfilling its imperatives—disclosed its others as "the part of no part" (Jacques Rancière); "the ungrievable" (Judith Butler); "the inarticulate" (Alain Brossat); "living animal"(Alain Badiou); "bare life" (Giorgio Agamben)[24]—is that, in my gesture of retrieval, I was symptomatically intuiting not only the time of the now (*ho nyn kairos*) as the radical essence of the human and the imperative of *care* as its mode of comportment—its logic of belonging—toward being from the vocational time of mastery and servitude into which the Western humanist tradition has devolved, but also humanity's plurality—the universality of its singularity—in which, as Edward Said declared by way of the voice of the Afro-Caribbean poet Aimé Césaire, one of Western humanism's superfluous others, as something like a final testament in *Humanism and Democratic Criticism*:

and no race possesses the monopoly of beauty,
of intelligence, of force, and there
is a place for all at the rendezvous
of victory

The posthumanist, from this perspective of the time of the now and its logic of belonging, is the non-humanist humanist.

8

What, then, are the theoretical and practical implications for contemporary educators of this retrieval of *ho nyn kairos* and its imperative of care as the essence of the human condition at large in this in-between world—this interregnum between a dying world and a new world struggling to be born? A definitive answer to this urgent but complexly polyvalent question is beyond the scope of this brief intervention. Further, since its purpose is to render the prevailing mastery/servitude system of belonging inoperative, the answer should take the form of opening the closed system in place to the question, to potentiality as such. Here, I will comment on four aspects of the question that have emerged since I wrote *The End of Education* as particularly urgent.

First and foremost, given the pervasive indifference to the question of the human and the secular as ontological categories in most divisions of the University, we oppositional educators in the humanities must, in the interregnum in which we exist, underscore the radical understanding of the human articulated above. This is because such an initiative will disclose to students, who are deeply inscribed by the vocational ethos, the positive possibilities of their anxiety-provoking human condition, which is represented not only by devotees of theology but also by professors of a supernaturalized humanism as fundamentally negative and thus to be transcended at all costs. It is also because this radical understanding of the human, in rendering the old binary between the positive and the negative of the human condition—its coercive mode of comportment to its others—inoperative, opens the transient world of time in which students actually exist to empowering potentiality.

Second, we must forcefully resist the neoliberal capitalist version of globalization and its dehumanizing instrumentalist—and neo-imperial—imperatives. The purpose of this resistance, however, is not to recuperate the binary logic of belonging of the now delegitimized nation-state but to proffer instead a radically different version of globalization that is indissolubly related to the radicalized de-centering of Man—that is, to a view of globalization that is consonant with the opening of the idea of humanity, to welcome "all at the rendezvous of victory."

More particularly, as teachers and scholars of the humanities, we must, third, not only resist the combined effort of university administrators and corporate capitalism to reduce the humanities to service departments that serve the needs of the global market (the most banalized form of the Higher Cause). We must also collectively work positively to re-structure the University in such a way as to render it adequate to the cultural, social, and political demands of the age of globalization. This means, above all, the de-structuring of the traditional disciplinary structure that, despite modifications compelled by the student and faculty protest movement in the 1960s and 1970s, remains vocational—an apparatus of capture that renders the young docile and useful to the larger (University and national) whole. It also means, not incidentally, breaking the insidious hold that the disciplinary structure (as ideology) continues to exert in the form of professional competition even on oppositional teachers and scholars. That is, we must work to establish a dialogic relation, or, more specifically, a loving strife not only between the humanities division and the sciences and social sciences, but also between the departments of the humanities, a relationship that, at least, would end the debilitating isolation of the faculties of these traditional disciplinary divisions.[25] The ultimate purpose of this de-structuring would be the inauguration of an authentic intellectual polity of the common that would become the model of the coming community.

Fourth, in calling for the globalization of the University according to the dis-closive—liberating—imperatives of the de-centering of Western Man, I am not recommending that we reject *tout court* the canonical approach to humanist literary studies that is intrinsic to the University under the aegis of the nation-state. As I have been suggesting, we live in an interregnum, an in-between time of potentiality, inaugurated by the self-destruction of the nation-state system, in which the local and the global have become inextricably related. As oppositional American humanist intellectuals, to invoke the area with which I am most familiar, we must, therefore, as a number of recent exemplary New Americanist scholars have been arguing, break the stranglehold that the American exceptionalist ethos has perennially had on American literary studies, and read the national canon from a global or, better, transnational perspective.[26] Whereas traditional American humanist scholars and teachers teach and read American literature from a nationalist perspective, the imperial exceptionalism of which blinds them to the negative effects of this canonical literature on the rest of the world, the globalization of the planet—the rendering of the West's others visible and vocal—has made that nationalistic mode obsolete. We are, therefore, compelled by this historically decisive opening of the local to the global to consider the impact that this canonical literature has made on America's global others. We must, that is, not only attend in our teaching and scholarship to what America's canonical writers have said about America but also to what they have left unsaid, what their American exceptionalism has blinded them to, what they have disavowed in the process of avowing its nationalist exceptionalism. In the inaugural terms Edward Said introduced to "trouble" the hegemonic status of the literature of the Western canon—I think, above all, of his revolutionary readings of Joseph Conrad's *Heart of Darkness* and Jane Austen's *Mansfield Park*—we must, in this in-between time, read and teach the American literary canon contrapuntally.

Given the power that neoliberal corporate capitalism wields over the state and the University, the scholarly and pedagogical imperatives of this interregnum are, needless to say, the most difficult of tasks. But they are not impossible, if we understand our present global occasion as an in-between time—a liminal time when the dominant Western vocational logic of belonging, in fulfilling itself by establishing the state of exception as the norm, has theoretically self-de-structed: disclosed a deeper understanding of the human and the possibility of a more humane human *polis*. Be that as it may, what is at stake in this in-between time of the now, in which we have, as it were, all become exiles from the Western homeland—is the very fate of the human itself. We must render the vision of a new, non-humanist humanity attractive to our students. If we don't succeed in this difficult undertaking, we leave the "higher law" of the global free market to continue doing its banalizing and dehumanizing work. It may be, as some critics have said, that Giorgio Agamben's assertion that the inexorable reduction of life (*bios*) under the aegis of modern humanist democracy to bare life (*zoé*) ends in the concentration camp is somewhat melodramatic. Be that as it may, what has become certain at this post-9/11 liminal point of the dehumanizing "progress" is that bare life—the life of *homo humanus* become *animal laborans*, in Hannah Arendt's apt language—is life not worth living.

2

Speaking the Lie of the Truth to Power

A Meditation on the Truth of Modernity by an Incorrigible Caviler

> In short with all sorts of cavilers, it was best [according to the Confidence Man] for them and everybody, that whoever has the true light should stick behind the secure Malakoff of confidence, nor be tempted forth to hazard skirmishes on the open ground of reason. Therefore, he deemed it unadvisable in the good man, even in the privacy of his own mind, or in communion with a congenial one, to indulge in too much latitude of philosophizing, or, indeed, of compassionating, since this might beget an indiscreet habit of thinking and feeling which might unexpectedly betray him upon unsuitable occasions. Indeed, whether in private or public, there was nothing which a good man was more bound to guard himself against, than, on some topics, the emotional unreserve of his natural heart; for, that natural heart, in certain points, was not what it might be, men had been authoritatively admonished.
>
> —Herman Melville, *The Confidence-Man*

Thanks to the poststructuralist revolution of the 1970s and '80s, particularly the de-centering of the "universal" discourse of the West by Michel Foucault's and Edward W. Said's epochal disclosure of the complicity between (Western) knowledge and power, we oppositional intellectuals, if not the intellectual deputies of the dominant liberal capitalist culture, have become acutely aware that the "Truth" that has presided over the building of the world at large is a fiction (or *re*-presentation) that has its origins in the period that the West has called the bourgeois "Enlightenment" or, to emphasize the accumulation of productive empirical knowledge intrinsic to its commitment to the (disinterested) "Truth," "modernity." Thus, for example, Foucault, invoking the "repressive hypothesis"—and anticipating his later identification of this disciplinary strategy with the biopoliticization of the human body—showed that the ultimate purpose informing the empirical (Anthropological) inquiry of the new, post-revolutionary bourgeois dispensation that superseded the divinely sanctioned truth of the monarchical regime was not to liberate the oppressed bodies of the multitude from the bondage of arbitrary (irrational) power as it claimed ("the truth shall set you free [from power]," as this repressive hypothesis has it). Rather, the purpose of this new dispensation was to harness its "disinterested" knowledge—its objectified or reified (spatialized) and "secular" "regime of truth"—in order to greatly minimize or render productive the economic and particularly political inefficiency of the old regime. By this last, Foucault means the material waste endemic to undisciplined human energy and the political insurrections endemic to the overt use of power, since it was this visibility of power that had resulted in the revolution that brought monarchical rule (the *ancien regime*) to its end. It was, we might say, to anticipate, the late, secularized moment of Western history that bore witness to the definitive fulfillment of the interpellative logic of the earlier transcendental calling in the establishment of the vocational ethic, the production of the *value of servitude*—and, ultimately, bare life—to an invisible "Higher Cause":

> The historical moment of the disciplines was the moment when an art of the human body was born, which was directed not only at the growth of its skills, nor at the intensification of its subjection, but to the formation of a relation that in the mechanism itself makes it more obedient as it becomes more useful, and conversely. What was then being formed was a policy of coercions that act upon the body, a calculated manipulation of its elements, it gestures, its behavior. The human body was entering a machinery of power that explores it, breaks it down and rearranges it. A "political anatomy," which was also a "mechanics of power," was being born; it defined how one may have a hold over other's bodies, not only so that they may do what one wishes, but so that they may operate as one wishes, with the techniques, the speed and the efficiency that one determines. Thus discipline [the spatialized and classified—i.e., textualized—diagram or "table"] produces subjected and practiced bodies, "docile"

> bodies. Discipline increases the forces of the body (in economic terms of utility) and diminishes these same forces (in political terms of obedience). In short, it dissociates power from the body; on the one hand, it turns it into an "aptitude," a "capacity," which it seeks to increase; on the other hand, it reverses the course of the energy, the power that might result from it, and turns it into a relation of strict subjection. If economic exploitation separates the force and the product of labour, let us say that disciplinary coercion establishes in the body the constricting link between an increased aptitude and an increased domination.[1]

Foucault distinguishes between a (monarchical) premodernity that exercised power arbitrarily and overtly in the name of a transcendental Higher Cause and a (bourgeois) modernity in which empirical—"disinterested" or "objective"—Truth was pitted against power. Similarly, Edward W. Said, following Foucault's directives *vis-á-vis* the relationality of knowledge and power in Western discourse and practice, disclosed, in *Orientalism*, the devastating disciplinary effects of Western modernity's spatializing Anthropological (empirical) "regime of truth": its reduction of the peoples of the Orient to "useful and docile bodies" serving the Occident. I am, of course, referring to that modern Western spatializing biopolitical initiative that begins with the "textual attitude" of such early "observers"/"visitors" to the Orient as Alphonse de Lamartine, François René Chateaubriand, Gustave Flaubert, Théophile Gautier, Gérard de Nerval, Sir Richard Burton, among many others—that schematic representational reduction of radical diversity and temporal motion to the whole picture to be looked upon at once:

> It may appear strange to speak about something or someone holding a *textual attitude*, but a student of literature will understand the phrase more easily if he will recall the kind of view attacked by Voltaire in *Candide*, or even the attitude to reality satirized by Cervantes in *Don Quixote*. What seems unexceptionable good sense to these writers is that it is a fallacy to assume that the swarming, unpredictable, and problematic mess in which human beings live can be understood on the basis of what books—texts—say; to apply what one learns out of a book literally to reality is to risk folly or ruin. One would no more think of using *Amadis of Gaul* to understand sixteenth-century (or present-day) Spain than one would use the Bible to understand, say, the House of Commons. But clearly people have tried and do try to use texts in so simple-minded a way, for otherwise *Candide* and *Don Quixote* would not still have the appeal for readers that they do today.[2]

Here, Said attributes this schematizing textual attitude to humans at large: "It seems a common human failing to prefer the schematic authority of a text to the disorientations of direct encounters with the human" (O, 93). But, like Foucault, *vis-á-vis* errancy within the European nation-states, he goes on to show at length and decisively that it came to prevail in Western modernity with the apotheosis of (Western) Man (the *Anthropologos*), when, more specifically, the West began its imperial penetration of the Orient, and the text of the observing Eurocentric visitor became the authoritative "Truth" of "objective" (i.e., Anthropological) empirical knowledge. I am, of course, referring to that uniquely modern Western imperial initiative—so different from (yet continuous with) the early Western crusades undertaken in the name of God's Word—inaugurated by Napoleon's invasion of Egypt (1798) with both an army of savants and warriors, apparatuses of knowledge production and power, and culminating in Silvestre de Sacy's "rational anthropology" and, above all, Ernest Renan's "philological laboratory" (123). I mean, the "secularism" or, more precisely according to Said, the "reconstituted theology" that, borrowing from M.H. Abrams, he called "natural supernaturalism" (O, 114)—the anthropological Truth of the West (the panoptic "objective" truth of the empirical scientific text)—which eventually enabled the West's domination of the Orient without its having to rely any longer, like Napoleon, on the violent apparatuses of power. I will return to Said's telling, but hitherto unnoticed, identification of Renan's secularism with a "reconstituted theology" or a "natural supernaturalism." Here, it will suffice for the historical purpose at hand to underscore the parallel between Foucault's and Said's highly influential, indeed, *paradigm-shifting diagnoses of modernity as something like an epistemic break* with the ("theological") Western past. I mean, to put it somewhat alternatively, the similarity between Foucault's identification of modernity, in opposition to the historical past (the *ancien regime*), as the moment in Western history when the "truth" of "disinterested" or "objective" observation (and its disciplinary tables of capture)—the truth that, according to the imperatives of the new bourgeoisie's "repressive hypothesis," exists to set humanity free from arbitrary power—becomes "hegemonic," the very powerful political apparatus of modern democratic/capitalist power, and Said's extension of Foucault's genealogy of Western modernity to encompass the geographical other of the Occident by way of the Orientalists' philological refinement of the "textual attitude." "Thus for Renan," Said writes about the latter's influential philological discriminations between Semitic and Indo-European languages:

> Semitic is a phenomenon of arrested development in comparison with the mature languages and cultures of the Indo-European group, and even with the other Semitic Oriental languages. The paradox that Renan sustains, however, is that even as he encourages us to see languages as in some way corresponding to "*êtres vivants de la nature* [living beings of nature]," he is everywhere else proving that his Oriental languages, the Semitic languages, are inorganic, arrested, totally ossified, incapable of self-regeneration; in other words, he proves that Semitic is not a live language, and for that matter, neither are Semites live creatures. Moreover, Indo-European languages and culture are alive and organic *because* of the laboratory, not despite it. But far from being a marginal issue in Renan's work, this paradox stands, I believe, at the very center of his entire work, his style, and his archival existence in the culture of his time. . . . To be able to sustain a vision that incorporates and holds together life and quasi-living creatures (Indo-European, European culture) as well as quasi-monstrous, parallel inorganic phenomena (Semitic, Oriental culture) is precisely the achievement of the European scientist in his laboratory. He *constructs*, and the very act of construction is a sign of imperial power over recalcitrant phenomena, as well as a confirmation of the dominating culture and its "naturalization." Indeed, it is not too much to say that Renan's philological laboratory is the actual locale of his European ethnocentrism; but what needs emphasis here is that the philological laboratory has no existence outside the discourse, the writings by which it is constantly produced and experienced. Thus even the culture he calls organic and alive—Europe's—is also a *creature being created* in the laboratory and by philology. (O, 145–146; emphasis in original)

Foucault's and Said's genealogy of modernity are persuasive. And in their name, a "post-colonial" dynamics of resistance to and liberation from the domination of a hegemonic Western modernity has emerged on a promising global scale not only at the site of theory, but also of political practice. Having said this, however, I also wish, in keeping with the argument of this book, to offer a long-standing caveat to this by now pretty much established Foucauldian/Saidian diagnosis of the relationship between truth and power in the present age. In overdetermining modernity (the Enlightenment) at the expense of the European past at large, in failing to perceive (or, perhaps more accurately, to underscore) the *continuity*, despite the drastic difference, between the Truth of Western (anthropological) modernity and the truth of the West's previous Onto-logy and Theo-logy, that is, in representing Enlightenment modernity as if it constituted an epistemic break with the Western past—*the displacement of a theo-logical regime by a secular or worldly dispensation*—

Foucault and Said, in turn, inadvertently enabled their Western and post-colonial "worldly" followers to overdetermine the ontic (or political) over the ontological site (the site of the truth of being) on the indissoluble continuum of being.[3] Indeed, this was especially true of Said, who, in underscoring the "worldlessness" of "textuality" and its "anti-humanism" in his insistent critique of poststructuralism,[4] "justified" his postmodernist and postcolonialist followers' putting of the political (worldly, secular) into a binary opposition with the ontological/textual, thus rendering ontological (and linguistic) inquiry, the truth of being, not simply irrelevant but an enemy of the political and its security.

This self-inflicted impasse of contemporary "worldly" criticism—this marginalization, if not entirely forgetting of the revolutionary essence of the poststructuralist moment—has been tacitly disclosed by the coming to its fulfillment and end of the Western onto-theo-logical tradition (understood as an indissoluble continuum ranging from the question of being as such, the human subject and its language, through the ecos, gender, ethnic, race, and class relations, to the economic, cultural, social, and political, national and transnational, sites) with the United States' inauguration of its unending polyvalent War on Terror in the aftermath of 9/11. And it is this self-inflicted impasse of contemporary "worldly criticism"—this betrayal, in Alain Badiou's appropriate language, of fidelity to the "eventality" of the poststructuralist "event"[5] in the face of a powerful "exceptionalist" (Chosen) Western state's liminal rendering of the state of the exception (in which anything is possible) as the global rule in the name of homeland security—that compels my genealogical retrieval (*Wiederholung*) of the origins of its concept of Truth.

2

Heidegger traces the origins of the prevailing modern concept of truth back to the very foundation of Western civilization. I am referring to the epochal moment in antiquity, when the Romans, in a strategic gesture of damage control intended to save their civilizational authority from the power-damaging errancy of their Greek forbearers, decisively distinguished their "Occidental"—*sedentary* (agricultural/metropolitan)—civilization from the *nomadism* of the "Oriental" tribes of the "*terra incognita*" at its periphery and thus inaugurated a universal discursive regime that justified its colonization of the latter in the name of this "Truth." More specifically, to ensure their dominion over the peripheric nomadic "tribes," they reduced the Greek understanding of truth—*alethéia* (unconcealment)—to *adaequatio intellectus et rei* (the adequation of mind and thing: correctness). In so doing, the Romans established *metaphysics*—thinking *meta ta physica*, from after, or beyond, or above *physis* ("things-as-they-are," i.e., the be-*ing*, the radical temporality, of being). This distancing gesture separating and privileging the panoptic eye—its *Logos* (Transcendent Word), as it were—over the other alienated "errant" senses in the pursuit of knowledge established a truth discourse *structured in domination*: a will to power over any thing and/or time that refused to conform to its panoptic and logocentric structuring imperatives. That is to say, this distancing gesture established a binary truth logic that privileged the *Logos*, Identity, the One, the Center, over (the errancy of) words, difference, the many, the periphery. Put alternatively, to introduce the essential significance of poststructuralist theory to the question at stake, this metaphysical mode of knowledge production—this Romanization of the errant Greek understanding of truth—*spatialized* or, more precisely, *structured* the unstructurable or unpresentable, the ontologically prior be-*ing* of being: radical temporality, the differences that time always disseminates, to render "it" "comprehensible" from the Latin *prehendere*: "to take hold of, to grasp."

All this, according to Heidegger, is borne witness to in the modern, anthropological era, when "philosophy comes to its end,"[6] to the fulfillment—and demise—of its teleologic by way of its final reduction of the temporality of being into a total "World Picture."[7] For at this liminal moment of the ontotheological tradition, what its truth logic has always—and increasingly—disavowed (has willfully "had nothing to do with")[8]—manifests itself in a decisive way: it discloses the nothing (*das Nichts*) that is, in actuality, ontologically prior to Being.

Heidegger's disclosure of this nothing of temporal being that has haunted the West's truth from its origins is at the heart of his epochal phenomenological analysis of Western speech in its "modern," *everyday* linguistic manifestation (the hegemonic speech of *das Man*, the they-self) in *Being and Time*.[9] But it is in his essay "What Is Metaphysics?," written with the coming to the fore of a global anxiety in the liminal post–World War I era in mind, that its full and inescapable force emerges. Pursuing the directives of the self-de-struction of the ontotheological tradition, he shows that the metaphysically oriented truth procedure has had as its purpose the psychological and sociopolitical at-homing (domestication) of an anxiety-ridden humanity (*Dasein*) that has been "thrown" (*Geworfen*) into the world (not put there by and in the name of a Higher

Cause). More fundamentally, he reveals that the function of this truth is to objectify—to make *something* of the radical nothingness of being (*das Nichts*) and by way of this reification to master, to impose Man's will to power over "its" dislocating unpresentability.

At the absent core of Heidegger's de-struction and his followers' deconstruction of the logocentric tradition is their revolutionary acknowledgment and affirmation of the *ontological priority of the nothing over Being*, difference over Identity, the many over the One. This disclosure of the de-centering or alienating spectrality of the prior nothing that has always and increasingly haunted Western humanity's constructed world is epitomized in Heidegger's phenomenological analysis of the "fundamental mood of anxiety [*Angst*]," which he distinguishes from fear (*Furcht*):

> Anxiety is indeed anxiety in the face of . . . , but not in the face of this or that thing [as in the case of fear]. Anxiety in the face of . . . is always anxiety for . . . but not for this or that. The indeterminacy of that in the face of which and for which we become anxious is no mere lack of determinacy but rather the essential impossibility of determining it. In a familiar phrase this indeterminateness comes to the fore.
>
> In anxiety, we say, "one feels ill at ease [*es ist einem unheimlich*]." What is "it" that makes "one" feel ill at ease? We cannot say what it is before which one feels ill at ease. As a whole it is so for one. All things and we ourselves sink into indifference. This, however, not in the sense of mere disappearance. Rather, in this very receding things turn toward us. The receding of beings as a whole that close in on us in anxiety oppresses us. We can get no hold on things. In the slipping away of beings only this "no hold on things" comes over us and remains.
>
> Anxiety reveals the nothing. (*WM*, 100–101)

What, in short, Heidegger and the poststructuralists disclosed by way of pointing to the "structuring" imperatives of the West's metaphysical truth is that the *Truth* of being it has bequeathed to or, rather, imposed on the world at large is a construct, a fiction—or, to put it bluntly—a paranoia or a lie.

3

I will return to this last formulation of the truth discourse of the Western ontotheological tradition later in the chapter. Here, in keeping with my thesis that Heidegger and his poststructuralist heirs inaugurated (if they did not accomplish) a revolution in thinking by way of their destructive or de-constructive genealogical hermeneutics, that implicated the truth of the West, from its origins, with political power, I want to briefly extend this genealogy through its three historical phases. In tracing the origins of the modern Western concept of truth as far back as Roman antiquity, in which, as it were, the human vocation (calling) becomes servitude to a Higher (transcendental) Cause—a Cause, it should be underscored, that is above, not only in the sense of "beyond the reach of [free] play," as Derrida abstractly puts it,[10] but also in the sense of being outside the infinitely finite and irreparable realm of temporal transience—Heidegger was enabled to identify its long differential yet ultimately continuous historical itinerary as the "onto-theo-logical tradition." I mean the tripartite historical identity structure—the Greco-Roman, in which the Metaphysical *Logos* as such prevailed; the Judeo-Christian era, in which the Theo-*Logos* prevailed; and the modern era of the humanist Enlightenment, in which the Anthropo-*Logos* (the Word of Man) prevails. It was, to be sure, a historical itinerary marked by significant differences, but one that, as the presiding *Logos* in each instance testifies, has ultimately been continuously metaphysical—or, in the deconstructive language of Jacques Derrida, "logocentric."

Let me return to my anticipatory reference to Edward Said's telling *but undeveloped* identification of Ernest Renan's modern—objective empirical scientific—philology, which, as he rightly claims, established a "justificatory discursive regime" that authorized the West's colonization of an "arrested Orient," with a "natural supernaturalism." The point I want to emphasize in this developing genealogy of the Western concept of the truth in the context of its remarkably unexamined status is that the (over-remarked) transformation of the West in the modern era from a theologically oriented to an ostensibly secular- or humanist-oriented world did not, as his (and Foucault's) followers all too easily assume, constitute an epistemic break that separated, overdetermined, and privileged secular politics from ontology and the immediate manifestations *vis-á-vis* truth at the sites of self, language, the ecos, and culture. Rather, the transformation constituted the *naturalization* of the Higher Theological Cause, its panoptic eye, and, by way of the disciplinary table, its will to power over the errant human body—which is to say, in Carl Schmitt's appropriate terms, the rendering of its liberal/secular/parliamentary/capitalist politics as "political theology."[11]

This continuity in modernity to which Heidegger, following Nietzsche, pointed at the beginning of the twentieth century, between the ontological truth of being (metaphysics in the anthropological mode) and the more overt political sites on the continuum of being (liberal parliamentary capitalism), as I have shown elsewhere,[12] is the event to which poststructuralist theory bore witness in the 1960s and 1970s, but, for whatever reasons, did not pursue with the fidelity it demanded. (My inclination is to attribute this unfortunate failure to the poststructuralists' quite understandable, if short-sighted, emphasis on the difficulty of agency implicit in a fictitious discourse that had become hegemonic—the truth.[13])

Whatever the reasons, however, it is, I believe, a serious mistake—indeed, a *damaging infidelity to the revolutionary imperatives of the event*—to represent, as so many recent "worldly" critics have, the poststructuralists as hopelessly "unworldly" and, thus, as sponsors of an ontological/textual discourse that constitutes a binary (and inferior) opposite to political practice. From the beginning of the poststructuralist revolution, as the examples of Heidegger's and Foucault's early genealogies especially testify, there is at least a strong intuition into the indissoluble relationality between knowledge and power: ontology (metaphysical truth) and the other more overtly political sites on the continuum of being as they have been represented in the Western tradition culminating in modernity. Thus, as I have shown in chapter 1, we find in Heidegger's massively studied "Letter on Humanism" the following telling (but insistently overlooked) passage on the genealogy of modern Western humanism that not only identifies its origins with the Roman translation of the Greek understanding of truth, *alétheia* (unconcealment) to *veritas* (the metaphysical adequation of mind a thing), but also, and in an indissolubly related way, to the *studia humanitatis* understood as *eruditio et institutio in bones artes* (scholarship and training in good conduct), that is to say, as a *paideia* (educational system/culture) intended to produce (in Foucault's later appropriate biopolitical language) "useful and docile bodies," bodies, that is, trained (disciplined) to obediently serve the Roman imperial metropolis:

> *Humanitas*, explicitly so called, was first considered and striven for in the age of the Roman Republic. *Homo humanus* was opposed to *homo barbarous*. *Homo humanus* here means the Romans, who exalted and honored Roman *virtus* [manliness, virtue, power] through the "embodiment" [read "biopoliticization"] of the *paideia* taken over from the Greeks. These were the Greeks of the Hellenistic age, whose culture was acquired in the schools of philosophy. It was concerned with *eruditio et institutio in bonas artes* [scholarship and training in good conduct]. *Paideia* thus understood

> was translated as *humanitas*. We encounter the first humanism in Rome: it therefore remains in essence a specifically Roman phenomenon, which emerges from the encounter of Roman civilization with the culture of late Greek civilization.[14]

But it is in the *Parmenides* lectures, delivered in 1942–43 during World War II, and, according to Éliane Escoubas, one of his most authoritative poststructuralist commentators, intended to come to terms with his National Socialist past, indeed, as his "reciprocal rejoinder" to Nazism,[15] that Heidegger articulates his proleptic genealogy of the truth of Enlightenment modernity in such a detailed and explicit way that once encountered can only be forgotten willfully. I am referring specifically to his disclosure of the complicity of the West's (metaphysical) truth with power (here, in terms of the Roman truth's [*veritas*] binary other, *falsum* ["the false"], the reductive counterpart of the Greek *pseudos*), and thus the subject of domination:

> The essential domain which prevails for the deployment of the Roman "*falsum*" is that of the "imperium" and of the "imperial." . . .
>
> To commanding as the essential foundation of sovereignty belongs "being on high" [or "above" *Obensein*]. That is only possible through constant surmounting [*Überhöhung*] in relation to others, who are thus inferior [*Unteren*]. In the surmounting, in turn, resides the constant ability to oversee [super-vise and dominate, *Übersehen-können*]. We say "to oversee something," which means "to master it [*beherrschen*]." To this commanding view, which carries with it surmounting, belongs the "always-being-on-the-lookout [*Auf-der-Lauer-liegen*]." That is the form of all action that oversees, but that holds to itself, in Roman the *actio* of the *actus*. The commanding overseeing is the dominating vision which is expressed in the often cited phrase of Caesar: *veni, vedi, vici*—I came, I oversaw [*übersah*], I conquered. Victory is already nothing but the consequence of the Caesarian gaze that dominates [*Übersehens*] and seeing [*Sehens*] which has the character of *actio*. The essence of the *imperium* reposes in the *actus* of the constant action [*Aktion*]. The imperial *actio* of the constant surmounting over others implies that the others, in the case where they raise themselves to a comparable or even identical height to command, are fallen [*gefällt werden*]—in Roman: *fallere* (particle: *falsum*, The "bringing-to-fall" [*das Zu-Fall-bringen*: "the occasioning of an ac-cident"] belongs necessarily to the domain of the imperial.

This resonant genealogy should suffice to validate my claim that Heidegger, early on, intuited the indissoluble relationality between the sites of truth (and its false: the unpresentable nothing) and imperial power on the continuum of being of the Western tradition founded by the Romans' inaugural identification of *veritas* (truth as correctness) with humanism. What is remarkable, however, is that Heidegger goes on in these *Parmenides* lectures to discriminate an early (*theo*-logical) and late (*anthropo*-logical, i.e., humanist) form of the truth/power relationship that uncannily anticipates Foucault's decisive historical distinction between knowledge and power relations in the monarchical era and in the modern era of the Enlightenment. Indeed, Heidegger's insight is, despite its brevity, so proleptic of Foucault's influential genealogical study of modern knowledge/power relations ("the repressive hypothesis") that it becomes difficult not to infer that Foucault, in fact, found the point of departure of *Surveiller et punir* (*Discipline and Punish*) in this passage about two related but temporally and qualitatively different forms of power—one dependent on war, the other on peace, that is, the *Pax Romana*—from Heidegger's *Parmenides* that immediately follows the above:

> The "bringing-to-fall" [*das Zu-Fall-bringen*] can be accomplished in a "direct" assault [*Ansturm*] and an overthrowing [*Niederwerfen*: literally "throwing down"]. But the other can also be brought to fall by being outflanked [*Um-gehung*] and tripped up from behind. The bringing-to-fall is now the way of deceptive circumvention [*Hinter-gehen*], of the trick—a word which not accidentally comes from the "English." Considered from the outside, going behind the back is a complicated, circumstantial and thus mediate "bringing-to-fall" as opposed to an immediate overthrowing [*Niederwerfen*]. In this way, what is brought to fall does not thereby become annihilated, but in a certain manner redressed within the boundaries [*in den Grenzen*] which are staked out by the dominators. This "staking out" [*Abstecken*] is called in Roman *pango*, whence the word *pax*, peace. This, thought imperially, is the firmly established condition of what has been brought to fall. In truth, the bringing-to-fall in the sense of deception [*Hintergehens*] and outflanking [*Umgehens*] is not the mediate and derived imperial *actio* but the imperial actio proper. *It is not in war, but in the* fallere *of deceptive outflanking* [hintergehenden Umgehens] *and its appropriation to the service of dominion that the proper and "great" trait of the imperial reveals itself*. . . . In the Roman *fallere*—to bring to fall as a going around resides the deceit [*Tauschen*]; the *falsum* is the insidiously deceptive: "the false."
>
> What happens when the Greek *pseudos* is thought in the sense of Roman *falsum*? The Greek *pseudos*, as what dissimulates and thereby also deceives is now no longer experienced and interpreted in terms of concealment [*Verbergen*], but from the basis of deception [*Hintergehen*]. The Greek

> *pseudos* [like the translation of the Greek *alétheia* to *veritas* (correctness)] through its translation into Roman *falsum* is *trans*ferred [*übergestzt*] into the imperial Roman domain of the bringing-to-fall.[16]

In short, from this modern Romanized understanding of truth as correctness, the nothingness of being (*das Nichts*)—and "its" polyvalent manifestations on the continuum of being, not least the (identityless) human (*Da-sein*: being-there)—which, in reality, is ontologically prior to Being (Presence, Identity), is represented by the Truth as both false and fallen—as the state of war of all against all—and thus rationally subject to correction in the name of its peace.

Heidegger's insight into the complicity between ontology (metaphysics) and the political, truth and domination, knowledge and power, in the Western ontotheological tradition, on the one hand, and the shift of emphasis from power (overt violence) to truth in Western modernity, on the other, was, despite the allegations of those critics who have put their "worldliness" in a binary opposition with the poststructuralists' "unworldly" and "agentless" "onto-textualitity," shared in some degree by all the other early poststructuralists. This is most obviously the case with Michel Foucault, as the central passage on the historical moment of the birth of the modern disciplinary society from *Discipline and Punish* quoted at the beginning to this chapter testifies. It is also reflected, however sporadically and unevenly, in Jacques Derrida's early poststructuralist criticism—not least in his insistent pointing to the power of the center of the "logocentric tradition" over the periphery,[17] and particularly in his very important political extension of his deconstructive project in *Specters of Marx*;[18] in Jean François Lyotard's reflections on the "postmodern sublime" and the "differend";[19] Philippe Lacoue-Labarthe's deconstructive analysis of Heidegger in *Heidegger, Art, and Politics*;[20] and in Jean-Luc Nancy's deconstructive meditations on the coming *polis* in *The Inoperative Community*.[21] Not least, in my mind, one perceives this onto-political insight in three related gestures of Louis Althusser's critique of modern capitalism: his disclosure of the metaphysical panopticism of the modern "disinterested" democratic capitalist "problematic" (frame of reference); his genealogical analysis of the ideological implications of the modern democratic capitalist "vocation" (interpellation) that produces the "subjected subject"; and his Gramscian-inflected collapsing of the orthodox Marxist Base/superstructure model of knowledge production to demonstrate that the hitherto secondary (marginalized and dependent) ontological/linguistic/cultural sites on the continuum of being are in fact characterized by a relative autonomy from the hitherto determining economic Base of both capitalist and Marxist modernity.[22]

Having all too briefly retrieved the early poststructuralist insight into the indissoluble relatedness of the ontological and ontic (political) sites on the continuum of being, and the ontological priority of the nothing over Being, it must be admitted, with Edward Said, that it was the failure of the poststructuralists to adequately perceive the polyvalent implications of this evental insight—to identify the Western truth of being as a continuum that, however unevenly developed at any particular historical moment, encompasses all the ontological and the political sites, and to think its directives concerning a practice of resistance and its positive possibilities concerning an alternative coming community.

4

It is in the light of this unfinished poststructuralist revolutionary initiative that, I suggest, one can best understand the itinerary of the radically innovative thought of such recent radically left theorists as Giorgio Agamben, Alain Badiou, Slavoj Žižek, Judith Butler, and Jacques Rancière, among others. For despite their various theoretical emphases, it is precisely this ultimately still existing hiatus in poststructuralist thinking between the ontological and the other more obviously worldly sites on the continuum of being—this failure to think both the implications for resistance and the positive possibilities for the political—that the radical polyvalent thought about the truth/power nexus of these "post-poststructuralists," as I call them, or "Left Heideggerians" as others have, would think in order to fulfill the revolutionary onto-political potential of the poststructuralist event.

As we have seen by way of their symptomatic genealogies of the "Truth" of modernity—its reliance on "the Nothing" that, as Heidegger tellingly observed, it will, at all costs, "have nothing to do with," for its global authority—poststructuralists, beginning with Nietzsche and Heidegger, have shown that this Truth that has come increasingly, until recently, to determine the subjective, linguistic, and sociopolitical "realities" of the various constituencies of global humanity is a "construct," a "fiction," an "imaginary" of the West that has been strategically imposed—staged for spectacular (ideological) effect, as it were—in the name of the perennially assumed practical superiority of its empirical knowledge about being on its inferior "others." I will return to this locution later in the book in the context of articulating my version of the post-poststructuralist ontological/ontic project. Here it will suffice to draw the irresistible conclusion of the symptomatic poststructuralist de-structive genealogies of the Truth of modernity. At the liminal point of the unerring development of its binary logic in modernity, the Truth that determines reality on the global scale turns out to be a lie.[23] But this de-structive project is not simply the urgent matter of calling the global Truth of (Western) modernity by its right name. As I have shown, the early poststructuralist genealogies of the Truth of modernity at the liminal point of the development of its binarist panoptic logic disclosed, contrapuntally, as it were, the latter's obsessive, indeed, paranoid representation of the temporal being of being as the ultimate negative—the Nothing (*das Nichts*). In so doing, they also made clear to the following generation, however tentatively, that the ontological disclosure of the Truth as a lie—and the lie as the truth—was polyvalent in its liminal manifestations: a hegemonic continuum that, to repeat, however unevenly developed at any particular moment in history, extended from being as such, through the ecos (earth) to the human subject, its language, culture, economy, and politics. And it was precisely this inadequately thought but heuristic insight into that which modernity perforce disavowed that provided the post-poststructuralist's contrapuntal directives for thinking both a practice of resistance adequate to the polyvalent hegemonic power and depredations of the Truth and, beyond that, of an alternative *polis*.

It is the pursuit of these unending indissolubly related ontological-ontic possibilities, I submit, that constitutes the pro-jective aspect of the de-struction (we can now read this linguistic term politically as "de-colonization") of the polyvalent Truth discourse of modernity being undertaken by the radical legatees of the poststructuralist revolution. Whatever the differences between their specific projects—and they are admittedly substantial—these post-poststructuralists share in common precisely an acute awareness (1) of the liminal—evental, in Badiou's apt term—nature of the de-centered contemporary occasion; (2) of the self-de-struction of the Truth discourse of the Western ontotheological tradition culminating in Anthropological modernity; (3) of the contrapuntal disclosure of the ontological priority—the (a-letheic/errant/nomadic) truth—of the nothing; (4) and, not least, of being not as a hierarchical disciplinary structure over which the *Logos* panoptically (commandingly) presides, but as an indissoluble polyvalent continuum ranging from the ontological as such to the other more obviously political sites. Which is to say, they are, as radical intellectual inheritors of the proleptic, if not clearly articulated poststructuralist legacy, committed to the articulation of a mode of political resistance against the modern nation-state/imperial identitarian logic of belonging (and its more recent extension in neoliberal globalism) that is "grounded," not in the modern (Anthropo) *Logos*, but precisely in the nothing that the modern *Logos* will, in virtually a paranoid way, have nothing to do with.

This inaugural and potential post-poststructuralist collapsing of the disabling distinction between the ontological and the ontic, being and politics, is testified by the paradoxical representation of its hitherto lowly marginalized protagonists. Following the directives of post-Heideggerians such as Hannah Arendt and Edward Said, who bore witness to the theoretical self-de-struction of Western modernity by way of bringing the "superfluous" or "stateless persons" (Arendt)[24] or "refugee," "migrant," "displaced person" (Said)[25] as the presiding demographic figure of the postmodern era, they take the point of departure of their intense contrapuntal meditations on political resistance in identifying and underscoring their human protagonists as precisely the counterparts—the "nobodies"—of the ontological nothing that the Truth of modernity will have nothing to do with. Thus, for example, Giorgio Agamben refers pointedly to his unlikely resistant protagonists—those whom the Truth of Western modernity in its biopolitical phase has reduced to "bare life" (*nuda vida*), "life that can be killed without it being called homicide"[26]—as unidentifiable "whatever beings";[27] Jacques Rancière as "the part of no part";[28] Alain Badiou as "the *inexistent* of the world"[29]; and Judith Butler as "the ungrievable."[30]

It is, I suggest, no accident that, despite the different names these post-poststructuralist thinkers give to their "lowly" protagonists, each is intended to point to its identification by the dominant culture as a lie—a violation of the Truth that threatens the peace (*Pax*) or, in its modern version, security—of the political order of the state and thus as an agent of crisis in need of correction (policing), on the one hand, and precisely as such an unnamable entity, a powerful paradoxical means of exposing the (imperial) violence intrinsic to but always disavowed by this Truth. Nor is it an accident that it is Herman Melville's proleptic enigmatic figure of Bartleby, the "nobody," who, having been invoked by prominent poststructuralists such as Maurice Blanchot, Gilles Deleuze, and Antonio Negri and Michael Hardt,[31] becomes the epitome of this paradoxical unnamable figure of resistance for many of the post-poststructuralists, not least, Agamben, Žižek, and Badiou.[32]

I could invoke a number of post-poststructuralist texts that overdetermine this unorthodox active passive mode of resistance grounded in the nothing, not least Badiou's *The Rebirth of History: Times of Riots and Uprisings* (2012), his profoundly suggestive reading of the un-namable revolts of the Arab Spring of 2010. But for the sake of brevity—and the continuity with the early poststructuralists' disclosure of the nothing for positive thought—it will suffice to restrict citation to Agamben's short but resonant Bartlebyan analysis of the event of Tiananmen Square. "What," Agamben begins, echoing Badiou, in order to underscore the identityless identities of his resistance protagonists, "could be the politics of whatever singularity, that is, of a being whose community is mediated *not by any condition of belonging (being red, being Italian, being Communist)* nor by the simple absence of conditions (a negative community, such as that recently proposed in France by Maurice Blanchot), but by belonging itself?" And, to underscore the proleptic essence of the event that has escaped the intellectual deputies of the Western nation-states, he goes on, "A herald from Beijing carries the elements of a response." As opposed to these Western observers, for the post-poststructuralist Agamben,

> What was most striking about the demonstrations of the Chinese May was the relative absence of determinate contents in their demands. . . . This makes the violence of the State's reaction seem even more inexplicable. It is likely, however, that the disproportion is only apparent and that the Chinese leaders acted, from their point of view, with greater lucidity than the Western observers who were exclusively concerned with advancing increasingly less plausible arguments about the opposition between democracy and communism.

Reading the predictable Western representations of the Tiananmen demonstrations (as a call for Western-style liberal nation-state democracy) contrapuntally, Agamben, invoking Badiou directly, not incidentally, argues:

> The novelty of the coming politics is that it will no longer be a struggle for the conquest or control of the State, but a struggle between the State and the non-State (humanity), an insurmountable disjunction between whatever singularity and the State organization. This is nothing to do with the simple affirmation of the social in opposition to the State that has often found expression in the protests movements of recent years. Whatever singularities cannot form a societas because they do not possess

> any identity to vindicate nor any bond of belonging for which to seek recognition. In the final instance the State can recognize any claim for identity—even that of a State identity within the State (the recent history of relations between the State and terrorism is an eloquent confirmation of this fact). What the State cannot tolerate in any way, however, is that singularities form a community without affirming an identity, that humans co-belong without any representable condition of belonging (even in the form of a simple presupposition). The State, as Alain Badiou has shown, is not founded on a social bond, of which it would be the expression, but rather on dissolution, the unbinding it prohibits. For the State, therefore, what is important is never the singularity as such, but only its inclusion in some identity, whatever identity (but the possibility of the whatever itself being taken up without an identity is a threat the State cannot come to terms with). (emphasis in original)

Following a telling gesture intended to show that the highly celebrated Western state "dogma of the sacredness of human life" and the "declaration of human rights" are fundamental aspects of the lying nature of its Truth in that they conceal their origins in the Roman State's inaugural reduction of the threatening "whatever being" to "*Sacer*" (bare life), "one who had been excluded from the human world and who, even though she or he could not be sacrificed, could be killed without committing homicide," Agamben concludes with a liminal (opening) finality:

> Whatever singularity, which wants to appropriate belonging itself, its own being-in-language, and thus rejects all identity and every condition of belonging, is the principle enemy of the State. Wherever these singularities peacefully demonstrate their being in common there will be a Tiananmen, and, sooner or later, the tanks will appear.[33]

As Agamben suggests at the outset of his analysis of Tiananmen Square, however, it is not only a mode of resistance adequate to the uniquely difficult conditions of modern power relations—its identification of the nothing as polyvalent lie—that the post-poststructuralists would project from their destruction of its Truth. Equally important, though understandably more tentative, it is also a coming *polis* that is "grounded" in the very contrapuntal nothing—or, to put this in terms of "its" temporal allotrope, "the time of the now" (*ho nyn kairos*), which, as Agamben has disclosed to us via Saint Paul and Walter Benjamin,[34] is the potentializing remainder of the teleological/panoptic/spatialized—structured—time of the Western tradition. I mean specifically the nothing/

time that, in its radically secular—that is, irreparably profane[35]—essence, is anathema not only to the sovereign Truth of the modern *Logos* and the identitarian—and total—logic of belonging of the nation-state but also to that of the Utopias of the traditional Marxists, who, in Agamben's language, would repair the irreparable human condition—that is, who in the end would do away with identity altogether in the name of the collective transcendental One.

Under the dispensation of the errant time of the now, Agamben insists, individual human beings and racial, gender, and ethnic groups of human beings will not be denied the identities that history has bestowed on them, but insofar as the ontological priority of the nothing prevails over identity, the devastating binarism—Friend/enemy—logic of belonging into which the Truth of the modern nation-state has compelled "it" will be, in Agamben's resonant term (which plays resonantly on the interpellative calling/vocation that produces the *subjected subject* of the nation-state), rendered *inoperative* (*inoperatisa; katergeo*).[36] These historical identities will remain intact; for example, women will remain women, males remain male, gays remain gay, straights remain straight, blacks remain black, whites remain white, Jews remain Jews, Palestinians remain Palestinian; and the relation of belonging will be, not the uneven war to the end of Us and Them as in the Western nation-state system, but a loving strife (*Auseinandersetzung*), in which, as Said put this resonant profane paradox, the "'complete consort danc[es] together' contrapuntally."[37]

Using the fraught instance of Jerusalem as his example, Agamben, following the directives of Hannah Arendt's inaugural post–World War notion of the "conscious pariah" as the figure of the nomadic "refugee" which is the "vanguard of its people"[38] (and, not incidentally, echoing Said's contrapuntal vision), puts this revolutionary inoperative community in the following way. It is no accident that, like Said, who uses music as his medium, Agamben resorts not to the language of Truth but to the marginalized nonverbal arts, in this case the metaphors of the Klein bottle and Möbius strip, in his effort to express the unnamable character of this coming *polis* without fixing it:

> Instead of two national states separated by uncertain and threatening boundaries, it might be possible to imagine two communities that would articulate each other via a series of reciprocal extraterritorialities in which the guiding concept would no longer be the *ius* (right) of the citizen but rather the *refugium* (refuge) of the singular. In an analogous way, we

> could conceive of Europe not as an impossible "Europe of the nations," whose catastrophe one can already foresee in the short run, but rather as an aterritorial or extraterritorial space in which all the (citizens and noncitizens) residents of the European states would be in a position of exodus or refuge; the status of European would then mean the being-in-exodus of the citizen (a condition that obviously could also be one of immobility). European space would thus mark an irreducible difference between birth [*nascita*] and nation in which the old concept of people (which, as is well known, is always a minority) could again find a political meaning, thus decidedly opposing itself to the concept of nation (which has so far unduly usurped it).
>
> This space would coincide neither with any of the homogeneous national territories nor with their *topographical* sum, but would rather act on them by articulating and perforating them, *topologically as in the Klein bottle or the Möbius strip, where exterior and interior in-determine each other* [emphasis added]. In this new space, European cities would rediscover their ancient vocation of cities of the world by entering into a relation of reciprocal extraterritoriality.[39]

Coda

It is, as I have suggested, the caviling post-poststructuralist commitment to speaking the lie of the Truth of Western modernity—the Malakoff, in Herman Melville's apt image, of the dominant culture's confidence—to power, this care-ful call, in Agamben's radically revisionary messianic Pauline language (*klēsis:* calling), for "the revocation of every vocation" that constitutes the calling of the oppositional intellectual in the liminal—irreparable in-between—time, the time of the now (*ho nyn kairos*), of the global world we all precariously inhabit:

> The messianic vocation is the revocation of every vocation. In this way, it defines what to me seems to be the only acceptable vocation. What is a vocation, but the revocation of each and every concrete factical vocation? This obviously does not entail substituting a less authentic vocation with a truer vocation. According to what norm would one be chosen over the other? No, the vocation calls the vocation itself, as though it were an urgency that works it from within and hollows it out, nullifying it in the very gesture of maintaining and dwelling in it. This, and nothing less than this, is what it means to have a vocation, what it means to live in the messianic *klēsis*.[40]

What is at stake, finally, in this unending post-poststructuralist vocation is not simply the articulation of an adequate mode of resistance to the dehumanizing "progressive" biopolitics of the Truth—the Malakoff—of modernity. It is also, I submit, the making of the inoperative community of the negative of this Truth: nobodies, the "whatever beings," the "inexistent," those who are "the part of no part," who "don't count," "the ungrievable," in which, as in the Möbius strip, "exterior and interior in-determine each other" or, in Said's language, the " 'complete consort' danc[es] together' contrapuntally"—like Said and Daniel Barenboim, non-Palestinian Palestinian and non-Jewish Jew, and the East–West Divan, the orchestra "composed" of Palestinian and Jewish youth, they imagined into collective being.

3

American Exceptionalism and the State of Exception

A Genealogy of the Contemporary Security State

"The criminal paid the penalty of his crime. The promptitude of the punishment has proved salutary. Nothing amiss is now apprehended aboard H.M.S. *Bellipotent*."

—From "an authorized naval chronicle,"
Herman Melville, *Billy Budd, Sailor*

The new historian, the genealogist, will know what to make of this masquerade. He will not be too serious to enjoy it; on the contrary, he will push the masquerade to its limit and prepare the great carnival of time where masks are constantly reappearing. No longer the identification of our faint individuality with solid identities of the past, but our "unrealization" through the excessive choice of identities. . . . In this, we recognize the parodic double of what the second of the *Untimely Meditations* called "monumental history": a history given to reestablishing the high points of historical development and their maintenance in a perpetual presence, given to the recovery of works, actions, and creations through the monogram of their personal essence. But in 1874 Nietzsche accused this history, one totally devoted to veneration, of barring access to the actual intensities and creations of life.

—Michel Foucault, "Nietzsche, Genealogy, History"

Taking their directives from Heidegger (his ontological insights into the enframing of being [*Ge-stell*] intrinsic to technological knowledge production that reduces life to "standing [or disposable] reserve"

[*Bestand*]);[1] Hannah Arendt (her bringing to center stage the "superfluous" or "stateless person" that is intrinsic to the logic of belonging of the nation-state);[2] and Michel Foucault (his disclosure of the biopolitics that has come to inform modern democratic politics),[3] Giorgio Agamben's genealogies of the liminal contemporary global political occasion bear witness not only to the state of exception becoming the rule and the consequent apotheosis of the security state in the post-9/11 era, on the one hand, but also to the rise of biopolitics and the normalization of "bare life"—life that can be killed without the killing being called homicide[4]—on the other. The debt of contemporary oppositional intellectuals to Agamben's genealogies is enormous. Though one may cavil about certain aspects of these disclosures, there can be no question that his witnesses to our fraught contemporary post-9/11 occasion have set an urgent, if not the only, agenda for thinking and practice. Thanks to Agamben and the theoretical tradition he is working in, we can no longer ignore the fact that the logic of the nation-state pursued to its limits has become the security state and that our vocation is to resist its dehumanizing momentum.

Having acknowledged this, however, I wish also to suggest that Agamben's genealogy of the contemporary security state remains Eurocentric. Though its point of departure in *The State of Exception* is the unending "War on Terror" inaugurated by the United States in the wake of *al Qaeda*'s bombing of the World Trade Center and the Pentagon on September 11, 2001, his genealogy of the contemporary security state is almost entirely restricted to the European jurisprudential history going back from the Weimar Republic and German National Socialism, through the Napoleonic to its origins in Roman *iustitia*. There is, of course, nothing invalid ultimately about this genealogy, as we shall see. But, I will argue, insofar as Agamben (and his followers) restricts the scope of his genealogy of the state of exception to European jurisprudential history, a restriction that includes the United States, he is blinded by his profound insight into the dehumanizing effects of the state of exception to what is "unique" about the contemporary American version of the security state (Homeland Security) and its globalized normalization of the state of exception. I am referring in general to the indissoluble relationship between the American exceptionalist ethos—the ethos the United States has perennially invoked since its founding by the Puritans to differentiate its polyvalent moral superiority from the decadent and tyrannical "Old World"—and the state of exception. Thus, in the following all too brief remarks, I will offer an alternative genealogy of the contemporary American version of the security state and its normalization of the state of exception, not to challenge Agamben's genealogy, but, in the spirit of *Auseinandersetzung*, to contribute a specific dimension that would enrich his general diagnosis of the global post-9/11 era—and contribute to the task of resistance he, as witness, calls for.

2

What a genealogy of the present post-9/11 historical global occasion that takes its point of departure from American history generally discloses, to put it provisionally, is that the state of exception—and its political allotrope, the Homeland Security State—is intrinsic to the *exceptionalist* logic of the United States' perennially avowed (and practiced) exceptionalist ethos. Such a genealogy reveals that its origin resides in the American Puritans' divinely ordained exodus from the decadent "Old World," which had abandoned God's Word and its redemptive imperatives—the world of "fleshpots," as their prefigural Hebrew "ancestors" put it in the Old Testament—and their providential "errand in the [New World] wilderness": to cultivate and domesticate it, and, in so doing, to build the "New Jerusalem," "the city on the hill," as John Winthrop inaugurally put it on board the Puritan flagship, the *Arabella*.[5] As God's "elect"—His chosen and convenantal people—they were thus enabled—indeed, compelled—to think of their divinely ordained vocation, their "calling," as a redemptive "errand" against a "fallen" condition that obstructed the enactment of God's "benign" providential design. Their divinely ordained exceptionalist logic, in other words, enabled them to dehumanize and demonize the native "inhabitants" of the wilderness—those who simply "roamed" rather than cultivated it[6]—if not exactly the wilderness as such. In the name of God's *Logos*, that is, they were justified in representing the natives as "bare life" and, as such, as a perpetual threat to God's providential design—a crisis—and thus, as the fate of the Pequots testifies, in enacting their extermination.

It is this *exceptional* element of the logic of the American Puritan exceptionalist ethos—this tendency to *extremism* intrinsic to the redemptive errand justified by the divine *Logos*—that needs to be highlighted for my purposes. For in the process of American history, as the New Americanist counter-memory has persuasively shown in recent years, most tellingly in the wake of the United States' inauguration of its unending War on Terror in the aftermath of 9/11, it became inscribed in the American national psyche. Thus, for example, after the decline of the Puritan theocracy and the emergence in the wake of the American Revolution of a constitutionalist government that separated church and state—that is, substituted a secular for a transcendental authority—the "new" secular dispensation did not abandon the Puritan covenantal structure, its exceptionalism, and its vocation—the errand in the wilderness—to build a "city on the hill." On the contrary, it naturalized this supernatural paradigm. Whereas under the aegis of the Puritans' theocracy it was God who chose the American Puritans to fulfill his creational purposes—endowed them with exceptionalist status—under the aegis of the new constitutional secularism, it was History. This is to say that the Puritan ideology of exceptionalism became, in Antonio Gramsci's sense of the word, hegemonic: a fiction that, for Americans, became in the process of the nineteenth century, during the era of westward expansion, "the way things really are": the Truth. It is, I suggest, this paradox—this American transformation of a lie into the ontological Truth of being—that needs to be underscored in the context of the present focus on the juridical/political in addressing the question concerning the normalization of the state of exception. For, by way of the indissoluble relationality of the ontological and the cultural, economic, and political, it suggests emphatically how deeply the exceptionalist ethos—and its violent practical imperatives—is inscribed in the American body politic and, therefore, how difficult it is to resist its deceptive mode of domination. Raymond Williams's resonant summary account of Gramsci's concept of hegemony—its difference from ideological consciousness—will convey both this inordinate difficulty and point to its hidden source:

> The concept of hegemony often, in practice, resembles these definitions [of ideology], but it is distinct in its refusal to equate consciousness with the articulate formal system which can be and ordinarily is abstracted as "ideology." It of course does not exclude the articulate and formal meanings, values and beliefs which a dominant class develops and propagates. But it does not equate them with consciousness, or rather it does not reduce consciousness to them. Instead it sees the relations of domination and subordination in their forms as *practical consciousness, as in effect a saturation of the whole process of living—not only of political and economic activity, not only of manifest social activity, but of the whole substance of lived identities and relationships, to such a depth that the pressures and limits of what can ultimately be seen as a specifically economic, political, and cultural system seems to most of us the pressures and limits of simple experience and common sense*. Hegemony is then not only the articulate upper level of "ideology,"

> nor are its forms of control only those ordinarily seen as "manipulation" or "indoctrination." It is a whole body of practices and expectations, over the whole of living: our senses and assignments of energy [what I call our vocation], our shaping perceptions of ourselves and our world. It is a lived system of meanings and values—constitutive and constituting—which as they are experienced as practices appear as reciprocally confirming. *It thus constitutes a sense of reality for most people in society, a sense of absolute because experienced reality beyond which it is very difficult for most members of the society to move, in most areas of their lives.* It is, that is to say, in the strongest sense a "culture," but a culture which has also to be seen as the lived dominance and subordination of particular classes.[7] (my emphasis)

The hegemonization of the American exceptionalist ethos—this gradual transformation of an initial vulnerable ideology into a virtually invulnerable hegemonic discourse that, however unevenly at any historical conjuncture, includes all the sites on the continuum of being from the ontological as such, to the sites of the subject, language, gender, race, the ecos, economics, culture, and politics—is borne witness to in the intermediary period of westward expansion. I am referring to the period when the United States inaugurated the policy of Indian removal (and later, detainment and extermination) and its appropriation of Mexican lands in the name of its exceptionalist ethos and civilizing errand or, more specifically, that aspect of this ethos/errand that enabled the Americans to represent the conditions of their relations to native Americans and the Spanish as a crisis/emergency state that threatened/obstructed the "Manifest Destiny" of the American people. John L. O'Sullivan, it is true, continues to invoke the Puritan deity and His providential design in his famous canonical essay "The Great Nation of Futurity," where he introduced the language of Manifest Destiny. But, given his rhetoric's patent overdetermination of the secular—the political equality that renders the "great American nation of futurity" radically different from and superior to the tyrannical Old World monarchies—this continuity between a divinely ordained Providence and a secularly ordained History, in fact, goes far to point to the hegemonizing direction that the exceptionalist Puritan ideology is heading in midcentury: the anthropologization of the *Theo-Logos*, the naturalizing of the supernatural and, thus, the representation of all obstacles in its unerring way as states of crisis that threaten the errand. Thus, in the exceptional name of (the lie of) this hegemonic Truth, O'Sullivan was justified in condemning the arbitrary violence of the Old World—"the oppression and injustice inflicted by ["monarchies and aristocracies"] on the masses of mankind"—and, *at the same time*, in *disavowing* (in the name of defense or security) the violence against humans the United States had committed in its past (the extermination of the Pequots, Indian removal) and was committing in the process of its westward Manifest Destiny to build the New Jerusalem—homeland—for (Anglo-Saxon) humanity:

> America is destined for better deeds [than the Old World]. It is our unparalleled glory that we have no reminiscences of battle fields, but in defence of humanity, of the oppressed of all nations, of the rights of conscience, the rights of personal enfranchisement. Our annals describe no scene of horrible carnage, where men were led on by hundreds of thousands to slay one another, dupes and victims to emperors, kings, nobles, demons in the human form called heroes. We have had patriots to defend our homes, our liberties, but no aspirants to crowns or thrones; nor have the American people ever suffered themselves to be led on by wicked ambition to depopulate the land, to spread desolation far and wide, that a human being might be placed on a seat of supremacy.[8]

This disavowal of the violence that the United States commits in the unerring name of the Truth—its natural supernaturally ordained westward errand (it is now, as in the case of John Gast's famous painting ["American Progress," 1872], tellingly represented as an unstoppable march)—becomes manifest in O'Sullivan's speech calling the Congress to enact the annexation of Texas in 1845.[9] As Quentin Youngberg forcefully puts O'Sullivan's exceptionalist claim, *without, however, noting the reciprocal relation in the latter's rhetoric between theological history (Puritan Providence) and secular history (Manifest Destiny), the ideological and the hegemonic*:

> Like the Puritans, who saw the very fact that they survived the voyage to the New World as evidence of their providential destiny, O'Sullivan appeals to the fact as justification for their taking over the entire territory of the New World [the western Mexican lands in this particular case]. His claim is that expansion is the inevitable and natural "fulfillment of our Manifest Destiny to overspread the continent allotted by Providence for the free development of our yearly multiplying millions." (*MMD*, 321–322)[10]

But, as Youngberg acutely observes, it is not simply the " 'natural' cause of our growing population" that O'Sullivan relies on to "justify the theft of Texas"—and the future incorporation of California. More fundamentally, he also relies on two essential and indissolubly related strategies, not, however, inaugurated by the Puritans, as Youngberg implies, but adapted by these "exceptionalists" from the historical origins of the West (when it defined its sedentary social existence in opposition to the nomadism of those non-human humans who "roamed" the "*terra incognita*" beyond *orbis terrarum* or the metropolitan City). These were (1) the concept of *terra nullius*, which implied not only the subhumanity of its inhabitants, as Youngberg implies, but also, it is important to add, *their threat to the Providential/Historical errand:*

> John Cotton, responding to the ethical concerns of his congregation, claims that one way God makes room for his people is by leading them to " 'uninhabited' space":
>
> > God makes room for a People in three ways. . . . When he makes a Countrey, though not altogether void of inhabitants, yet the void in the place where they reside. Where there is a vacant place, there is liberty for the Son of *Adam* or *Noah* to come and inhabit, though they neither buy it, nor ask their leaves. (4)

Likewise, O'Sullivan implies that the separation of Texas from Mexico was inevitable because the territory had primarily an Anglo-American, not a Mexican, population. Moreover, it was by no fault of the American government that the squatters came to be there but by the tacit invitation of the Mexican government (Texas, 3). Aside from his obliviousness to historical fact, in this reasoning, O'Sullivan recycles the Puritanical justification of territorial theft in order to legitimate squatters' rights (*MMD*, 321). And (2) the "husbandry," that is, the cultivation of the empty land:

> If they [the Mexicans] are not tending the land, then it can be rightfully taken away. Again, like John Cotton—who states that "in a vacant Soyle, he hath taken possession of it, and bestoweth culture and husbandry upon it, his Right it is"—O'Sullivan legitimated the annexation of Mexican territory on the premise that the Mexican government could not properly care for it and the American government could:
>
> > Imbecile and distracted, Mexico never can exert any real governmental authority over such a country [O'Sullivan is referring here not to Texas but to California.] The impotence of the one and the distance

> of the other, must make the relation one of virtual independence; unless, by stunting the province of all natural growth, and forbidding that immigration [of the Anglo-American] which can alone develop its capabilities and fulfill the purpose of its creation, tyranny may retain military dominion, which is no government in the legitimate sense of the term. (*MMD*, 232)[11]

3

What I have said thus far about the genealogy of the state of exception that has become the global rule in the post-9/11 era under the aegis of the American exceptionalist ethos is indisputable, but nevertheless inadequate in its generality. Though my affirmation of the indissoluble relation between the logic of American exceptionalism and the state of exception is essentially self-evident and goes far to modify Agamben's exclusive genealogical focus on the European juridical history of the state of exception, it still lacks the specific American onto-cultural dimension of its genealogy: that which gives the relationship its inescapable, distinguishing, and abiding force. I am referring to the American jeremiad, the Puritan ideological strategy that, as Sacvan Bercovitch has decisively shown in *The American Jeremiad*, his radical revision of Perry Miller's representation of American Puritanism, became in the course of American historical expansion hegemonic: a defining cultural ritual of the American national identity and thus its truth discourse.

The genealogy of the American jeremiad, according to Bercovitch, had its activating origins in the post-covenantal period of Puritanism (which he calls the "Halfway Covenant"), the crisis period inaugurated, not incidentally, by the insurrection of the American natives that the Puritans called "King Philip's War." This was the period when the second generation of Puritans, having gained temporal distance from the immediate crisis conditions of the first generation of settlers—the conditions that enabled both the covenantal character and the concomitant youthful energy that were the supreme requisites for the fulfillment of their divinely ordained errand—began backsliding or, in the prefigural language they adopted from their Old Testament Israelite precursors, "murmuring,"[12] thus threatening the covenant, which is to say, both the unity of the Puritan community and the will to fulfill its divinely ordained vocation. In other words, the Puritans, in the aftermath of their inaugural encounter with the rejuvenating New World wilderness, were confronted with the apparently irreconcilable paradox of their civilizing mission: insofar as civilizing—

cultivating, taming, domesticating ("bettering" is the term appropriated by their pioneer heirs)[13]—was necessarily accompanied by the fruit of their labor in the vineyard of the Lord—that is, physical and psychic satisfactions, comfort, the well-being, the repose of the laborers—it also threatened to entropically void the very dynamic energy and dissolve the community that was the prerequisite of the errand. At this post-covenantal moment, in other words, the American Puritans were compelled to confront the inescapable paradox of civilizational recidivism: the danger of their exceptional New World regressing to an old World, that is, back to the very unexceptional—lethargic, self-satisfied, decadent—type ("flesh-pots") that they, like their Old Testament Israelite prefigurations, had defined themselves against and that had instigated their Exodus.

The Puritans' "solution" to this dilemma, as Bercovitch enablingly (though partially) observed, was the jeremiad: the recurrent ritualized reminder to the covenantal community not only of the dangers to the errand of backsliding, but also, and even more important, the simultaneous instigation of a *perpetual sense of crisis* intended to instigate in the individual members the *perpetual anxiety* that would always already rejuvenate and reunify the covenantal community. This is how Bercovitch, using Samuel Danforth's classic election-day address "Brief Recognition of New England's Errand into the Wilderness" (May 1670, "exactly forty years after the *Arabella*")[14] as his exemplary text, puts the Puritans' fateful "solution" to the problem of recidivism:

> In effect, Danforth [is] reinforcing [John] Cotton's analogy and [John] Winthrop's model of vocation by reminding his audience that the prophecies they inherited, their promised future, entailed "the values of piety, frugality, and diligence in one's worldly calling."[15] Economically as well as figurally, it was their mission to leave a "soft" Old World order, with its "courtly pomp and decay," for a "purer" kind of society, one that would provide them with the proper means for both "respectable competence in the world and eternal salvation in the world to come."
>
> So understood, the nature of the errand goes far toward explaining the distinctive form and function of the American Puritan jeremiad. The European jeremiad *developed within a static hierarchical order*; the lessons it taught, about historical recurrence and the vanity of human wishes, amounted to a massive ritual reinforcement of tradition. Its function was to make social practice conform to a completed and perfected social ideal. The American Puritan jeremiad was the ritual of a culture on an errand—which is to say, a culture based on a faith in process. Substituting teleology for hierarchy, it discarded the Old World ideal of stasis for a New World vision of the future. Its function was to create a climate of anxiety that

> helped release the restless "progressivist" energies required for the success of the venture. The European jeremiad also thrived on anxiety, of course. Like all "traditionalist" forms of ritual, it used fear and trembling to teach acceptance of fixed social norms. But the American Puritan jeremiad went much further. *It made anxiety its end as well as its means. Crisis was the social norm it sought to inculcate.* The very concept of errand, after all, implied a state of *un*fulfillment. The future, though divinely assured, was never quite there, and New England's Jeremiahs set out *to provide the sense of insecurity that would ensure the outcome*. Denouncing or affirming, their vision fed on the [perpetual] distance between promise and fact. (*AJ*, 22–23; my emphasis)

Bercovitch did not perceive the radical implications of his otherwise decisive diagnosis of the American jeremiadic aspect of Puritan exceptionalism and his proleptic insight into the origins of the American national identity in 1978 for two related reasons. First, he did not clearly perceive that the particular structure of the Puritan jeremiad, itself, had its enabling origins in the deeper concept of the Protestant *felix culpa*, which distinguished the Protestant worldly vocation from that of "prelatical" Old World Catholicism, the concept that interpreted Adam's eating of the fruit of the tree of knowledge, not as catastrophe as such, but paradoxically as a "fortunate fall," in that, in exiling him from Paradise into the world of temporal history—that is, to anticipate, the world of *perpetual crisis*—he was deprived, as John Milton puts the thesis of *Paradise Lost* in the "Areopagitica," of his easy "cloistered virtue" and rendered him a dynamic agent of God's creative errand in the world:

> I cannot praise a fugitive and cloister'd vertue, unexcercis'd & unbreath'd, that never sallies out and sees her adversary, but slinks out of the race, where that immortal garland is to be run for, not without dust and heat. Assuredly we bring not innocence into the world, we bring impurity much rather: *that which purifies us is trial, and trial is by what is contrary*. The vertue therefore which is but a youngling in the contemplation of evill, and knows not the utmost that vice promises to her followers, and rejects it, is but blank virtue, and not pure; her whiteness is but an excremental whiteness.[16]

Second, and in a related way, it was, as I have observed elsewhere,[17] Bercovitch's failure to historicize the resonant abstractions—"anxiety," "crisis," "insecurity"—he thematized and foregrounded. To be more specific, he failed to clearly identify the crisis condition that instigated the rejuvenating and mobilizing anxiety as the nomadic native *enemy* (those who "roamed" rather than inhabited the wilderness) that "threatened" their divinely ordained errand, or, to put it alternatively, as the *frontier* between "Civilization" and "savagery" (Paradise and the fallen world). Indeed, Bercovitch, in *American Jeremiad*, affirms the "Puritan thesis" about the origins of the American national identity against the "frontier thesis" first posited by the historian Frederick Jackson Turner at the time of the official announcement of the closing of the frontier by the U.S. Census Bureau at the end of the nineteenth century—the thesis sponsored by the Myth and Symbol School of American Studies in the 1950s on behalf of America's cause in the Cold War against communism. In so doing, Bercovitch was prevented from perceiving the indissoluble continuity of his revisionary Puritan theological thesis, which overdetermined its unifying function, and the reigning Myth and Symbol School's secular frontier thesis—the American national identity's need for a perpetual frontier/enemy, which overdertermined its rejuvenating function. As I observed in *American Exceptionalism in the Age of Globalization*:

> In pointing to Bercovitch's overdetermination of the unifying potentialities of the American jeremiad at the expense of its rejuvenating effects—the solidarity of the community in behalf of the errand at the expense of renewal that would render its civil life immune to decay—I am not opting for the "frontier" thesis about the development of the American national identity. Rather, I am suggesting that Bercovitch's thesis about the role played by the American jeremiad needs to incorporate and emphasize the "fact of the frontier" instead of minimizing it. Bercovitch is right in singling out the jeremiad as that cultural ritual that more than any other explains the development of the American national character and the elect's domestic and foreign policies. But this cultural ritual—this communal agency for the renewal of the commonweal's covenant with God—must, I suggest, be understood not simply in domestic terms (as the solidarity of civil society), but also, and simultaneously in terms of its "foreign" relations (the threatening "Other" beyond the American frontier). In the wake of the demise of the Puritan theocracy and the constitutional separation of church and state, the "fact of the frontier" came to dominate the discourse of an ever-westward expanding America, but it is the jeremiad—the concept of providential/optimistic history on which it is founded—not in a purely secular form, as liberals have erroneously assumed, but in a religio-secular—"natural supernaturalist"—form, that has determined the meaning of its various and fluid historical manifestations. And, as in the case of the Puritans, though increasingly as America rationalized and banalized the "wilderness," its purpose has been not to close the frontier and terminate the errand, but to keep it perpetually open, even after the

> farthest western reaches of the continent had been settled and colonized. Its purpose has been to *always already produce crisis and the communal anxiety crisis instigates* not simply to mobilize the national consensus and a flagging patriotism, but also to inject by violence the American body politic with antibiotics against decay. (AE, 197–198)

In short, what Bercovitch, in the central passage from *American Jeremiad* quoted above, is intuiting about the ritual structure of the Puritan jeremiad without naming it, as his own rhetoric bears remarkable witness—the "anxiety" that energizes and unifies, the "crisis" as "the social norm it sought to inculcate," the "insecurity" that overdetermines the value of [homeland] security—is this: In "solving" the problem of generational recidivism, the loss of the defining exceptionalist status, inhering in their civilizing errand in the wilderness—by invoking the concept of Protestant *felix culpa*—the need for a perpetual crisis-provoking, reunifying, and rejuvenating frontier/enemy—the founding American Puritans implicitly *identified their exceptionalist ethos (their Election by a transcendental Logos) with the normalization of the state of exception, the suspension of the Law (in order, ostensibly, to preserve it), the establishment of the permanent security state, and ultimately with the dehumanizing (bio)cultural and political imperatives intrinsic to the state of exception*: what Giorgio Agamben encapsulates in the term "bare life," life that can be killed without the killing being called homicide.

It is this American *onto-political* version of the normalization of the state of exception, however, that needs to be emphasized for the purpose of the argument of this chapter. Agamben's genealogy of the normalization of the state of exception in the post-9/11 age of globalization, is, as I stated at the outset, restricted to the European history of jurisprudential law and is thus Eurocentric in essence (the United States is simply included in its orbit). This modified version of Bercovitch's genealogy of the American national identity, on the other hand, reveals that the normalized state of exception and the accompanying biopolitics of the security state are not only constitutional/juridical categories, which are thus easily identifiable and, theoretically at least, subject to resistance, but also ontological—the "Truth" of a Higher Cause (first, The Puritan Deity, and then History (Manifest Destiny). In this version, that is, the ontological dimension, the logic of American exceptionalism is prior to, indeed, justifies the constitutional and the juridical. It is, to repeat, hegemonic, and thus far more difficult to perceive, let alone resist.

4

Understood in the context of this revision of Bercovitch's Puritan genealogy of the American national identity—this disclosure of the indissoluble complicity between the logic of the American exceptionalist state and the state of exception—the "secular" history of the United States that follows the Puritan founding unerringly reveals not only the intrinsic need for a rejuvenating frontier/enemy. In thus rendering the state of exception (crisis) the rule, this history also discloses—contrapuntally, as it were—the recurrent aggressive (offensive) violence the United States has always disavowed in the name of (defensive) security: the counterhistory of the spectacular monumentalized history[18] that has perennially represented the United States as "redeemer nation."[19]

This increasing secularization (and hegemonization) of the theologically ordained "Puritan jeremiad" (and the state of exception it normalizes) is, as Bercovitch's genealogy has shown, mirrored in the "American jeremiad" it eventually became, and is patently manifest in the discursive (cultural) and political history of the United States following the decline of the Puritan theocracy. I refer to the post-Revolution history of the "pioneering" era of westward expansion and, as we have seen by way of the notorious example of John O'Sullivan, Manifest Destiny, to the extension of the continental frontier, first, into the Pacific (the Hawaiian and the Philippines) after its official closing at the end of the nineteenth century with the settlement of California, and then, as we shall see, under the aegis of President John F. Kennedy and America's Cold War crisis, to Southeast Asia (Vietnam)—the "New Frontier," in the prevailing language of his administration.

I cannot, of course, in the limited space available, do justice to this unerring, however uneven, American exceptionalist history, in which the perennial paradoxical search for an enemy and the state of emergency are determinative. It will have to suffice simply to point briefly to a few relatively self-evident exemplary moments of this cumulative history, and then amplify at greater length on its culminating or, more precisely, disclosive liminal moment. I mean the moment when, in the wake of 9/11, *al Qaeda*'s traumatizing attack on the American homeland, President George W. Bush, as Commander in Chief, proclaimed his unending War on Terror in the name of the American exceptionalist ethos and overtly decreed the state of exception as the global rule.

Given the jeremiad's ability to resolve the essential problem of the Puritans' historical condition, it is no accident, then, that, following their modification of the exceptionalist ethos to include the jeremiad—the need for an anxiety-provoking frontier/enemy—this solution became, in Edward Said's terms, a "textual attitude"[20] for their more secular, post-revolutionary descendants, who undertook their "pioneering," that is, westward expansionist (ethnic cleansing and imperial) project, according to its paradoxical dictates. This, for example, is the essential witness of the cultural historian Richard Slotkin, one of the precursors, like Bercovitch, of the New American studies, in the three volumes of his magisterial series on the counter-history of American canonical cultural production from the Puritan era to the period of the Vietnam War, from the Puritan apologists and Mary Rowlandson's captivity narrative (*The Sovereignty and Goodness of God* [1682]) through James Fenimore Cooper's Leatherstocking novels, Ralph Waldo Emerson's prose, and Walt Whitman's poetry, to William J. Lederer and Eugene Burdick's *Ugly American* (1958) and beyond. Anticipating Bercovitch in his inaugural volume, Slotkin, in the context of the Vietnam War, shows with great force, if not with the precision of the former, thus pointing to the relationality between American exceptionalism and the state of exception, that the celebrated civilizing pioneering enterprise was a myth—a "textual attitude"—that in reality was, as he puts it in the title and in the introduction, a matter of "regeneration through violence":

> It is by now a commonplace that our adherence to the "myth of the frontier"—the conception of America as a wide-open land of unlimited opportunity for the strong, ambitious, self-reliant individual to thrust his way to the top—has blinded us to the consequences of the industrial and urban revolutions and to the need for social reforms and a new concept of individual and communal welfare. Nor is it by a far-fetched association that the murderous violence that has characterized recent political life has been linked by poets and news commentators alike to the "frontier psychology" of our recent past and our heritage. *The first colonists saw in America opportunity to regenerate their fortunes, their spirits, and the power of their church and nation; but the means to that regeneration ultimately became the means of violence, and the myth of regeneration through violence became the structuring metaphor of the American experience.* How that myth evolved and gained credence and power is the subject of this study.[21] (emphasis in original)

This literary search for a unifying and rejuvenating enemy and the tacit normalization of the state of exception by nineteenth-century exceptionalist American poets and novelists is also everywhere evident in the monumental (canonical) nineteenth-century histories of the United States by Francis Parkman and George Bancroft. Indeed, these celebratory spectacular histories tacitly repeat the centrality of the exceptionalist (Protestant) New World ethos and the History-ordained success of the errand (the "doomed Indian"), the anxiety over the waning of the frontier, and the American jeremiadic theme of the frontier/enemy (rejuvenation through violence) in their contents. Thus, for example, Parkman summarily writes—triumphantly and anxiously—in the context of the *accomplished* "Conquest of Canada," which he represents as "an event of momentous consequence in American history":

> It changed the political aspect of the continent, prepared for the independence of the British colonies, rescued the vast tracts of the interior from the rule of military despotism [the Old World French], and gave them, eventually, to the keeping of an ordered democracy. Yet to the red natives of the soil its results were wholly disastrous. Could the French have maintained their ground, the ruin of the Indian tribes might long have been postponed; but the victory of Quebec was the signal of their swift decline. Thenceforth they were destined to melt and vanish before the advancing waves of Anglo-American power, which now rolled westward unchecked and unopposed. They saw the danger and, led by a great and daring champion [Pontiac], struggled fiercely to avert it. The history of the epoch, crowded as it is with scenes of tragic interest . . . has been as yet unwritten, buried in the archives of governments, or among the obscurer records of private adventure. To rescue it from oblivion is the object of the following work. *It aims to portray the American forests and the American Indian at the period when both received their final doom.*[22] (my emphasis)

Equally, if not more important, as the exemplary anxiety of the last sentence of the above quotation testifies, these scholarly nineteenth histories of American westward expansion, like O'Sullivan's ideological journalistic prose, are themselves, in Bercovitch's terms, patently American jeremiads *in form*, published, like the Puritans' election-day sermons two centuries before, to instigate anxiety—and a collective sense of crisis (emergency)—in an Eastern American body politic that, having grown civilizationally soft, was in danger of reverting to Old World decadence.

One could invoke many other telling examples prior to the liminal post-9/11 occasion of this obsessive American jeremiadic search for a rejuvenating frontier/enemy in the face of an over-civilization that threatened to annul America's exceptionalism—and the inevitable, if tacit, establishment of the state of exception and the national security state as the norm it entailed. Two resonant *fin-de-siècle* instances immediately come to mind: Mark Twain's celebrated end-of-the-century jeremiadic novel, *A Connecticut Yankee in King Arthur's Court* (1889), which, by way of the Connecticut Yankee's contrasting self-reliance, New World practicality, and empirical knowledge (as opposed to Merlin's Old World magic), points to the corruption of the democratic American pioneering spirit by the end-of-the century industrialist magnates, appropriately called "robber barons" to suggest their reversion to Old World tyranny and decadence—and thus to the urgent need for the rejuvenation (through violence) of the covenantal people;[23] and Frederick Jackson Turner's "The Significance of the Frontier in American History" (1893), which anxiously calls for a new frontier in the face of the official closing of the American frontier, a closing that, for Turner, meant, above all, the atrophy of the pioneering spirit that defined the American, "New World" national identity.[24] But for the sake of brevity and exemplary historical scope, I will restrict my remarks to William J. Lederer's and Eugene Burdick's *Ugly American* (1958), the mediocre but extremely influential novel published early in the Cold War era in response to Grahame Greene's devastating criticism of the American exceptionalist ethos in *The Quiet American* (1954),[25] because, like Parkman's and Bancroft's histories a century before, this novel, so reminiscent of what Said calls "the textual attitude," is a quintessential American jeremiad both in its content and in its form. That is, its essential ideological intention is not only to underscore America's post–World War II recidivist complacency in the face of what it refers to, with almost paranoid force, as the emergence of the Soviet Union's bid for global hegemony, epitomized by its alleged intention to gain control over all of Southeast Asia (the "Domino Theory"), but also to point to the urgency of the need of a new frontier and the permanent crisis- or emergency-situation that would renew the decaying American body politic, that, literally, would recuperate the youthful and self-reliant exceptionalist pioneering spirit.

Lederer and Burdick accomplish this crude ideological end of their American jeremiad by first depicting the American diplomatic corps—epitomized first by the mediocre Ambassador Louis Sears and the representatives of the American media (Joe Bing)—in Sarkhan (the fictitious name of a Southeast Asian country intended to recall the post-colonial Vietnam) as having become effete and thus oblivious to the redemptive American calling (vocation)—to the exceptionalist ethos of the heroic American past and the errand. Indeed, aided and abetted by their ventriloquized fictitious natives (Ruth Jyoti, for example), the authors characterize the American establishment in Southeast Asia as having reverted perilously close to the arrogant, self-satisfied Old World colonial predecessors (the French), who live their positions of authority in the colonial country as a sinecure, an opportunity for easy luxurious living, and, of course, blindly indifferent to the needs of and dangers facing the vulnerable native people, above all, to the highly sophisticated and insidious machinations of the neighboring communist countries.

Then, to counter this recidivist state, the authors introduce a variety of minority Americans who, unlike their jaded superiors, have not been adulterated by the virus of overcivilization. Like the self-reliant pioneers of the frontier era, they embody the American exceptionalist ethos. Patently reminiscent of Daniel Boone, Davy Crockett, Kit Carson, James Fenimore Cooper's Natty Bumppo, and other mythic American stereotypes who have been perennially represented as fleeing from the encroaching civilized settlement into the wilderness, these figures, enacting the American calling, disdain the sedentary existence of their superiors in the capitals of these "vulnerable" Southeast Asian countries, preferring, like their legendary pioneer ancestors, to leave the comforts of the city and to mingle with—and learn from—the natives in the wilderness.

What Lederer and Burdick's jeremiad disavows in thus emphasizing the "benign" intent of these American exceptionalist figures, however, is that their real purpose in staging this fictional opposition between American officials and American "mavericks" was to instigate the complacent post–World War II American government in Washington into recognizing Southeast Asia as a critical new frontier: a global crisis zone between democracy and communism, good and evil, civilization and barbarism, that would recharge America's (neo)imperial errand in the world's wilderness. And this recognition is precisely what Lederer and Burdick's jeremiadic novel contributed enormously toward accomplishing. (As the caption under the title of the 1999 reissue puts it: "The multi-million-copy best seller whose title became a synonym for what was wrong with American foreign policy.") Given the deeply inscribed historical background I have all too briefly touched upon and its ideological appropriation by Lederer and Burdick in *The Ugly American*, it is no accident, that, despite the muted references to the Cold War occasion, John F. Kennedy identified his future, new, and youthful Cold War presidential administration, in his speech accepting his nomination in

1960, as "The New Frontier." "Facing west" (his speech was delivered in the Memorial Coliseum in Los Angeles), bemoaning the old-age complacency of the immediate American past, and underscoring his youth, he re-called the erring American people to their original vocation, the errand in the new New World wilderness, in the following, by now familiar, jeremiadic way:

> There has been a change—a slippage—in our intellectual and moral strength. Seven lean years of drouth and famine have withered a field of ideas. Blight has descended on our regulatory agencies—and dry rot, beginning in Washington, is seeping into every corner of America—in the payola mentality, the expense account way of life, the confusion between what is legal and what is right. Too many Americans have lost their way, their will and their sense of historic purpose.
>
> It is time, in short, for a new generation of leadership—new men with new problems and new opportunities. . . . For I stand tonight facing west on what was the last frontier. From the lands that stretch three thousand miles behind me, the pioneers of old gave up their safety, their comfort and sometimes their lives to build a new world in the West. They were not the captives of their doubts, the prisoners of their price tags. Their motto was not "every man for himself"—but "all for the common cause." They were determined to make that new world strong and free, to overcome its hazards and its hardships, to conquer the enemies that threatened from without and within.
>
> Today some would say that those struggles are all over—that all the horizons have been explored—that all the battles have been won—that there is no longer an American frontier.
>
> But I trust that no one in this vast assemblage will agree with those sentiments. For the problems are not all solved and the battles are not all won—and we stand today on the edge of a New Frontier—the frontier of the 1960's—a frontier of unknown opportunities and perils—a frontier of unfulfilled hopes and threats. . . .
>
> But I believe the times demand new invention, innovation, imagination, decision. I am asking each of you to be pioneers on the New Frontier. My call is to the young in heart, regardless of age—to all who respond to the Scriptural call: "Be strong and of good courage; be not afraid, neither be thou dismayed."[26]

Kennedy's jeremiad, we now know, in hindsight, was a gesture, which, in fact, inaugurated a decade or more of crisis, during which the state of exception and the security state became the tacit norm, and, as the pervasive obscene practice of the "body count" as the determinant of progress in the war testifies ("A dead Gook is a VC"), human life was reduced to bare life. That is to say, for the purpose of the argument of this chapter, the United States' brutal conduct of the war, undertaken against a people seeking independence from colonial rule, in the exceptionalist name of the New Frontier, inaugurated what I am calling the *liminal* point of the development of the exceptional logic of the American expectionalist ethos. What was hitherto tacit—and disavowable—under the benign aegis of domesticating the wilderness, began to manifest itself overtly: the will to power and violence informing the divinely or History-ordained errand. This, for example, is the inescapable testimony of the reporter Michael Herr in the "dispatches" he sent from "Indian country" back to the United States, forcefully epitomized by the following reference to the Tet Offensive (1968):

> Our worst dread of yellow peril became realized; we saw them now dying by the thousands all over the country, yet they didn't seem depleted, let alone exhausted, as the Mission was claiming by the fourth day. We took space back quickly, expensively, with total panic and close to maximum brutality. Our machine was devastating. And versatile. It could do everything but stop. As one American major said, in a successful attempt at attaining history, "We had to destroy Ben Tre in order to save it." That's how most of the country came back under what we called control, and how it remained essentially occupied by the Viet Cong and the North until the day years later when there were none of us left.[27]

This disclosive liminal period extended from the Vietnam War through the first Gulf War and, after the bombing of the World Trade Center and the Pentagon on September 11, 2001, to the second Gulf War: George W. Bush's invasion of Afghanistan and Iraq. And it bears overt witness, however unevenly and incrementally, to what was inauguratively disclosed during the Vietnam War: the indissoluble relationship, hitherto tacit and disavowable in the American past, between the logic of American exceptionalism and the state of exception.

5

From this cultural perspective on the modern history of the United States, one of the two most significant enabling recent events was the implosion of the Soviet Union (1989–1991) and the termination of the

Cold War. For this end not only facilitated the marginalization of the memory of the humiliating defeat of the United States in Vietnam but gave credence to the dominant culture's recuperative effort to represent the protest movement during the war as a symptom of a national neurosis (the "Vietnam Syndrome"). It also, as the example of Francis Fukuyama's euphoric *The End of History* (1994) testifies,[28] enabled the United States to recuperate its damaged American exceptionalist ethos. But, it is important to add, the end of the Cold War was also significant in this context because, as we shall see, it signaled, like the closing of the American frontier at the end of the nineteenth century to Frederick Jackson Turner, the closing of the New Frontier, or, to invoke its allotrope, the demise of exceptionalist America's rejuvenating enemy.

The second enabling event in the post-Vietnam era was, of course, the September 11, 2001, bombing by *al Qaeda* of the World Trade Center and the Pentagon, the symbols of the economic and political system that, to the dominant American culture, made the United States exceptional. For, as we now know, this unprecedented attack on American soil provided the George W. Bush administration with both the rejuvenating enemy it had lost with the end of the Cold War, and the justification to finish what the first Gulf War did not: not simply the achievement of military and political hegemony in the Middle East, but also what, in the name of American exceptionalism, the neoconservative intellectual deputies of the Bush administration (Project for the New American Century [PNAC]) unabashedly referred to, long before the invasion, as the global *Pax Americana*.[29]

What was predictable about President Bush's response to the foreign attacks on American soil was, of course, his repeated invocation of the American exceptionalist ethos, which, echoing the periodic calls of the dominant Anglo-Protestant culture for "a Great Awakening,"[30] took the precise form of appeals to the perennial American calling and the intrinsic ritual of the American jeremiad in his addresses to the covenantal American people. For example, in the State of the Union speech delivered in the wake of his declaration of the United States' War on Terror (the invasion of Afghanistan), Bush, echoing the Puritan founders' jeremiad, concluded: "We can't stop short. If we stop now—leaving terror camps intact and terrorist states unchecked—our sense of security would be false and temporary. History has called America and our allies to action, and it is both our responsibility and our privilege to fight freedom's fight."[31] What, however, was unprecedented in Bush's responses was his unilateral declaration, as Commander in Chief of the U.S. Armed

Forces, not, as in former times, of war against a namable nation, but his administration's "War on Terror," a sovereign decision, undertaken in the name of the American exceptionalist ethos, that in the indefiniteness of its object, implied both its global scope and its unending nature:

> States like these ["rogue states" such as North Korea, Iraq, and Iran] and their allies constitute an axis of evil, arming to threaten the peace of the world. By seeking weapons of mass destruction [the reference is to Iraq, which, according to the Bush administration's (deliberately false) representation, was manufacturing the atomic bomb and thus subject to invasion], these regimes pose a grave and growing danger. They could provide these arms to terrorists, give them the means to match their hatred. They could attack our allies or attempt to blackmail the United States. In any of the cases, the price of indifference would be catastrophic.
>
> We will work close with our coalition to deny terrorists and their state sponsors the materials, technology, and expertise to make and deliver weapons of mass destruction. We will develop and deploy effective missile defenses to protect America and our allies from sudden attack. *And all nations should know: Americans will do what is necessary to ensure our nation's security.* [my emphasis]
>
> We'll be deliberate, yet time is not on our side. *I will not wait on events, while dangers gather.* I will not stand by, as peril draws closer. The United States of America will not permit the world's most dangerous regimes to threaten us with the world's most destructive weapons.
>
> Our war on terror is well begun, but it is only begun. This campaign may not be finished on our watch—yet it must be and will be waged on our watch.

In thus pushing the logic of American exceptionalism to its liminal point, President Bush rendered the state of exception, which hitherto was undeclared, patently manifest as the global norm:

> The security environment confronting the United Sates today is radically different from what we have faced before [when, during the Reagan administration, "containment" was the fundamental policy]. Yet the first duty of the United States Government remains what it always has been: to protect the American people and American interests. It is an enduring American principle that this duty obligates the government to anticipate and counter threats, using all elements of national power, before the threats can do grave damage. The greater the threat, the greater the risk of inaction—and the more compelling the case for taking anticipatory action to defend ourselves, even if uncertainty remains as to the time and

> place of the enemy's attack. There are few greater threats than a terrorist attack with WMD [weapons of mass destruction].
>
> To forestall or prevent such hostile acts by our adversaries, the United States will, if necessary, act preemptively in exercising our inherent right of self-defense. The United States will not resort to force in all cases to preempt emerging threats. Our preference is that nonmilitary actions succeed. And no country should ever use preemption as a pretext for aggression. (*AN*)

In the domestic sphere, as the above example of "The Bush Doctrine" implies, this evental sovereign executive decision took the form of the Homeland Security State, in which the government assumed the power to police the private lives of American citizens at the expense of the First Amendment on behalf of the security of the state. In the global contest, this sovereign decision manifested itself in the unprecedented—and internationally illegal—adoption of the policies of preemptive war against what President Bush unilaterally deemed "rogue states"; "regime change," which entailed the imposition of American-style governments (ventriloquized puppet regimes) on the subdued people; the establishment of extralegal detention centers such as Guantánamo and other sites of "extraordinary rendition," where terrorist suspects could be incarcerated without recourse to the law and tortured (or, as the euphemism employed by the legal counsel of the Bush administration put it, undergo "enhanced methods of interrogation") with impunity; and the staging of the spectacle—the "shock and awe" military tactics reminiscent of the tactics employed by the early colonizers of the "uncivilized" non-Western world, intended to strike the "backward" spectators dumb: bereave them of speech and the polity speech implies. Justified by the exceptionalist redeemer state that ironically normalizes the violence of the state of exception (blurs the border between human life and politics), all these exceptionalist tenets of the liminal "Bush Doctrine" are manifestly oriented toward the biopolitics that, as Agamben, following the directives of Michel Foucault and Hannah Arendt, observes, reduces human life to bare life, life that can be killed without the act being called homicide. And, in thus recalling the inexorable metamorphosis of the Weimar Republic into the Nazis' totalitarian Third Reich, they point ominously to the (detention) camp as the paradigm of the future city:

> Along with the emergence of biopolitics, we can observe a displacement and gradual expansion beyond the limits of the decision on bare life, in the state of exception, in which sovereignty consisted. If there is a

> line in every modern state marking the point at which the decision on life becomes a decision on death, and biopolitics can turn into thanatopolitics, this line no longer appears today as a stable border dividing two clearly distinct zones. This line is now in motion and gradually moving into areas other than that of political life, areas in which the sovereign is entering into an ever more intimate symbiosis not only with the jurist but also with the doctor, the scientist, the expert, and the priest. . . . [C]ertain events that are fundamental for the political history of modernity (such as the declaration of rights), as well as others that seem instead to represent an incomprehensible intrusion of biologico-scientific principles into the political order (such as National Socialist eugenics and its elimination of "life that is unworthy of being lived," or the contemporary debate on the normative determination of death criteria) acquire their true sense only if they are brought back to the common biopolitical (or thanatopolitical) context to which they belong. From this perspective, the camp—as the pure, absolute, and impassable biopolitical space (insofar as it is founded solely on the state of exception)—will appear as the hidden paradigm of the political space of modernity, whose metamorphoses and disguises we will have to learn to recognize. (*HS*, 122–123)

At this liminal point of the unerring incremental development of its logic, to put this analysis of the post-9/11 Bush Doctrine alternatively, the American exceptionalist ethos (theoretically) self-de-structs. The hegemonic status it achieved after the secularization of the Puritan theological errand reverts to the (conscious) ideology it was at its origin. In other words, this post-9/11 liminal point discloses the hitherto concealed complicity of the American exceptionalist ethos with the state of exception as the norm—the violence it has always disavowed in the name of the redemptive errand. But in so doing, it is necessary to point out, it also unconceals the potential of an alternative *polis* to that of the security state.

6

The preceding New Americanist genealogy tracing the post-9/11 security state and its normalization of the state of exception to the American Puritan jeremiad could, of course, be interpreted as an ideological imposition on American history from a radical leftist perspective. But the ironic fact is that my argument derives as much from one of the most influential neoconservative intellectual deputies of the George W.

Bush administration as it does from Sacvan Bercovitch's studies of the Puritan heritage of the American national identity. I am referring to Samuel P. Huntington, the neoconservative exponent of the notorious "clash of civilizations" thesis about the contemporary world,[32] who, in 2004, undertook a systematic justification of President Bush's flagging War on Terror in a book anxiously entitled *Who Are We? Challenges to the American National Identity*. Since I have written elsewhere at length on Huntington's book,[33] here I will only briefly underscore those aspects of this liminal, post-9/11 justification of the Bush Doctrine that demonstrate its kinship with the American jeremiad and its crisis-producing structural apparatuses.

What, in fact, is remarkable about *Who Are We?* is that, unlike its many post-Puritan predecessors, which, as we have seen, were unconscious American jeremiads, Huntington's version, in keeping with the liminality of the post-9/11 occasion, is, like its original, a conscious jeremiad both in its content and structure. In justifying President Bush's preemptive wars against Afghanistan and Iraq as harboring terrorists, he proffers a historical narrative of the formation of the American national identity that, remarkably like Bercovitch's thesis, but from a celebratory perspective, not only locates its origins in the Puritans' divinely ordained exodus from the Old World and their exceptionalist errand in the New World's wilderness, but also in their insistent employment of the jeremiad to resolve the paradox of the civilizing process: the backsliding that threatened to erode their self-defining exceptionalism. Thus, after Huntington establishes the *raison d'être* of his timely meditation on the American national identity—the crisis of the recidivism of the American public in the face of the disclosure of the Bush administration's prevarications on the issue of Saddam Hussein's weapons of mass destruction—he goes on, like Bercovitch, to locate the origins of the exceptionalist American identity in the Puritans' divinely ordained Massachusetts Bay Colony. All too reminiscent, not incidentally, of Foucault's devastating Nietzschean parody of the traditional historian—the liminal monumentalist who, in willfully "reestablishing the high points of historical development and their maintenance in a perpetual presence," produces a history that, in its total devotion to veneration, "bars access to the actual intensities and creations of life"—Huntington writes:

> The settling of America was, of course, a result of economic and other motives, as well as religious ones. Yet religion still was central. . . . Religious intensity was undoubtedly greatest among the Puritans, especially

> in Massachusetts. They took the lead in defining their settlement based on "a Covenant with God" to create "a city on a hill" as a model for all the world, and a people of other Protestant faiths soon also came to see themselves and America in a similar way. In the seventeenth and eighteenth centuries Americans defined their mission in the New World in biblical terms. They were a "chosen people," on an "errand in the wilderness," creating "the new Israel" or the "new Jerusalem" in what was clearly "the promised land." America was the site of a "new Heaven and a new earth, the home of justice," God's country. The settlement of America was vested, as Sacvan Bercovitch put it, "with all the material, spiritual, and intellectual appeal of a religious quest." The sense of holy mission was easily expanded into millenarian themes of America as "the redeemer nation" and "the visionary republic." (*WAW*, 64)[34]

What is noteworthy about Huntington's summary monumentalist history, however, is not simply its focus on the exceptionalist origins of the American national identity. As Huntington's repeated identification of the Puritans, or as he puts the national identity they founded, the "Anglo-Protestant core culture," as "settlers" of the New World pointedly suggests, he is also defining the crucial essence of their covenantal society in anticipation of the particular form the threat of recidivism will take in contemporary America. This becomes manifestly clear in the crude, anti-democratic distinction Huntington makes between the early settlers and the later, to him, essentially parasitical "immigrants." Taking his structural directives from the jeremiad—and, not incidentally, the Puritans' concept of *terra nullius*—he asserts, in a way that makes the normally hidden undemocratic violence of the exceptionalist ethos patent:

> Settlers and immigrants differ fundamentally. Settlers leave an existing society, usually in a group, in order to create a new community, a city on the hill, in a new and often distant territory. They are imbued with a sense of collective purpose. Implicitly or explicitly they subscribe to a compact or charter that defines the basis of the community they create and their collective relations to their mother country. Immigrants, in contrast, do not create a new society. They move from one society to a different society. Migration is usually a personal process, involving individuals and families. The seventeenth and eighteenth-century settlers came to America because it was a *tabula rasa*. Apart from Indian tribes, which could be killed off or pushed westward, no society was there; and they came in order to create societies that embodied and would reinforce the culture and values they brought with them from the origin country. Immigrants came later because they wanted to become part of the society

> the settlers created. Unlike settlers, they experienced "culture shock" as they and their offspring attempted to absorb a culture often much at odds with that which they brought with them. Before immigrants could come to America, settlers had to found America (*WAW*, 40)

It was, above all, according to Huntington's neoconservative reading, and in keeping with the anxiety-producing dictates of the jeremiad, what he exaggeratedly called "the deconstructionist movement" in the 1970s, which, in encouraging these hitherto quiescent late "immigrant cultures" to assert their multiple identities—"subnational," he calls them derisively—threatened to disintegrate the covenantal Anglo-Protestant settler core culture ("people") and to atrophy the exceptionalist energy of the nation necessary to carry out its errand in the global wilderness:

> The deconstructionists promoted programs to enhance the status and influence of subnational racial, ethnic, and cultural groups. They encouraged immigrants to maintain their birth country cultures, granted them legal privileges denied to native born Americans, and denounced the idea of Americanization. They pushed the rewriting of history syllabi and text books so as to refer to the "peoples" of the United States in place of the single people of the Constitution. They urged supplementing or substituting for national history the history of subnational groups. They downgraded the centrality of English in American life and pushed bilingual education and linguistic diversity. They advocated legal recognition of group rights and racial preferences over the individual rights central to the American Creed. They justified their actions by theories of multiculturalism and the idea that diversity rather than unity or community should be America's overriding value. The combined effect of these efforts was to promote the deconstruction of the [exceptionalist] American identity that had been gradually created over three centuries and the ascendance of subnational identities. (*WAW*, 143)

It is at this ominous climactic point in his jeremiadic narrative that Huntington re-introduces the idea of the frontier or enemy—the "fault-line" between civilizations is his immediate term—which he has strategically kept in abeyance from the beginning. Unlike his fellow neoconservative Francis Fukuyama, who celebrated the end of the Cold War as the "end of History"—in the Biblical language of "good news"—Huntington, truer to the Puritan tradition, paradoxically, though predictably, emphasizes its negative ideological implications. Following his predecessor American Jeremiahs' fundamental and enabling awareness of the paradox that civilizational advance is always accompanied by decline, he thus represents the loss of the Soviet enemy—peace—as a looming threat to America's exceptionalist status—its unity and youthful energy—and its redemptive errand:

> At the end of the twentieth century, Democracy was left without a significant secular ideological rival, and the United States was left without a peer competitor. Among American foreign policy elites, the results were euphoria, pride, arrogance—and uncertainty. The absence of an ideological threat produced an absence of purpose. "Nations need enemies," Charles Krauthammer commented as the Cold War ended. "Take away one, and they find another." The ideal enemy for America would be ideologically hostile, racially and culturally different, and militarily strong enough to pose a credible threat to American security. The foreign policy debates of the 1990s were already over who might be such an enemy. (*WAW*, 262)

Following the dramatic emergence of the problem of the absent frontier/enemy, Huntington, in a staging for effect worthy of Mark Twain in his novelistic jeremiad *A Connecticut Yankee in King Arthur's Court*, orchestrates a scenario, in a chapter bizarrely entitled "The Search for an Enemy," intended to culminate in a spectacular reference to America's discovery of its "new enemy." With the bombing of the World Trade Center and the Pentagon in mind from the outset, he lists the hypothetical candidates for this role—from Slobodan Milošević and China to the more satisfying threats: Iraq, Iran, Sudan, and Libya. And then, in a rhetoric seemingly implying euphoric relief of a disturbing anxiety, he brings his staged jeremiad to a dramatic conclusion by returning to the spectacular event of 9/11 (and the clash of civilizations thesis) that has been waiting off stage from the beginning:

> The cultural gap between Islam and America's Christian and Anglo-Protestantism reinforces Islam's enemy qualifications. And on September 11, 2001, Osama bin Laden ended America's search. The attacks on New York and Washington followed by the wars with Afghanistan and Iraq and the more diffuse "war on terrorism" make militant Islam America's first enemy of the twenty-first century. (*WAW*, 264–265)

The result of this jeremiadic search for an enemy that would instigate the rejuvenating and reunifying anxiety on which the success of the covenantal peoples' errand in the world's wilderness depended—it can now be called paranoid—was President George W. Bush's establishment of the state of exception and the Homeland Security State as the norm and the accompanying lawless policies of preemptive war, regime change, the primacy of the spectacle (as opposed to speech) as agency of the truth, and, not least, the detention camp: all informed by a biopolitics that reduces human life to bare life, life that can be killed with impunity.

7

There have been, of course, however rare, critical American voices in the past that have intimated the indissoluble relationality between the American exceptionalist ethos and the state of exception. One thinks, for example, of Herman Melville's counter-mnemonic fiction, particularly *Billy Budd, Sailor*. This proleptic novella, written in his late style at the end of the nineteenth century, is, as I have shown elsewhere,[35] a cautionary tale warning the dominant nineteenth-century American capitalist culture against its arrogant imperial will to extend the American frontier into the Pacific by way of the catastrophic example of imperial Britain's conflict with Napoleonic France over naval control of the high seas, an imperial conflict, as in the case of the *H.M.S. Bellipotent*, the *mis en scène* of the novella, that renders the state of exception and the security state the global rule. Under the aegis of the state of exception, the criminal master-at-arms, Claggart, as Melville's shows, inevitably becomes the real master of the ship of state, and the innocent common seaman, Billy, the criminal. But, ironically, the fate of Melville's very witness to the complicity of the American exceptionalist ethos with the state of exception proves its logic's inordinate power. Inconceivable to most pre-9/11 Americans, even the most conscious intellectuals, that violence is intrinsic to the redeemer nation, Melville's counter-mnemonic tale, we know, was interpreted by and large as his "testament of acceptance," his abandonment in his old age of his earlier quarrel with his country and his reconciliation with its redemptive tenets.

To return in the end to my beginning, it is this inordinate power of the American exceptionalist truth—and the fact that it is the policies of the exceptionalist United States of America that have established the state of exception and the security state as the global norm—that has compelled me to supplement Giorgio Agamben's Eurocentric jurisprudential genealogy of the contemporary state of exception, which includes America, by way of distinguishing his from my American genealogy.

Of course, ultimately there is no difference in this respect between the United States and Europe, since both adhere to the nation-state system, which is ontologically grounded on the logic of exception: Friend/foe, Us/them, as Carl Schmitt puts it. As American history testifies, however, there is a difference within this ultimate same. And it is this difference that Agamben fails to perceive.

As I have observed, Agamben's overdetermination of the history of Western law, as seminal and revelatory as its results have been, is a focus on a (*conscious*) ideological apparatus of capture that, in its visibility, is thus ultimately resistible. What I have shown in the process of this alternative American genealogy of the contemporary 9/11 occasion, on the other hand, is that the American exceptionalist ethos is invisible, ontologically prior to the more apparently worldly juridical realm, which is to say, is hegemonic: a fiction or lie that has become the reality, the Truth. It is, to recall Raymond Williams's impeccable summary account of Gramsci's enabling concept, "a lived system of meanings and values—constitutive and constituting—which as they are experienced as practices appear as reciprocally confirming. It thus constitutes a sense of reality for most people in the society, a sense of absolute because experienced reality beyond which it is very difficult for most members of the society to move, in most areas of their lives." As such a realization of a lie, it is, as even the post-Bush American era testifies, difficult to resist. But not impossible: if, that is, we take our directives from this American genealogy of the present occasion, which, as I have shown, has been enabled by the visible theoretical, cultural, and political violence, hitherto effectively disavowed, disclosed in the post-9/11 era, at the liminal point of the development of the logic of the American exceptionalist ethos.

4

The Human in Modernity

A Genealogy of Bare Life

But where danger is, grows
The power also . . .

—Friedrich Hölderlin, "Patmos"

Giorgio Agamben's term "bare life" (Italian: *vida nuda*) has achieved a remarkable, if contested, currency in theoretical, literary critical, and political discourse in the last decade, testimony to a reluctant but growing awareness of the dehumanizing logic intrinsic to the knowledge-producing apparatuses of Western modernity. But this growing awareness of the term remains academic and by and large restricted to the thinking of its coiner. What I want to offer in this chapter is a genealogy of Agamben's concept of bare life to show that it has resided at the hidden core of contemporary theory's critical diagnosis of Western modernity since its origins in Nietzsche and Heidegger, through Hannah Arendt and Michel Foucault, to the present in Judith Butler, Alain Badiou, Jacques Rancière, Slavoj Žižek, and, above all, Giorgio Agamben. Such a genealogy is a timely untimeliness because, I suggest, it demonstrates both the pervasiveness of this dark diagnosis of the human in modernity and the global urgency of rethinking this modern human as it has evolved in the last two and half centuries, since, that is, the secularization of the *Theologos* to the *Anthropologos*, during which Man became the measure of all things (Humanism). More specifically, I mean by "modernity" that all-encompassing hegemonic truth structure that constitutes an indissoluble continuum from metaphysics (thinking from after or above things as they are) in its late empirical scientific mode (ontology), to the subject as individual, language as a materially productive instrument (technology as a mode of knowing), the nation-state, capitalist democracy, and the alleged superiority (exceptionalism) of the West.

2

For the sake of brevity, I will begin this genealogy of bare life produced by the Truth of Western modernity with that modern (anthropological) aspect of Martin Heidegger's interrogation of metaphysics—the prevailing mode of Western knowledge production in what he called the "onto-theo-logical tradition," that, in thinking being from above things-as-they-are, that is, teleologically, privileges a hierarchical binary logic that prioritizes Spatiality over temporality, Identity over difference, the One over the many, that is, spatializes and quantifies (structures) the temporality—*die Zeit* (or nothing: *das Nichts*), that, in reality, is ontologically prior to thingness. More specifically, I will begin by thinking the meaning of that metaphysical structuring mode of revealing (truth production), which, in contrast to *a-lethéia* (unconcealing), which acknowledges the ontological priority of time, Heidegger calls technology or, more tellingly, "Enframing" (*Ge-stell*): "Enframing means the gathering together of the setting-upon that sets upon man, i.e. challenges him forth, to reveal the actual, in the mode of ordering, as disposable reserve [*Bestand*]. Enframing means the mode of revealing that holds sway in the essence of modern technology and that itself is nothing technological."[1]

Heidegger begins his inquiry into the present relationship between Being and time established by the pursuit of the binary logic of metaphysics by way of his de-struction [*Destruktion*] of the banal everyday language of *das Man* (the They-self), which is to say, the modern human being whose language, determined as it is by the "dictatorship of the public realm,"[2] has forgotten the question of (the be-ing of) being. This is how he puts this reduction in "Letter on Humanism":

> The widely and rapidly spreading devastation of language not only undermines aesthetic and moral responsibility, in every use of language; it arises from a threat to the essence of humanity. A mere cultivated use of language is still no proof that we have as yet escaped the danger

> to our essence. These days, in fact, such usage might sooner testify that we have not yet seen and cannot see the danger because we have never yet placed ourselves in view of it. Much bemoaned of late, and much too lately, the downfall of language is, however, not the grounds for, but already the consequence of, the state of affairs in which language under the dominance of the modern metaphysics of subjectivity almost irremediably falls out of its element. Language still denies us its essence: that it is the house of the truth of Being. Instead, language surrenders itself to our mere willing and trafficking as an instrument of domination over beings. We encounter beings as actualities in a calculative businesslike way, but also scientifically and by way of philosophy, with explanations and proofs. (*LH*, 222–223)

Taking his directives from this modern de-humanized figure (*das Man*) and its reduced language—the paradoxical fulfillment of the Western humanist tradition—Heidegger extends his inquiry into the forgetting of the question of being in modernity in his famous but still to be adequately understood essay "The Question Concerning Technology" (QCT), in which he interprets technology—Enframing—as a mode of knowledge production that, in "challenging forth," reduces the phenomena of being to *Bestand*, usually translated as "standing reserve," but as Heidegger's developing interpretation suggests, can be more precisely—and proleptically—rendered as "disposable reserve":

> What kind of unconcealing is it, then, that is peculiar to that which results from the setting upon that challenges? Everywhere everything is ordered to stand by, to be immediately on hand, indeed, to stand there just so that it may be on call for a further ordering. Whatever is ordered about in this way has its own standing. We call it disposable reserve [Bestand]. The word expresses here something more, and something essential, than mere "stock." The word "disposable reserve" assumes the rank of an inclusive rubric. It designates nothing less than the way in which everything *presences* that is wrought upon by the revealing that challenges. Whatever stands by in this sense of disposable no longer stands over against us as object. (QCT, 322; trans. modified)

What needs to be remarked, in a way it has not been, about this term *Bestand* is that the existence of the referent—"everything everywhere" (on the continuum of being)—is guaranteed as long as it has utility—that when it no longer has use value, it can be disposed of without afterthought.

The anticipatory affiliation of this passage from "The Question Concerning Technology" with Agamben's idea of bare life (and, as we shall see, not incidentally, Judith Butler's appropriation of the concept of the "frame" to account for who is grievable in modernity and who is not) is thus clearly apparent. But insofar as Heidegger's analysis of *Bestand* focuses on the "object" of man's Enframing perspective, it leaves the all-important question of the status of modern humanity open. What follows this account of the effects of the (teleo)logic of Enframing as a mode of knowledge production that challenges forth, however, establishes the relationship between this spatializing technological apparatus of unconcealing (Enframing as a mode of knowledge production) in a decisive way. Indeed, in pursuing the binarist logic of Enframing to its liminal end at which it has arrived in late modernity, Heidegger discloses what Enframing has always, throughout the history of modernity, disavowed: the paradox, prefigured, not incidentally, in his analysis of *das Man* in *Being and Time*, that, in the end, the reifying logic of Enframing (the naming of the unnamable phenomena of being)—later, it will come to be called, first, by Hannah Arendt (via Karl Marx), man's "metabolism with nature," and then, by Michel Foucault, "biopolitics"—inexorably reduces man, the master, himself, to disposable reserve:

> Yet when destining reigns in the mode of enframing, it is the supreme danger. This danger attests itself to us in two ways. As soon as what is concealed no longer concerns man [in the sense of care (*Sorge*)] even as object, but exclusively as disposable reserve, and man in the midst of objectlessness is nothing but the ordered of the disposable reserve, then he comes to the very brink of a precipitous fall; that is, he comes to the point where he himself will have to be taken as disposable reserve. Meanwhile, man, precisely as the one so threatened, exalts himself and postures as lord of the earth. In this way the illusion comes to prevail that everything man encounters exists only insofar as it is his construct. This illusion gives rise in turn to one final delusion: it seems as though man everywhere and always encounters only himself. Heisenberg has with complete correctness pointed out that the actual must present itself to contemporary man in this way. *In truth, however, precisely nowhere does man today any longer encounter himself; i.e. his essence.* Man stands so decisively in subservience to the challenging-forth of Enframing that he does not grasp Enframing as a claim, that he fails to see himself as the one spoken to, and hence fails in every way to hear in what respect he ek-sists, in terms of his essence, in a realm where he is addressed, so that he can *never* encounter himself. (QCT, 332; emphasis in original)

Heidegger's overdetermination of the ontological site on the polyvalent continuum of being he gave us to think against the modern Enframing unfortunately marginalized the other more political sites. I mean specifically the regime of truth that has reduced the temporal dynamics of being to a disciplinary table and knowledge production to a matter of disciplinary study. As a result of this overdetermination of the ontological site, Heidegger obscured the radical political implications of his critique of modern technology and its Enframing apparatus of capture. One of the unfortunate results of his failure to think being beyond the site of ontology to the more political sites was to open himself up to the charge of being indifferent to the human by his traditional humanist critics. I am, of course, referring to their notorious invocation of Heidegger's "equation" of the modern transformation of agriculture into "a mechanized food industry" with the Nazi gas chambers:

> Agriculture is now a mechanized food industry. As for its essence, it is the same thing as the manufacture of corpses in the gas chambers or death camps, the same as blockades and reduction of countries to famine, the same as the manufacture of the hydrogen bomb. (QCT)[3]

Understood in terms of this analysis of Heidegger's disclosure of the consequence of Enframing at the liminal point of the development of its logic—the indissoluble relationship between the reduction of the phenomena of being and humanity (*Dasein*) to disposable reserve—Heidegger's apparently troublesome relating of the modern technologically oriented "modern food industry" and the Nazi gas chambers takes on a far more different and justifiable meaning than that attributed to it by his accusers, who have invoked the analogy as indicative of his crude Nazi mindset—a meaning, in fact, that will resonate in a fundamental way in the work of thinkers who have diagnosed modernity as a dehumanizing momentum of its version of humanism that at its liminal point ends in the production of "bare life"—life that can be killed without the killing being called homicide.

3

It was, I suggest, Hannah Arendt's fundamental purpose in all her work to radicalize Heidegger's, her mentor's, symptomatic—resonant but inchoate—ontological insight into the dehumanizing consequences of thinking being *meta ta physica* (from after or above things as they are) or, to anticipate, panoptically, in its modern anthropological mode: that is, to thematize its radical political significance. One realizes this if one reads Arendt's masterpiece, *The Human Condition* (1958), not as it has been read by the Habermasian school of political scientists, who have identified Arendt's thought with the liberal democratic tradition,[4] but precisely as a radicalized extension of Heidegger's sustained ontological insight into the dehumanized and dehumanizing essence of modern anthropological man (*das Man*) and his banalized language.

In that book, it will be recalled, Arendt takes her directives from her mentor's de-struction of the means/end logic of knowledge production privileged by the teleological concept of time intrinsic to metaphysical thinking, particularly in its modern anthropological mode. She undertakes a de-structive critique of the prevailing idea of the human in modernity: "*homo faber*," man the maker, who, like the technological man of Heidegger's account of modernity, in assuming the means/end logic of teleology, reduces all it encounters to utilitarian status: disposable reserve. To accomplish this urgent task of retrieval, Arendt inaugurates her destructive-projective project by returning, like Heidegger, to the ancient Greeks, though now with an emphasis on the idea of the *polis* (the public sphere) enabled but unthought in Heidegger's interpretation of truth as *a-lethéia* (unconcealing) as opposed to the truth of Western civilization inaugurated by the Romans (*adaequatio intellectus et rei*: the correspondence of mind and thing, correctness). According to Arendt, the ancient Greeks drew an impenetrable boundary between the *oikos*, the private household, and the *polis*, the public sphere. The *oikos*, under the aegis of the father (*pateras*), was organized for the sole purpose of biological survival—what Arendt, drawing from Marx, calls "man's metabolism with nature:"

> When Marx defined labor as "man's metabolism with nature," in whose processes "nature's material [is] adapted by a change of form to the wants of man," so that "labour has incorporated itself with its subject," he indicated clearly that he was "speaking physiologically" and that labor and consumption are but two stages of the ever-recurring cycle of biological life. Whatever labor produces is meant to be fed into the human life process almost immediately, and this consumption, regenerating the life process, produces—or rather, reproduces—new "labor power," needed for the further sustenance of the body.[5]

Under the dispensation of the *oikos*, then, man, according to Arendt, is an "*animal laborans*," the "*worldless*" entity whose vocation is to labor for the sake of keeping the family alive. On the other hand, the *polis*—the public realm—is a space where the human potential of humanity becomes possible: *zoé* (life as such) becomes a *bios politikos*. This is because it is a space that enables speech and action—the *initiation* of a world, the *sine qua non* of the *vita activa* (life of action), that is to say, a public space that, in opposition to the *oikos*, the domain of necessity the vocation of which is mere survival—"life's metabolism with nature"—is a space of freedom, of a beginning freed from the subservience to an end, and calls for the dialogic intercourse of individual human beings that *always already* enables individual human (his)tory, but also (political) history: the two conditions constituting the fully human:

> With word and deed we insert ourselves into the human world, and this insertion is like a second birth, in which we confirm and take upon ourselves the naked fact of our original physical appearance. This insertion is not forced upon us by necessity, like labor [*animal laborans*], and it is not prompted by utility, like work [*homo faber*]. It may be stimulated by the presence of others whose company we may wish to join, but it is never conditioned by them; its impulse springs from the beginning which came into the world when we were born and to which we respond by beginning something new on our own initiative. To act, in its most general sense, means to take an initiative, to begin (as the Greek word *Archéin*, "to begin," "to lead," and eventually "to rule," indicates), to set something into motion (which is the original meaning of the Latin *agere*). Because they are *initium*, newcomers and beginners by virtue of birth, men take initiative, are prompted into action. [*Initium*] *ergo ut esset, creatus est homo, ante quem nullius fuit* (that there is a beginning, man was created before whom there was nobody), said Augustine in his political philosophy. This beginning is not the same as the beginning of the world; it is not the beginning of something but somebody, who is a beginner himself. With the creation of man, the principle of beginning came into the world itself, which, of course, is another way of saying that the principle of freedom was created when man was created but not before. (*HC*, 176–177)

In the modern age, to put Arendt's complex diagnosis all too simply, the *oikos* (the private realm or household)—under the aegis of the means/end logic of *homo faber*—has been almost entirely socialized; that is, the private realm of biological necessity has penetrated the public realm of freedom and transformed the humanizing worlding space of speech/act (the *polis*) into the nation-state understood as a "national household." This transformation had its origins in modernity, when, under the sway of the calculative means/ends logic, anthropological man became *homo faber*, the maker of utilitarian objects for consumption. And in the unerring process of transforming the *polis* into a consumer society—a national household—it threatens to reproduce man as *animal laborans* on a global scale. I quote at length to underscore not only the remarkable continuity of Arendt's diagnosis of modernity with Heidegger's analysis of technological Enframing (*Ge-stell*)—the reduction of man to "disposal reserve" (*Bestand*)—but also to her uncanny anticipation of Michel Foucault and, above all, Giorgio Agamben. I am referring primarily to the former's analysis of the disciplinary apparatuses of the late modern panoptic society that produce "useful and docile bodies," and to the latter's analysis of the apparatuses that level the play of human life to "bare life":

> Tools and instruments [the prostheses of *homo faber*] ease pain and effort and thereby change the modes in which the urgent necessity inherent in labor once was manifest to all. *They do not change the necessity itself; they only serve to hide it from our senses.* Something similar is true of labor's products, which do not become more durable through abundance. The case is altogether different in the corresponding modern transformation of the work process by the introduction of the principle of the division of labor. Here the very nature of work is changed and the production process, although it by no means produces objects for consumption, assumes the character of labor. Although machines have forced us into an infinitely quicker rhythm of repetition than the cycle of natural processes prescribes—and this specifically modern acceleration is only too apt to make us disregard the repetitive character of all laboring—the repetition and the endlessness of the process itself put the unmistakable mark of laboring upon it. This is even more evident in the use objects produced by these techniques of laboring. Their very abundance transforms them into consumer goods. The endlessness of the laboring process is guaranteed by the ever-recurrent needs of consumption; the endlessness of production can be assured only if its products lose their use character and become more and more objects of consumption, or, if, to put it in another way, the rate of use is so tremendously accelerated that the objective difference between use and consumption, between the relative durability of use objects and the swift coming and going of consumer goods, dwindles to insignificance.
>
> In our need for more and more rapid replacement of the worldly things around us, we can no longer afford to use them, to respect and preserve their inherent durability; we must consume, devour, as it were, our houses and furniture and cars as though they were the "good things" of nature which spoil uselessly if they are not drawn swiftly into the never-ending cycle of man's metabolism with nature. *It is as though we had forced open the distinguishing boundaries which protected the world, the human artifice,*

> *from nature, the biological process which goes on in its very midst as well as the natural cyclical processes which surround it, delivering and abandoning to them the always threatened stability of the human world.* (my emphasis)

It is this collapsing of the distinction between the human artifice and the biological process by way of the inevitable overdetermination of consumption, according to Arendt, that ends in the reversion of man the fabricator to *animal laborans*:

> The ideals of *homo faber*, the fabricator of the world, which are permanence, stability, and durability, have been sacrificed to abundance, the ideal of *animal laborans*. We live in a laborer's society because only laboring, with its inherent fertility, is likely to bring about abundance; and we have changed work into laboring, broken it up into minute particles until it has lent itself to division where the common denominator of the simplest performance is reached in order to eliminate from the path of human labor power—which is part of nature and perhaps even the most powerful of all natural forces—the obstacle of the "unnatural" and purely worldly stability of the human artifice. (*HC*, 125–126; my emphasis)

The dark political implications of Arendt's diagnosis of *homo faber* and its modern means/end (teleo)logic that, at the liminal point of its development, reproduces *animal laborans* as the predominant figure of the late modern age, becomes patently manifest in her "controversial" analysis of the liminal figure of Adolph Eichmann, the synecdochical calculative and quantifying human being produced by Nazi Germany, the polity of which she interprets as the fulfillment of the logic of belonging of the modern Western nation-state.[6] All too often—particularly by Zionists, who fanatically represent the holocaust as an utterly unique event—Eichmann, the facilitator of the rounding-up and transportation of European and Eastern Jews to the Nazi gas chambers and death camps, has also been represented as an utterly unique phenomenon—the monstrous antithesis of the ideal human of modern Western humanity. But if we attend to the insistent and pervasive poststructuralist interrogation of modernity, it will be seen that Eichmann, like the practices of Nazism itself, constitutes, not a monstrous anomaly but the fulfillment—the dis-closive liminal point—of the dehumanizing logic of belonging of the Western nation-state system and its means/end mode of knowledge production. To be more specific, it will be seen that Arendt's provocative representation of Eichmann's language at his trial in Jerusalem in 1964 as "a report on the banality of evil," which outraged and continues to outrage the Zionists, constitutes a radicalization of the itinerary that led Heidegger (among others such as Theodor Adorno and Max Horkheimer and Walter Benjamin)[7] from the critique of *das Man* and its banalized language (the "idle talk" that servilely accommodates itself to "the dictatorship of the public realm)" to the exposure of modern man's reliance on technological Enframing, the modern mode of revealing (the truth) that has reduced being all across its continuum to disposable reserve (*Bestand*):

> The trouble with Eichmann was precisely that so many were like him, and the many were, *and still are*, terribly and terrifyingly normal. From the viewpoint of our legal institutions and of our moral standards of judgment, this normality was much more terrifying than all the atrocities put together, for it implied . . . that this new type of criminal, who is in actual fact *hostis generis humanis*, commits his crimes under circumstances that make it well-nigh impossible for him to know or to feel that he is doing wrong.[8]

Lest this conclusion be taken to restrict Arendt's judgment to the Nazi occasion, I remind the reader of the introduction to her unfinished *The Life of the Mind*, published posthumously a decade after *Eichmann in Jerusalem*, in which, despite her ostracism from the Jewish community,[9] she continues to implicate Western modernity at large with the Eichmann mentality and passionately articulates the urgency of rethinking the way Western moderns think the humanity of the human:

> Factually, my preoccupation with mental activities [*The Life of the Mind*] has two rather different origins. The immediate impulse came from my attending the Eichmann trial in Jerusalem. In my report of it I spoke of "the banality of evil." Behind that phrase, I held no thesis or doctrine, although I was dimly aware of the fact that it went counter to our tradition of thought—literary, theological, or philosophic—about the phenomenon of evil. Evil, we have learned, is something demonic; its incarnation is Satan, a "lightning fall from heaven" (Luke 10:18); or Lucifer, the fallen angel ("The devil is an angel too"—Unamuno), whose sin is pride ("proud as Lucifer"), namely, that *superbia* of which only the best are capable: they don't want to serve God but to be like Him. Evil men, we are told, act out of envy; this may be resentment at not having turned out well through no fault of their own (Richard III) or the envy of Cain, who slew Abel because "the Lord had regard for Abel and his offering, but for Cain and his offering he had no regard." Or they may be prompted by weakness (Macbeth). Or, on the contrary, by the powerful hatred wickedness feels for sheer goodness (Iago's "I hate the Moor: my cause is hearted"; Clag-

> gart's hatred for Billy Budd's "barbarian" innocence, hatred considered by Melville a "depravity according to nature"), or by covetousness, "the root of all evil" (*Radis omnium malorum cupiditas*). However, what I was confronted with was utterly different and still undeniably factual. I was struck by a manifest shallowness in the doer that made it impossible to trace the incontestable evil of his deeds to any deeper level of roots or motives. The deeds were monstrous, but the doer—at least the very effective one now on trial—was quite ordinary, commonplace, and neither demonic nor monstrous. There was no sign in him of firm ideological conviction or of specific evil motives, and the only notable characteristic one could detect in his past behavior as well as in his behavior during the trial and throughout the pre-trial examination was something entirely negative: it was not stupidity but *thoughtlessness*.[10]

4

The next figure in this genealogy of the concept of bare life is the poststructuralist Michel Foucault, who, as I have shown elsewhere at length,[11] took the directives of his decisive critique of modernity (the panopticism of the disciplinary society) from Nietzsche's and Heidegger's destruction of Western metaphysical thinking, particularly in its modern anthropological phase. I am, of course, referring primarily to his great book *Surveiller et punir* (inadequately translated into English as *Discipline and Punish*, thus obscuring the ocularcentrism that had its origins in the metaphysical thinking that founded the West), which constitutes a decisive genealogy of the post-Enlightenment era: what, reminiscent of Heidegger's identification of the modern age as "the age of the world picture," he perspicuously calls alternatively the "panoptic age" and the "disciplinary society" to underscore the indissoluble relationship between the modern anthropological allotrope of metaphysical thinking and power. I mean, of course, that bourgeois capitalist apparatus of capture that Foucault called the "repressive hypothesis."[12] This was the apparatus of power relations that, in opposition to that of the *ancien regime* (symbolized by the spectacular function of the guillotine), which, as the French Revolution testifies, in using overt force as a means of preventing resistance, actually provoked it, harnessed knowledge—particularly the instrumental means/end knowledge of empirical (observational) science—to the purpose of disciplining the bodies of all types of deviants who threatened the stability or impeded the progress of the new bourgeois order. In a formulation that is remarkably reminiscent of Heidegger's characterization of the result of Enframing as "disposable reserve" and Arendt's characterization of Eichmann's "thoughtless" thought as a banalization that could not distinguish between trucks and human beings in the pursuit of his horrific logistic project, Foucault characterized this knowledge/power apparatus of modernity as one that produced not only "docile" but also "useful" *bodies*:

> The historical moment of the disciplines was a moment when an *art of the human body was born*, which was directed not only at the growth of its skills, nor at the intensification of its subjection, but at the formation of a relation that in the mechanism itself makes it more obedient as it becomes more useful, and conversely. What was then being formed was a policy of coercions *that act upon the body, a calculated manipulation of its elements, its gestures, its behavior. The human body was entering a machinery of power that explores it, breaks it down and rearranges it. . . . Thus discipline produces subjected and practised bodies, "docile" bodies.* Discipline increases the forces of the body (in economic terms of utility) and diminishes these same forces (in political terms of obedience). In short, it dissociates power from the body; on the one hand, it turns it into an "aptitude," a "capacity," which it seeks to increase; on the other hand, it reverses the course of the energy, the power that might result from it, and turns it into a relation of strict subjection. If economic exploitation separates the force and the products of labour, let us say that disciplinary coercion establishes in the body the constricting link between an increased aptitude and an increased domination.[13] (my emphasis)

Foucault goes on to overdetermine Jeremy Bentham's Panopticon as a practical manifestation of this apparatus of capture, an overdetermination that led all too many early commentators to mistakenly minimize, if not entirely overlook, the ontological foundation of this political panoptic apparatus in the metaphysical discourse of the Western tradition and thus of its polyvalent applications. I mean, above all, Foucault's sustained emphasis on the *biopoliticization* of the human body at large. That he is alluding to this "new [polyvalent] political anatomy" of the human body throughout *Surveiller et punir* is, in fact, underscored by him at the end of his analysis of the particular operations of the panoptic prison:

> The Panopticon . . . must be understood as a generalizable model of functioning; a way of defining power relations in terms of the everyday life of men. No doubt Bentham presents it as a particular institution, closed in upon itself. Utopias, perfectly closed in upon themselves, are common enough. As opposed to the ruined prisons, littered with mechanisms of

> torture, to be seen in Piranesi's engravings, the Panopticon presents a cruel, ingenious cage. *The fact that it should have given rise, even in our time, to so many variations projected or realized, is evidence of the imaginative intensity that it has possessed for almost two hundred years.* But the Panopticon must not be understood as a dream building: *it is a diagram of a mechanism of power reduced to its ideal form;* its function, abstracted from any obstacle, resistance or friction, must be represented as a pure architectural and optical system: it is in fact a figure of political technology that may and must be detached from any specific use.
>
> It is polyvalent in its applications; it serves to reform prisoners, but also to treat patients, to instruct school children, to confine the insane, to supervise workers, to put beggars and idlers to work. It is a type of location of bodies in space, of distribution of individuals in relation to one another, of hierarchical organization, of disposition of centres and channels of power, of definition of the instruments at modes of intervention of power, which can be implemented in hospitals, workshops, schools, prisons. Whenever one is dealing with a multiplicity of individuals on whom a task or a particular form of behaviour must be imposed, the panoptic schema may be used. It is—necessary modifications apart—applicable "to all establishments whatsoever, in which, within a space not too large to be covered or commanded by buildings, a number of persons are meant to be kept under inspection." (DP, 205–206; my emphasis)

Understood in the context of the polyvalency of this panoptic apparatus of capture, Foucault's analysis not only recalls Heidegger's diagnosis of modernity as a time that, under the aegis of technological Enframing, is reducing being all along its continuum to "disposable reserve," and Arendt's diagnosis of modernity as producing the "banality of evil." In focusing on the birth of "an anatomy of the human body," it overtly introduces the idea of biopolitics—hitherto latent in the means/end, potential/act logic exposed by his predecessors—as a pervasive polyvalent initiative of Western modernity. In so doing, he also points proleptically to Giorgio Agamben's more specific and complete political analysis of this historical momentum, which, by way of the biopoliticization of the political realm, threatens to reduce human life on a global scale to bare life: life that can be killed with impunity.

5

The genealogy of Western modernity—the reduction of human life to bare life—I have been attempting to articulate culminates, then, in the resonant thought of Giorgio Agamben, which, as in the cases of Arendt and Foucault, radicalizes and politicizes the ontological thought of Nietzsche and Heidegger. Like Arendt, Agamben was a student of Heidegger. Taking his directives, far more than Nietzsche and Heidegger, from the recognition that being is an indissoluble continuum from the ontological sites—being as such, the ecos, the subject, languages—to the apparently more political sites—gender and race relations, the family, the nation, the global community—he begins his genealogy of Western modernity, like Heidegger, with the Greeks, particularly—and significantly—with Aristotle's inaugural epistemological meditation on the relationship between *Zoé*, life as such, and *Bios*, conscious life. Heidegger, following the Greek concept of truth (*a-lethéia*), interpreted the human as an ek-sistent in-sistent entity, a conscious being capable of thought—of imagining alternatives to mere thingness—but also, it is important to underscore, irreparably tethered to the finite realm of things. With that epistemological interpretation in mind, Agamben begins his genealogy of modernity with his interpretation of Aristotle's more political formulation of the human. In distinction to living entities, which Aristotle identifies with *zoé* (a living entity: flora, fauna), the human being was a *bios* or, more to the point, a *bios politikos*: a life, recalling Hannah Arendt's definition of the *vita activa*, capable of speech and of the organization of the *polis*: the human city understood on the basis of an open-ended community consonant with the open-endedness of human language: *a-lethéia*, an unending process of unconcealing/concealing.

The moment in antiquity that established the identity of the West—and sealed its fate, Agamben implies—is when, consonant with the teleology of metaphysical thinking, it put the potentiality of conscious humanity at the service of the Act, a decisive gesture of subordination that in the name of mastery (the will to power) rendered the means/end logic the privileged agency of human knowledge production, of the organization of human life, and of the human comportment toward the polyvalent phenomena of being. Under the aegis of this teleological logic, man's vocation, which he understands as mastery of all he surveys, becomes, in fact, recalling Heidegger, servitude to a future End (or Higher Cause)—and, to introduce a phrase that epitomizes Agamben's alterative to the means/end logic, thus negates the "time of the now" (*ho nyn kairos* in Saint Paul's language; *Jetztzeit*, in Walter Benjamin's)—the fundamental and irreparable condition of humanity's being-in-the-world, or, in Heidegger's formulation, his thrownness (*Geworfenheit*). Furthermore, and, not least, as I will show, it is this means/end logic that, in privileging the *Telos*, and interpreting any gesture threatening its sovereignty as a state of emergency, established the ground for the normalization of the state of exception.

All this begins to surface, according to Agamben, in late modernity. Prior to the advent of the modern occasion, the means/end logic was competing with older versions of teleological thinking, not least, of course, Christian theology and its monarchical political allotrope, for sovereign dominance. But with the advent of "objective," empirical thinking in the Enlightenment period, this logic achieved hegemony in the West and became the means of justifying its global imperial project ("the white man's burden"). As long as this means/end logic of modernity produced ameliorative results, the dominant culture could disavow the violence it necessarily perpetrated against being in the name of human progress as "collateral damage." It was when this sovereign means/end logic arrived at its fulfillment in what Heidegger called "the age of the world picture (*Weltbild*)—when, that is, its spatializing/reifying imperatives reached their liminal point—that what the West had always disavowed, from the ontological nothing/temporality through the phenomena of the ecos, to humans this logic exploited by way of reducing them to bare life, became visible and opened for positive thought. Referring, in his genealogy of bare life, enabled by the arrival of the sovereignty of this means/end logic at its liminal point, to his earlier identification of the idea of the sovereignty of the state as the origin of the state of exception that provided it with the means of capturing the human being in a system of inclusive exclusion—and thus, not incidentally, revealing the hypocrisy of the nation-state concept of human rights—Agamben writes:

> We have already encountered a limit sphere of human action that is only ever encountered in a relation of exception. This sphere is that of the sovereign decision, which suspends law in the state of exception and thus implicates bare life within it. We must therefore ask ourselves if the structure of sovereignty and the structure of *sacratio* might be connected, and if they might, from this perspective, be shown to illuminate each other. We may even advance a hypothesis: once brought back to his proper place beyond both penal law and sacrifice, *homo sacer* presents the originary figure of life taken in to the sovereign ban and preserves the memory of the originary exclusion through which the political dimension was first constituted. The political sphere of sovereignty was thus first constituted through a double exclusion as an excrescence of the profane in the reli-

> gious and of the religious in the profane, which takes the form of a zone of indistinction between sacrifice and homicide. *The sovereign sphere is the sphere in which it is permitted to kill without committing homicide and without celebrating a sacrifice, and sacred life—that is, life that may be killed but not sacrificed—is the life that has been captured in this sphere.*[14] (my emphasis)

Agamben, of course, is very much aware that the democratic nation-states of the West that had fought the Nazi regime in a bloody world war that lasted a decade are to be distinguished from their fascist enemy. However, to him, this difference is not a difference in kind, as these democratic nation-states vociferously claim, but a matter of degree. Like Arendt, who read Eichmann and the Germany that produced him as the liminal manifestation of a logic oriented in that direction, Agamben, supplementing Arendt's diagnosis of modernity with Foucault's, reads the Nazi concentration camp as a liminal manifestation of a symptomatic biopolitical momentum that is inherent in the Western idea of sovereignty and is becoming increasingly manifest in every facet of the modern Western nation-state:

> Along with the emergence of biopolitics, we can observe a displacement and gradual expansion beyond the limits of the decision on bare life, in the state of exception, in which sovereignty consisted. If there is a line in every modern state marking the point at which the decision on life becomes a decision on death, and biopolitics can turn into thanatopolitics, this line no long appears today as a stable border dividing two clearly distinct zones. *This line is now in motion and gradually moving into areas other than that of political life, areas in which the sovereign is entering into an even more intimate symbiosis not only with the jurist but also with the doctor, the scientist, the expert, and the priest.* In the pages that follow, we shall show that certain events that are fundamental for the political history of modernity (such as the declaration of rights), as well as others that seem instead to represent an incomprehensible intrusion of biologico-scientific principles into the political order (such as National Socialist eugenics and its elimination of "life that is unworthy of being lived," or the contemporary debate on the normative determination of death criteria), acquire their true sense only if they are brought back to the common biopolitical (or thanatopolitical), context to which they belong. From this perspective the camp—as the pure, absolute, and impassable biopolitical space (insofar as it is founded solely on the state of exception)—will appear as the hidden paradigm of the political space of modernity, whose metamorphoses and disguises we will have to learn to recognize. (*HS*, 122–123; my emphasis)

Finally, but by no means least, the coming to its logical fulfillment of the means/end logic in late modernity, according to Agamben, insofar as it thrives on crisis, manifests itself in the normalization of the state of exception, in which the (democratic) law is annulled in the name of saving it. The inevitable consequence is the exacerbation of the biopolitical state apparatuses that produce bare life: the state information-gathering agencies, public surveillance, the informer mentality, illegal detention, torture, the apotheosis of the spectacle ("shock and awe"). The post-9/11 era under the aegis of the United States' exceptionalist, and necessarily unending, War on Terror ("Infinite Justice" in the George W. Bush administration's spectacular language) in the name of Homeland Security bears chilling witness to this present biopolitical momentum that increasingly threatens to reduce human life to bare life on a planetary scale. In the end, according to Agamben, following and radicalizing Arendt's narrative about the modern human condition, this view of human life that renders the means/end logic humanity's vocation—this biopoliticization of the human polity—will become, as it did in Nazi Germany, a thanatopolitics.

6

It would be possible to extend this genealogy of bare life to include, in an indissolubly related way, such prominent contemporary post-post-structuralist theorists as Judith Butler, Alain Badiou, Slavoj Žižek, and Jacques Rancière. But, for the sake of brevity, I will limit reference to that aspect of their thought that addresses the biopolitical means/end logic of democratic capitalist modernity that it has always disavowed, but which, as we have seen, the arrival at the limits of its operations has dis-closed. I mean the political figure at the other end of the continuum of being, who, like the ontological nothing (*das Nichts*) that this binarist logic "will have nothing to do with,"[15] yet absolutely relies on, is captured in a system of exclusion/inclusion that reduces "it," in some degree or other, to a non-being that at the same time serves the dominant culture, that is to say, to "disposable reserve" (Heidegger), "useful and docile body" (Foucault) and, ultimately to a "superfluous" entity (Arendt) or "bare life" (Agamben): life, to reiterate, that can be killed, as the Nazis killed the Jews, with impunity.

Thus, for example, Judith Butler, in a gesture remarkably reminiscent of Heidegger's analysis of that technological mode of comportment toward being he calls Enframing (*Ge-stell*), interprets late modernity, particularly the fulfillment of the logic of belonging of the nation-state, as a "frame of war," that is, a permanent state of exception, that determines those who, in one way or another, do not adhere to the imperatives of the frame, as "ungrievable," which is to say, as expendable (bare life):

> The shared condition of precariousness implies that the body is constitutively social and interdependent. . . . Yet, precisely because each body finds itself potentially threatened by others who are, by definition precarious as well, forms of domination follow. This standard Hegelian point takes on specific meanings under contemporary conditions of war: the shared condition of precariousness leads not to reciprocal recognition, but to a specific exploitation of targeted populations, of lives that are not quite lives, cast as "destructible" and "ungrievable." Such populations are "lose-able," or can be forfeited, precisely because they are framed as being already lost or forfeited; they are cast as threats to human life as we know it, rather than living populations in need of protection from illegitimate state violence, famine, or pandemics. Consequently, when such lives are lost they are not grievable, since, in the twisted logic that rationalizes their death, the loss of such populations is deemed necessary to protect the lives of "the living."[16]

In the case of Badiou, the "others" of the nation-state in its modern, parliamentary capitalist mode are those "who don't count" in a quantitative truth system in which "what counts" is determined by those who own the means of production.[17] But it is, above all, in his book on the Arab Spring, *The Rebirth of History* (2012), so reminiscent of Agamben's analysis of Tiananmen Square,[18] that Badiou most clearly specifies his sense of these "non-existents" and their affiliation with the non-beings of the other theorists I have invoked. There he writes:

> The state can virtually be defined as an institution with the means for imposing norms on a whole population that prescribe what pertains to this state, the duties it imposes and the rights it confers. In the context of this definition the state fictionalizes an *identitarian object* (for example, the "French person") that individuals and groups have a duty to resemble as closely as possible, if they are to merit positive attention from the state. Anyone declared unduly dissimilar from the identitarian object will also be entitled to the attention of the state, but in a negative sense (suspicion, police checks, internment, expulsion, and so on).
>
> A separating name refers to a particular way of not resembling the fictive identitarian object. It enables the state to separate certain groups

> from the collectivity, who therefore call for particular repressive measures. These can range from "immigrant," "Islamist," "Muslim," and "Roma" to "youth from the banlieues." Let us note that "poor" and "mentally ill" are in the process of being constructed before our very eyes as separating names.[19]

Similarly, in Jacques Rancière, this "no one" or "non-existent" *of* the dominant culture is the "part" that becomes "the part of no part," which, when it "institutes" itself, constitutes authentic politics. Returning to the question of the political that troubled the Greek "*demos*," he writes:

> It must be emphasized that the Ancients, much more than the Moderns, acknowledged that the whole basis of politics is the struggle between the poor and the rich. But that's just it: what they acknowledged was a strictly political reality—even if it meant trying to overcome it. The struggle between the rich and the poor is not social reality, which politics then has to deal with. It is the actual institution of politics itself. There is politics when there is a part of those who have no part, a part or party of the poor. Politics does not happen just because the poor oppose the rich. It is the other way around: politics (that is, the interpretation of the simple effects of domination by the rich) cause the poor to exist as an entity. The outrageous claim of the demos to be the whole of the community only satisfies in its own way—that of a *party*—the requirements of politics. Politics exists when the natural order of domination is interrupted by the institution of a part of those who have no part. This institution is the whole of politics as a specific form of connection.[20]

This collectivization of the theorists I have invoked for the purpose of my genealogy of the troubling phenomenon of bare life is by no means to deny the differences between their diagnoses of Western modernity. The differences are very significant. It is, rather, to bring to urgent presence from this diversity what has not been adequately done by a disciplinary profession largely driven by competition rather than collaboration in the name of the abiding question. I mean, as I observed at the beginning, that, at bottom, what these diverse theoreticians' thinking at the liminal point of the logic of modernity have in some significant degree in common is the awareness of the pervasive biopoliticization of the human *polis* and their underscoring of the unerring momentum in late modernity toward the reduction of human life to bare life. I offer this diagnosis not for its own sake but to suggest some adequate directives for thinking an alternative mode of resistance than that ineffective one tolerated by the liberal protocols of democratic capitalist modernity and of the *polis* to come.

7

As it has become abundantly evident, my reiteration of the present historical occasion as a liminal point in the development of the logic of modernity is not accidental. It is intended to reveal that the logic of modernity has come to its fulfillment—and demise—and thus to show that at this liminal point, as the contemporary theorists I have invoked commonly testify, this logic also dis-closes the positive possibilities of its self-de-struction. Again, as the foregoing genealogy has suggested, we are compelled to return to Heidegger's Nietzschean disclosure—when "philosophy [the metaphysical thinking of the Western tradition] has come to its end [fulfillment and demise]" in the "age of the world picture"—of the ontological priority of the Nothing (*das Nichts*) over the *Summum Ens* (Total Thing)—and to his resonant disturbing question: "How is it with the nothing [that "modern science will have nothing to do with]?" (WIM, 101). This is the question that, though Heidegger did not pursue it beyond its ontological implications, has become, I am claiming, the supreme political theme of contemporary theory. For it is precisely to the political implications of this retrieval of the ontological Nothing from the oblivion to which the binary logic of science would relegate "it" that a contemporary theory has turned at the dis-closive liminal point of modernity's forwarding itinerary in its belated effort to think both a mode of resistance adequate to counter the depredations of democratic capitalist modernity and an alternative *polis*.

Both aspects of this dual agenda—resistance and the envisioning of a coming community—have their beginning in the refugee, the de-centered, homeless (stateless) figure that constitutes the political allotrope of the emergence of the nothingness of being. Hannah Arendt was the first to identify this "superfluous," "stateless" figure (the "conscious pariah")[21] as the potential precipitate of the self-de-struction of the nation-state system in World War II, and, as such an "outlaw" figure, as the "vanguard of [its] people":

> History has forced the status of outlaws upon both, upon pariahs and parvenus [assimilated Jews] alike. The latter have not accepted the great wisdom of Balzac's "*On ne parvient pas deux fois*" [One does not arrive/

> succeed twice]; thus they don't understand the wild dreams of the former and feel humiliated in sharing their fate. Those refugees who insist upon telling the truth, even to the point of "indecency," get in exchange for their unpopularity one priceless advantage: *history is no longer a closed book to them and politics is no longer the privilege of gentiles*. They know that the outlawing of the Jewish people in Europe has been followed closely by the outlawing of most European nations. *Refugees driven from country to country represent the vanguard of their peoples—if they keep their identity*. For the first time Jewish history is not separated but tied up with that of all other nations. The comity of European peoples went to pieces when, and because, it allowed its weakest member to be excluded and persecuted.[22]

But it was Edward Said, Arendt's exilic Palestinian counterpart, who first articulated the specific dynamics of the potential of this pervasive post-nation-state and -imperial exilic "outlaw"—this stateless, superfluous, nomadic figure of the contemporary interregnum—as the paradoxical agency of the dual task of resistance and the envisioning of a coming community:

> Yet it is no exaggeration to say that liberation as an intellectual mission, born in the resistance and opposition to the confinements and ravages of imperialism has now shifted from the settled, established, and domesticated dynamics of culture to its unhoused, decentered and exilic energies, energies whose incarnation today is the migrant, and whose consciousness is that of the intellectual and artist in exile, the political figure between domains, between forms, between homes, and between languages. From this perspective then all things are indeed, counter, original, spare, strange. From this perspective also, one can see the "complete consort dancing together" contrapuntally.[23]

At the site of resistance, to separate for the sake of convenience the indissoluble relationship of his revolutionary dual task, I will cite the paradoxical special specie of the refugee that these poststructuralist theorists have almost universally invoked as the agent adequate in some significant degree to the task of resisting a world structured in domination:[24] the literary figure, proleptically imagined by Herman Melville in the middle of the American nineteenth century, who brings the operations of the Wall Street lawyer he works for (and the capitalist system he symbolically represents) to a standstill, not by the direct counter-action expected (and prepared for) by the exponents of modernity, but by way of the very non-existent condition ("separating names") to which he has been relegated by the capitalist apparatuses, by, that is, his refusal to be answerable to his Wall Street boss's (interpellative) call: "I would prefer not to."[25] I could cite several examples of this appeal to Melville's uncannily proleptic story about the potent potentiality inhering in the condition of impotence to which Western modernity has reduced the vast majority of humanity. For the purpose of this essay, however, it will suffice to briefly cite Agamben's *Coming Community*, where, in a brief but resonant and decisive chapter entitled "Bartleby," he anticipates the opening conclusion of that richly suggestive book by way of invoking the event of Tiananmen Square as the "herald" of this alternative mode of resistance, in the process of which he pointedly demonstrates the blindness to its essential reality of Western observers:

> What could be the politics of whatever singularity, that is, of a being whose community is mediated not by any condition of belonging (being red, being Italian, being Communist) nor by the simple absence of conditions (a negative community, such as that recently proposed in France by Maurice Blanchot), but by belonging itself? A herald from Beijing carries the elements of a response.
>
> What was most striking about the demonstrations of the Chinese May was the relative absence of determinate contents in their demands (democracy and freedom are notions too generic and broadly defined to constitute the real object of a conflict, and the only concrete demand, the rehabilitation of Hu Yao-Bang, was immediately granted). This makes the violence of the State's reaction seem even more inexplicable. It is likely, however, that the disproportion is only apparent and that the Chinese leaders acted, from their point of view, with greater lucidity than the Western observers who were exclusively concerned with advancing increasingly less plausible arguments about the opposition between democracy and communism.
>
> The novelty of the coming politics is that it will no longer be a struggle for the conquest of the State, but a struggle between the State and the non-State (humanity), an insurmountable disjunction between whatever singularity and the State organization. This has nothing to do with the simple affirmation of the social opposition to the State that has often found expression in the protest movements of recent years. Whatever singularities cannot form a *societas* because they do not possess any identity to vindicate nor any bond of belonging for which to seek recognition. In the final instance the State can recognize any claim for identity—even that of a State identity within the State (the recent history of relations between the State and terrorism is an eloquent confirmation of this fact). What the State cannot tolerate in any way, however, is that the

> singularities form a community without affirming an identity, that humans co-belong without any representable condition of belonging (even in the form of a simple presupposition). The State, as Alain Badiou has shown, is not founded on a social bond, of which it would be the expression, but rather on the dissolution, the unbinding it prohibits. For the State, therefore, what is important is never the singularity as such, but only its inclusion in some identity, whatever identity (but the possibility of the whatever itself being taken up without an identity is a threat the State cannot come to terms with). . . .
>
> Whatever singularity, which wants to appropriate belonging itself, its own being-in-language, and thus rejects all identity and every condition of belonging, is the principal enemy of the State. Wherever these singularities peacefully demonstrate their being in common there will be a Tiananmen, and, sooner or later, the tanks will appear.[26]

Turning finally from the potential of resistance intrinsic to the Bartleby figure to the positive political implications of the retrieval of the relay of nothings disclosed by the coming to its end of modernity at the site of the coming *polis*, it is no accident that in virtually every version of contemporary theory it is, as with the question of resistance, the nothing or nobody, the identityless identity—the very bare life—produced by the means/end logic of modernity, that constitutes the point of departure of its coming into being. This is the testimony, for example, of Said, of Badiou, of Rancière, of Žižek, of Butler. But because Agamben, more than any of the others, consistently, if not systematically, refers insistently to the genealogy of bare life that it is my purpose to bring to visible presence in the post 9/11 era, it is again to him I turn for my all too brief account of the structureless structure of the coming *polis*.

At the ontological base of this "coming community"—which, it is important to point out, unlike the teleological Western nation-state, is always already coming—is the pure potentiality intrinsic to the radical temporality (the nothingness) of being. In this context, the members of the coming community, unlike the identitarian inhabitants of the old nation-state, are identityless identifies—what Agamben calls "whatever singularities." This is not to say that they are without identities, but rather that their identities are historically constructed: fictions, "separating names," in Badiou's terms. As such displaced persons, we might say, employing a highly relevant example to which I will return, the Jew becomes a "non-Jewish Jew" and the Palestinian, a "non-Palestinian Palestinian." That is to say, to invoke a key term of Agamben's discourse—one he derives from his radicalized readings of Saint Paul's epistles (*katergeo*)[27]—the binary identitarian and biopolitical logic of the nation-state system is rendered "inoperative" (Italian, *inoperatisa*): the identities remain, but the former negative consequences of the original binarist logic intrinsic to this essentialist idea of identity are not annulled but transformed into positive possibilities.

This potential for the coming *polis* of the non-identical identity becomes especially manifest in Agamben's meditation on the fraught—and synecdochical—contemporary question of Palestine. Taking his directives from Hannah Arendt's affirmation of the figure of the nomadic refugee of the nation-state as the "vanguard" of his or her people, Agamben imagines a future of this apartheid state in which Jerusalem becomes the extraordinary capital of a state in which each people coexist in a creative tension. As in the case of the non-identical identical subjects of the coming *polis*, the collectives, Palestinians and Jews, maintain their historically constructed identities. However, under the imperatives of the unhomed and nomadic figure of the refugee—this in-between figure of the post-liminal interregnum—they (and the former deadly Friend/foe binary) are rendered inoperative. In the wake of this dis-operating process, the boundaries produced by the binary logic of belonging of the nation-state come to "indetermine each other," as in the metaphors of the Klein bottle or the Möbius strip. The "non-orientable" space precipitated by the deterritorialization of the nation, Agamben writes,

> would coincide neither with any homogeneous national territories nor with their topographical sum, but would rather act on them by articulating and perforating them topologically as in the Klein bottle or the Möbius strip, where exterior and interior indetermine each other. In this new space, European cities would rediscover their ancient vocation of cities of the world by entering into a relation of reciprocal extraterritoriality.[28]

What, finally, the foregoing genealogy of bare life has disclosed is that, in the end—at precisely its liminal point—the very biopolitical logic that has reduced human life to bare life, has also disclosed the potentiality-as-such that is the essence of the ek-sistent in-sistent human. I mean, to underscore its urgent imperatives, the "thrown" being who lives in the time of the now (*ho nyn kairos*) and whose vocation, in Agamben's radicalized retrieval of Saint Paul's epiphany on the road to Damascus, is the "revocation of all vocations" (*TR*, 23). It is, I submit, this vocation, this dis-operating imperative, that we who would resist the biopolitics that are increasingly reducing human life to bare life have been called to think in the post-9/11 interregnum that is our occasion. It is not an exaggeration to say that what is at stake in this precarious in-between time is the very being of the human species.

5

Revoking the Vocational Imperative

Post-poststructuralist Theory and the Interrogation of the Interpellative Call

In the wake of the George W. Bush administration's declaration of its spectacular "War on Terror" following September 11, 2001, oppositional criticism in the United States has fallen into disarray. The reasons for this impasse are complexly multiple, but, it seems to me, they are tethered to one fundamental condition: the failure to perceive America's exceptionalist global War on Terror as an epochal event that has rendered the traditional (Enlightenment) political means of opposition inadequate to the urgent task of resisting the neoconservative usurpation of state power and its anti-historical dehumanizing global project. More specifically, oppositional intellectuals have failed to perceive that the Bush regime, in monomaniacally pursuing the redemptive logic of American exceptionalism to its liminal point—its inauguration of the United States' unilateral global and unending War on Terror and its tacit rendering of the state of exception the rule—constituted its *fulfillment*—and theoretical demise—in disclosing not only the predatory identity of the "New World" and the "Old," but also the violence intrinsic to exceptionalism's redeeming mission that America has perennially disavowed. To invoke Alain Badiou's post-poststructuralist language, American oppositional intellectuals have failed to perceive that the Bush regime's liminal declaration of America's War on Terror (including its commitment to the doctrines of "pre-emptive war" and "regime change," and to a "shock and awe" representational and military tactics) was an "event" that revealed the "void" at the bottom of its avowed plenary totality:

> We might say that since a situation is composed by the knowledges circulating within it, the event names the void inasmuch as it names the not-known of the situation. To take a well-known example: Marx is an event for political thought because he designates, under the name "proletariat," the central void of early bourgeois societies. For the proletariat—being entirely dispossessed, and absent from the political stage—is that around which is organized the complacent plenitude established by the rule of those who possess capital.
>
> To sum up: the fundamental ontological characteristic of an event is to inscribe, to name, the situated void of that for which it is an event.[1]

Put alternatively, what American oppositional intellectuals have failed adequately to register—or, perhaps more accurately, been unfaithful to—is that the neoconservative Bush regime's Ahabian pursuit of the logic of American exceptionalism to the liminal point has precipitated an interregnum: not simply a time between the decline of the old capitalist/democratic dispensation and a new world struggling to be born, but also between the old—Enlightenment—and a new, post-Western, yet to be articulated concept of being-in the-world. In other words, they have failed adequately to understand that the post-9/11 era has rendered the exilic condition the occasion of all of humanity.

All this—both the negative and the positive—was the proleptic witness of Edward W. Said's historical analysis of the post-imperial moment in the concluding pages of his magisterial *Culture and Imperialism*, published in the immediate aftermath of the Cold War and anticipating the United States' reactionary neo-imperial effort to achieve global hegemony. Invoking the poststructuralist theoretical insights into the nomadic of Paul Virilio and Gilles Deleuze and Félix Guattari, Said meticulously and forcefully summarizes the "evental" consequences of the self-de-struction of the Western nation-state/imperial project in the aftermath of World War II. I quote at length not only to underscore Said's proleptic polyvalent insight into the self-destructive nature of the identitarian logic of Western exceptionalism, but also to draw attention to his remarkable anticipation of certain cardinal critical gestures concerning resistance and the coming community, hitherto gone unnoticed, that affiliate Said with those post-poststructuralists—Giorgio Agamben, Alain Badiou, Slavoj Žižek, Jacques Rancière, Judith Butler, among others—who have been represented as his intellectual opponents:

> For surely it is one of the unhappiest characteristics of the age to have produced more refugees, migrants, displaced persons, and exiles than ever before in history, most of them as an accompaniment to and, ironically enough, as afterthoughts of great post-colonial and imperial conflicts. As the struggle for independence produced new states and new boundaries, it also produced homeless wanderers, nomads, and vagrants, unassimilated to the emerging structures of institutional power, rejected by the established order for their intransigence and obdurate rebelliousness. And insofar as these people exist between the old and the new, between the old empire and the new state, their condition articulates the tensions, irresolutions, and contradictions in the overlapping territories shown on the cultural map of imperialism.
>
> There is a great difference, however, between the optimistic mobility, the intellectual liveliness, and "logic of daring" described by the various theoreticians on whose work I have drawn, and the massive dislocations, waste, misery, and horrors endured in our century's migrations and mutilated lives. Yet it is no exaggeration to say that liberation as an intellectual mission, born in the resistance and opposition to the confinements and ravages of imperialism, has now shifted from the settled, established, and domesticated dynamics of culture to its unhoused, decentered, and exilic energies, energies whose incarnation today is the migrant, and whose consciousness is that of the intellectual and artist in exile, the political figure between domains, between forms, between homes, and between languages. From this perspective then all things are indeed counter, original, spare, strange. From this perspective also, one can see "the complete consort dancing together" contrapuntally. And while it would be the rankest Panglossian dishonesty to say that the bravura performances of the intellectual exile and the miseries of the displaced person or refugee are the same, it is possible, I think, to regard the intellectual as first distilling then articulating the predicaments that disfigure modernity—mass deportation, imprisonment, population transfer, collective dispossession, and forced immigration.

To summarize Said's overlooked indissolubly related anticipatory gestures, they include (1) the idea of the event itself; (2) the de-centering of anthropological Man; (3) the naming of the void (the refugee or migrant) concealed by the "plenary" discourse of the dominant culture; (4) the obsolescence of the traditional "settled and domesticated" means of resistance to imperial confinement; (5) the recognition of this post-imperial occasion as an interregnum—an in-between time, or, to retrieve his virtually forgotten meditation on beginnings in *Beginnings*, the radically secular now time that remains as the consequence of the implosion of teleological—end-oriented—time;[2] (5) the precipitation of exile from a homeland as the essence of the present global human condition;

(6) the putting under erasure of the Schmittian Friend/foe opposition; and, not least, (7) the opening up in the wake of the theoretical demise of the idea of the nation-state of the possibility of a radically different logic of belonging (the *polis*), one "grounded" in the irreparably decentered or exilic condition of humanity.

Said not only announces the potential for a radically new kind of resistance precipitated by this interregnum and the exilic consciousness it activates. In an eighth resonant gesture, he also suggests its essential paradoxical positive character: what I will call, despite his acknowledgment of its source in Theodor Adorno, the "Bartleby factor." Immediately following the passage quoted above, Said writes:

> "The past life of émigrés is, as we know, annulled," says Adorno in *Minima Moralia*, subtitled *Reflections from a Damaged Life*. . . . Why? "Because *anything that is not reified, cannot be counted and measured, ceases to exist" or, as he says later, is consigned to mere "background*." Although the disabling aspects of this fate are manifest, its virtues or possibilities are worth exploring. Thus the émigré consciousness—a "mind of winter" in Wallace Stevens's phrase—discovers in its marginality that "a gaze averted from the beaten track, a hatred of brutality, a search for fresh concepts not yet encompassed by the general pattern, is the last hope for thought." Adorno's general pattern is what in another place he calls the "administered world" or, insofar as the irresistible dominants in culture are concerned, "the consciousness industry." There is then not just the negative advantage of refuge in the émigré's eccentricity; there is also the positive benefit of challenging the system, describing it in language unavailable to those it has already subdued:
>
>> *In an intellectual hierarchy which constantly makes everyone answerable, unanswerability alone can call the hierarchy directly by its name.* The circulation sphere, whose stigmata are borne by intellectual outsiders, opens a last refuge to the mind that it barters away, at the very moment when refuge no longer exists. He who offers for sale something unique that no one wants to buy, represents, even against his will, freedom from exchange.[3] (CI, 333; my emphasis)

If we read Adorno's reference to the "intellectual hierarchy's" demand that everyone be answerable to its systemic imperatives as the "calling" of the administered society, we can then say that, according to this dominant cultural dispensation, the *vocation* (calling) of those who belong to it is to sacrifice their existential present in the name of service—servitude—to a "higher" cause. To anticipate, they become interpellated, means to an End, *subjected* subjects. Thus we can also say alternatively that those who are not reified, named, "counted" in and by the administered society and its teleological time frame—those who "cease to exist"—are enabled to refuse being answerable to the calling—or, in Bartleby's phrase in response to the lawyer boss's call, "would prefer not to"—thus exposing the vocational (administered) society as a fundamentally coercive one.

These eight indissolubly related Saidian revocational gestures, I suggest, not only anticipate the self-destruction of the administered/vocational society in the wake of the United States' declaration of its unending War on Terror in the aftermath of the bombings of the World Trade Center and the Pentagon on September 11, 2001: the establishment of the state of exception and the security state as the global norm. They are also proleptic of the radical diagnosis of the post-9/11 global occasion—and the paradoxical politics of resistance articulated by a number of contemporary thinkers whom I call post-poststructuralists in this book. What I mean by this term, to put it provisionally and all too simply, is the critical orientation of those "Heideggerians of the left"—Giorgio Agamben, Alain Badiou, Slavoj Žižek, Jacques Rancière, Judith Butler—who closed the divide between ontology and worldliness that their textual-oriented poststructuralist predecessors, particularly the deconstructionists, as Said rightly claimed, left disablingly intact. In what follows, I will argue that these theorists, including Said, constitute a constellation that, in radicalizing the poststructuralists' de-centering of Man (as *Anthropologos*), has inaugurated an ontological/worldly oppositional discourse that is more adequate than both the oppositional discourse of the Enlightenment (Anthropological) era and the poststructuralism of the postcolonial period to the radically changed global terrain precipitated by the United States' declaration of its unilateral global War on Terror, its establishment of the Homeland Security State, its commitment to achieving hegemony over the planet in behalf of neoliberal capitalism, and its consequent self-righteous use of militarist means of achieving this global goal: pre-emptive war, regime change, and the spectacular "shock and awe" tactics that strikes the spectator dumb—bereaves him or her of language, the *sine qua non* of a polity.

2

Before directly addressing the revolutionary thought of this post-poststructuralist constellation, however, it will be useful to briefly recall the genealogy of its provenance. Its origins, as we have seen earlier in this book, lies, above all, in the radicalization, via the mediation of Hannah Arendt and Michel Foucault, of certain revolutionary ontological and worldly disclosures emanating from Martin Heidegger's inaugural de-struction (*De-struktion*) of metaphysics—that ontology, endemic to the West (the "onto-theo-logical tradition"), that thinks being *meta ta physica* (from after or above or beyond things as they are: panoptically), thus establishing a binary teleological logic that privileges Identity over difference and, in its latest allotrope (the anthropological phase), endows human being (Man) with the right of mastery over the other phenomena of being. The main ontological disclosures precipitated by the destruction of the onto-theo-logical tradition and that anticipate the post-poststructuralists are, above all, (1) the exposure of the Truth of the metaphysical interpretation of being as a fiction and the consequent ontological de-centering of Man; (2) the delegitimization of the prevailing teleological—or panoptic/spatialized—concept of time in favor of an existential temporality; (3) the unhoming of the humanistic *Anthropos* by way of asserting humanity's primordial "thrownness" (*Geworfenheit*) into the nothingness of being (*das Nichts*): homelessness or exile as the human species' primordial mode of being-in-the-world; (4) the de-centering of Man as the center and measure of all things—the rejection of the servitude of mastery as humanity's essential mode of comportment toward the phenomena of being—his vocation (or calling) as a being-in-the-world—in favor of "care" (*Sorge*): the recognition of his privileged status among the phenomena of being—his "ontological/ontic" or "ek-static/in-sistent" (outside-inside, in between) being-in-the-world—as a *responsibility* rather than a right of mastery.

The principal worldly disclosure precipitated by Heidegger's destruction of the ontotheological tradition that is remarkably proleptic of the post-poststructuralist moment has its origins in Heidegger's critique of *das Man* (in *Being and Time* and "Letter on Humanism"): the "they-self" that is the consequence of the progressive reification and eventual forgetting of the question of being in modernity, that is, the reduction of thinking and language to instrumental calculation under the aegis of the "dictatorship of the public realm": what, to anticipate, Hannah Arendt would later rephrase as the "banalization of evil":

> The widely and rapidly spreading devastation of language not only undermines aesthetic and moral responsibility, in every use of language; it arises from the threat to the essence of humanity. A mere cultivated

> use of language is still no proof that we have as yet escaped the danger to our essence. These days, in fact, such usage might sooner testify that we have not yet seen and cannot see the danger because we have never yet placed ourselves in view of it. Much bemoaned of late, and much too lately, the downfall of language is, however, not the grounds for, but already a consequence of, the state of affairs in which language under the dominance of modern metaphysics of subjectivity almost irremediably falls out of its element. Language still denies us its essence; that it is the house of being. Instead, language surrenders itself to our mere willing and trafficking as an instrument of domination over beings. We encounter beings as actualities in a calculative businesslike way, but also scientifically and by way of philosophy, with explanations and proofs.[4]

This is a telling indictment of the calculative language of modernity. But, as I have shown in chapter 4, it is in "The Question Concerning Technology" that Heidegger exposes that horrific aspect of the banalization of language and thinking under the dictatorship of the public realm and anticipates the post-poststructuralists' underscoring of the dehumanization of humanity under the aegis of "disinterested" Enlightenment (anthropological) thinking. I am referring, more particularly, to Giorgio Agamben's diagnosis, following Hannah Arendt's critique of *homo faber* (man as maker) and his means/end logic, and Michel Foucault's identification of modern disciplinary politics as a biopolitics, of the dehumanizing momentum of modernity that ends in the reduction of *bios* to *zoé*, the life of man as political animal to bare life. In that remarkable essay, which, despite the archive of commentary it has solicited, has yet to be adequately understood, Heidegger refers to the liminal condition of the technological vocation—the modern (spatializing) mode of knowledge production (*Ge-stell*, Enframing) that operates as a "challenging forth"—as the reduction of the phenomena of being to *Bestand*, usually rendered into English as "standing reserve," but which, to underscore its proleptic status, I have translated as "disposable reserve," a reserve that is "on call" only as long as it has exchange value. When this latter requisite no longer exists, the life that has been reduced to "standing by" can, in Agamben's more political language, as we shall see, be killed with impunity. I requote this inaugural passage from Heidegger to underscore its cardinal importance in this study:

> What kind of unconcealment is it, then, that is peculiar to that which comes to stand forth through this setting-upon that challenges? Everywhere everything is ordered to stand by, to be *immediately at hand, indeed to stand*

> *there just so that it may be on call for a further ordering.* Whatever is ordered about in this way has its own standing, We call it the standing-reserve [*Bestand*]. The word expresses here something more, and something more essential, than mere "stock." The name "standing-reserve" assumes the rank of an inclusive rubric. It designates nothing less than the way in which everything presences that is wrought upon by the challenging revealing. Whatever stands by in the sense of standing-reserve no longer stands over against us as object.[5] (my emphasis)

In this passage, Heidegger identifies the "disposable reserve" as the phenomena of being that modern humanity's masterly vocation—its "enframing" mode of revealing (knowledge production)—is to put on call. But in thus reducing being at large to disposable reserve in keeping with its vocational imperatives ("attendance"—servitude—to the call of technological enframing), Heidegger goes on to say, humanity, the master, not only becomes the slave of the "higher" call, but, as we have seen, also, anticipating Agamben, paradoxically exposes itself to the dehumanizing dynamics of enframing, becomes himself "disposable reserve":

> Yet when destining reigns in the name of Enframing, it is the supreme danger. This danger attests itself to us in two ways. As soon as what is unconcealed no longer concerns man even as object, but does so, rather, exclusively as standing-reserve, and man in the midst of objectlessness is nothing but the orderer of the standing-reserve, then he comes to the very brink of a precipitous fall; that is, he comes to the point where he himself will have to be taken as standing-reserve. Meanwhile man, precisely as the one so threatened, exalts himself to the posture of lord of the earth. In this way the impression comes to prevail that everything man encounters exists insofar as it is his construct. This illusion gives rise in turn to one final delusion: It seems as though man everywhere and always encounters only himself. . . . *In truth, however, precisely nowhere does man today any longer encounter himself, i.e. his essence.* Man stands so decisively *in attendance on the challenging forth of Enframing as a claim*, that he fails to see himself as the one spoken to, and hence also fails in every way to hear in what respect he ek-sists [is an ontic-ontological, outside-insider, between the transcendental and the secular worlds], from out of his essence, in the realm of an exhortation or address, and thus *can never* encounter only himself. (QT, 26–27; second emphasis is mine)

The work of Hannah Arendt, Heidegger's student, was, it could be said, undertaken not only to bring to light some of the worldly realities to which Heidegger was blinded by his overdetermination of his ontological insights, but also, and perhaps more fundamentally, to politically radicalize her mentor's fundamentally ontological disclosure of the will to power—the coerciveness—informing the metaphysical mode of knowledge production of the onto-theo-logical tradition, that is, to demonstrate what Heidegger theoretically asserted but in practice failed to (adequately) think: that the (nothingness of) being he retrieved from this spatializing tradition constitutes an indissoluble continuum, however unevenly developed at any moment in history, extending from the ontological site and the site of the subject, through the sites of the ecos, culture, race, and gender, to those of the economy, the domestic order, and global politics, that is, from its abstract to its more *worldly* manifestations. More specifically, Arendt, in keeping with her effort to radicalize Heidegger's critique of the Western tradition, sought not only to show that the Enlightenment, far from inaugurating a humanist revolution in announcing the hegemony of the secular realm, constituted a naturalization of the will to power inhering in the supernatural/teleological perspective, a dispensation in which the *Theo-logos* of the former age was replaced by the *Anthropo-logos* as sovereign center of the continuum of being, in which, that is to say, the metaphysics (thinking *meta ta physica*: from after or beyond or above things as they are) of the former age—and its teleological conception of time—remained intact. Taking her directives from Heidegger's de-centering of Man and his retrieval of Greek "errancy," that is, the radicalization of the idea of beginning—and her own condition as a "conscious pariah" (as opposed to the assimilated Jewish "parvenu")—she also sought to think a new *polis* based not on the identity endemic to the nation-state, but, anticipating post-poststructuralist theorists such a Giorgio Agamben, Alain Badiou, Slavoj Žižek, Jacques Rancière, and Judith Butler, on the identityless identity of the exilic condition, the human species' thrownness in the world. I cannot do justice in this limited space to Arendt's wide and deep-ranging ontological/political thought as it pertains to these post-poststructuralist issues, but by retrieving her Heideggerian origins from the oblivion to which they were relegated by the Habermasian school of political thinking that usurped her work, the importance of this affiliation will become clear.

As I have noted above, the point of departure of this Heideggerian version of the origins of Arendt's thought is precisely the exilic condition that the Habermasian school (and the Jewish intellectuals reacting to her *Eichmann in Jerusalem*) almost entirely overlooked: her status as a "conscious pariah"[6]—as an in-between, outside/inside, figure, who is both an ontological exile and a worldly Jew conscious of and resisting her victimization by anti-Semitism. As in the case of Edward Said, Arendt's acknowledgment of her onto-political exilic condition—her "non-Jewish Jewishness"[7]—precipitated, despite its ravages, a productive estranging perspective. It enabled her to perceive, contrapuntally as it were, the polyvalent violence against the other that those, like the Hippias of Plato's *Hippias Major* (and Adolf Eichmann),[8] who are total insiders (*das Man*), are blinded to by this vocational mode of belonging.

Further, and equally important, Arendt, as conscious pariah or non-Jewish Jew, was enabled to free herself from the spatialized teleological (end-oriented) time to which the Western metaphysical tradition has reduced the transient temporality of being. For her, this Heideggerian ontological insight had, above all, two related radical worldly political consequences: (1) It demoted *homo faber* (man the maker)—the presiding figure of man in anthropological modernity, who, in entirely socializing the ancient private sphere (rendering the *oikos* a national "household economy" or, in Adorno's term, an "administered society") where *animal laborans* presides, threatens to reduce humanity at large to the latter—in favor of man, the *bios politikos* (political animal: "ek-sistent/in-sistent" in Heidegger's language); (2) It retrieved a notion of time affiliated with this *bios politikos* in which the beginning (like Said's)[9] is untethered to its consummation in an End (a notion of time that, in opposition to Heidegger's privileging of death—*Sein-sum-Tode)* as the determinant of existential life, she insistently associates with natality. By the first, the demotion of *homo faber*, I mean, more specifically, the delegitimization of the prevailing means/end or possibility/act dyad that is intrinsic to the logic of the teleological concept of time that has enjoyed hegemonic status in Western secular modernity.

> The actual work of fabrication is performed under the guidance of a model in accordance with which the object is constructed. This model can be an image beheld by the eye of the mind or blueprint in which the image has already found a tentative materialization through work. In either case, what guides the work of fabrication is outside the fabricator and precedes the actual work process in much the same way as the urgencies of the life process within the laborer precedes the actual process.[10]

To anticipate her affiliation with Giorgio Agamben, Arendt's displacement of *homo faber* by man as *bios politikos* constitutes a rejection of the *vocation* imposed on the human species by the West's privileging of a teleological concept of time: the dehumanizing *calling* that renders humanity the willing servant of a "higher," *other-worldly* cause—or, to put this in a more recent language, the "interpellation" that reduces the human self to a "subjected subject."[11] Put alternatively to suggest its possible source in her fellow conscious pariah, Walter Benjamin—and this is the second consequence of Arendt's Heideggerian de-struction of teleological time—in refusing to be answerable to the master/slave imperatives of the Western calling, Arendt is enabled to retrieve the "time of the now" (*ho nyn kairos*, *Jetztzeit*) of which humanity has been deprived under the aegis of the means/end imperative intrinsic to *homo faber*. This is the in-between time—*inter esse*—that precipitates "interest" (Kierkegaard) or, in Heidegger's formulation, care (*Sorge*), the profane time, that is, which, in breaking the relationship between potentiality and act, instigates the "active life" (*vita activa*)—the careful speech or saying/doing or, what is the same thing, the human agency that initiates (not once and for all, but always already) that is the *sine qua non* of *bios politikos*:

> With word and deed, we insert ourselves into the human world, and this insertion is like a second birth, in which we confirm and take upon ourselves the naked fact of our original physical appearance. This insertion is not forced upon us by necessity, like labor [*animal laborans*], and it is not prompted by utility like work [*homo faber*]. It may be stimulated by the presence of others whose company we may wish to join, but it is never conditioned by them; its impulse springs from the beginning which came into the world when we were born and to which we respond by beginning something new on our own initiative. To act, in its most general sense, means to take an initiative, to begin (as the Greek word *archein*, "to begin," "to lead," and eventually, "to rule," indicates), to set something into motion (which is the original meaning of the Latin *agere*). Because they are *initium*, newcomers and beginners by virtue of birth, men take initiative, are prompted into action. *Initium ergo ut esset, creates est homo, ante quem nullius fuit* [that there is a beginning, man was created before whom there was nobody], said Augustine in his political philosophy. This beginning is not the same as the beginning of the world; it is not the beginning of something but of somebody, who is a beginner himself. With the creation of man, the principle of beginning came into the world itself, which, of course, is only another way of saying that the principle of freedom was created when man was created but not before. (*HC*, 176–177)

The socialization of the private realm (the *oikos* of *animal laborans*) by *homo faber* in the nation-state of Enlightenment modernity, according to Arendt, also precipitated the massive and unprecedented category of the person who doesn't count in a system of belonging tethered to nativity/citizenship/territory: the human to whom which, we have seen, she variously refers to as "the superfluous," "the displaced," "the refugee," "the stateless person," "the outlaw," "the emigrant," "the émigré," and, above all, "the pariah"—to underscore its non-existent existence. This not only means the denial of speech and action, which is to say, a polity, to these countless countless. Reminiscent of Heidegger's critique of the technological mode of knowledge production that threatens to transform the human species to "disposable reserve" (*Bestand*), it also means their dehumanization, or, to anticipate, the subjection of their bodies to the biopolitics that reduces *bios* to *zoé*, what after Arendt, Agamben calls bare life (*vida nuda*). In the proleptic chapter of *The Origins of Totalitarianism* entitled "The Decline of the Nation-State and the End of the Rights of Man," in which she inaugurates the now focal critique of the nation-state version of human rights, Arendt puts this epochal dehumanizing consequence of the "socialization" of the private sphere (of *animal laborans*) in modernity in the following resonantly radicalized way:

> Yet in light of recent events [the institutionalization of the concentration camp and the gas chamber in Nazi Germany] it is possible to say that even slaves still belonged to some sort of human community. . . . To be a slave was after all to have a distinctive character, a place in society—*more than the abstract nakedness of being human and nothing but human*. Not the loss of specific rights, then, *but the loss of a community willing and able to guarantee any rights whatsoever, has been the calamity which has befallen ever-increasing numbers of people*. Man, it turns out, can lose all so-called Rights of Man without losing his essential quality as man, his human dignity. *Only the loss of a polity itself expels him from humanity*. (*OT*, 197; my emphasis)

The vocational means/end logic of *homo faber* manifests itself in modernity in the socialization of the public sphere—the rendering of the private, biopolitically organized *oikos* a "national household" economy. At the end point of the development of its logic of belonging, it reproduces the "worldless" *animal laborans*—the utterly unworldly entity that labors for no other purpose than to keep the body alive—as the defining figure of the post–World War II occasion, now, however, in its liminal avatar: what Agamben was to call "bare life," life that, like the Jews under the aegis of Nazism, can be killed without the killing being called murder.

As dark as Arendt's reading of post–World War II modernity is, it nevertheless, as in the case of Edward Said's diagnosis of the post-imperial era, points, *precisely in its darkness*—its "expulsion of man from humanity," its utter denial of language to the vast population of the exilic "superfluous" precipitated by the fulfillment of the logic of belonging of the nation-state—to the positive possibilities of this enforced exilic—dehumanized—condition. For in reducing this vast population of stateless pariahs to silence (their deprivation of saying/doing, a polity), the exilic silence, at this disclosive liminal point, becomes—or points to—an alternative language to the plenary vocational/interpellative language of the nation-state, a spectral subversive one—that of the "*conscious* pariah," which, like Said's Adornian version, in refusing to be answerable to the hierarchy's call, can "call the hierarchy by its [oppressive] right name." More specifically, in calling into question the means/end language of the nation-state under the sway of *homo faber*, this alternative language precipitated by the fulfillment of the logic of the nation-state, Arendt implies, no doubt with her fellow Jewish exile Walter Benjamin in mind, has its point of departure in the radically transient, that is, profane, "time of the now," the exilic "in-between" time of the interregnum that, it will be recalled, Said was to posit as the locus of the new, post-colonial form of resistance: "liberation as an intellectual mission has now shifted from the settled, established, and domesticated dynamics of culture to its unhoused, decentered, and exilic energies, energies whose incarnation today is the migrant, and whose incarnation is that of the intellectual and artist in exile, the political figure between domains, between forms, between homes, and between languages."

This liberating potential of the (conscious) pariah disclosed by the coming to its end of the logic of belonging of the nation-state is implied throughout *The Origins of Totalitarianism*, particularly in the second volume, "Imperialism," which, as in the case of Said's diagnosis of the post-colonial moment in *Culture and Imperialism*, focuses on the reduced status of the vast population of stateless people precipitated by the (contradictory) combination of imperialism (the precipitation of racism and the administration of human bodies as means of domesticating their threat) and the binarist logic of belonging of the nation-state in the wake of World War II. But for a reason that will become clear in the sequel I will cite Arendt's earlier proleptic biographical essay "We Refugees," where, in distinguishing between the "parvenu" and the "conscious pariah," she identifies the refugee not only as the defining figure of the post-war global occasion but also as the "vanguard of their people":

> History has forced the status of outlaws upon both, upon [conscious] pariahs and parvenus alike. The latter have not yet accepted the great wisdom of Balzac's "*On ne parvient pas deux fois*" [One does not arrive/

> succeed twice]; thus they don't understand the wild dreams of the former and feel humiliated in sharing their fate. Those few refugees who insist upon telling the truth, even to the point of "indecency," get in exchange for their unpopularity one priceless advantage: *history is no longer a closed book to them and politics is no longer the privilege of Gentiles*. They know that the outlawing of the Jewish people in Europe had been followed closely by the outlawing of most European nations. *Refugees driven from country to country represent the vanguard of their people—if they keep their identity* [refuse to be assimilated]. For the first time Jewish history is not separated but tied up with that of all other nations. The comity of European peoples went to pieces when, and because, it allowed its weakest member to be excluded and persecuted.[12]

In this passage, Arendt, it is important to register, not simply envisions the exilic refugee, understood as conscious pariah—or, in Said's formulation, following Isaac Deutscher, as "non-Jewish": the nobody who, in becoming conscious of its superfluity, is enabled, like Bartleby, to use its in-betweenness—its identityless identity—against the oppressor—as the paradoxical figure that promises liberation. From the exilic vantage point of the time of the now, the refugee as conscious pariah in the interregnum, as I will show later by way of invoking Agamben's reading of Arendt's "We Refugees," she also, like Said, however indirectly, envisions a coming *polis* that, in its refusal of the trinity intrinsic to the structure of the nation-state ("State, Nation [nativity], Territory")[13]—or, more accurately, in rendering that metaphysical structure "inoperative"—is proleptic of the radically different—de-centered, structureless—structure of the *polis* being envisioned by post-poststructuralists like Agamben, Badiou, Žižek, Rancière, Butler, and others.

The third figure in this genealogy of post-poststructuralist theory is Michel Foucault. Indeed, it could be said that Foucault is this post-nation-state/colonial constellation's main inspiration insofar as he contributed significantly (however tentatively) to the process of bridging the gap between being and world (ontology and the ontic)—specifically, his disclosure of the complicity between the panoptic (metaphysical) mode of knowledge production and worldly power-relations in the anthropological phase of the Western (onto-theo-logical) tradition—and his consequent inaugural study of the biopolitics that has increasingly characterized this anthropological era. I mean specifically (1) his critique of the modern disciplinary mode of knowledge production he calls "panopticism"—the disciplinary mode that, in *seeing being from above*, spatializes or reifies all the sites, from the abstract to the more worldly, on its continuum: from being as such and the subject; through race, gender, and culture; to the ecos, the economy, domestic politics, and international political relations, and (2) his critique of panopticism's most advanced mode: that biopolitical form of knowledge production, that, following Heidegger's critique of technology, the mode of thinking *meta ta physica* Heidegger calls *Ge-stell*, the "challenging forth" or "Enframing," which, as we have seen, ends in the dehumanization of man: his reduction to "disposable reserve" (*Bestand*). This constellation is at the heart of Foucault's masterpiece, *Surveiller et punir* (I use the original title of *Discipline and Punish* to draw attention to the provenance of this interpellative/disciplinary mode of knowledge production), which, in distinguishing between the *ancien regime*'s use of overt power from the new bourgeoisie's use of knowledge about the human body to domesticate the amorphous, unruly, and threatening multitude (the "repressive hypothesis"), inaugurates his decisive analysis of the biopolitics that has become the dehumanizing politics of the modern era. The first, the indissoluble relationality between panoptic ontology (perceiving being *meta ta physica*) and a polyvalent world structured in domination—the movement from the Panopticon to "panopticism"—is epitomized by the following summary passage on the technology of Jeremy Bentham's Panopticon from *Surveiller et punir*:

> The Panopticon . . . *must be understood as a generalizable model* of functioning; a way of defining power relations in terms of the everyday life of men. No doubt Bentham presents it as a particular institution, closed in upon itself. Utopias, perfectly closed in upon themselves, are common enough. As opposed to ruined prisons, littered with mechanisms of torture, to be seen in Piranesi's engravings, the Panopticon presents a cruel, ingenious cage. *The fact that it should have given rise, even in our own time, to so many variations, projected or realized, is evidence of the imaginative intensity that it has possessed for almost two hundred years.* But the Panopticon must not be understood as a dream building: it is the *diagram of a mechanism of power reduced to its ideal form; its functioning, abstracted from any obstacle, resistance or friction, must be represented as a pure architectural and optical system: it is in fact a figure of political technology that may and must be detached from any specific use.*
>
> *It is polyvalent in its applications; it serves to reform prisoners, but also to treat patients, to instruct school children, to confine the insane, to supervise workers, to put beggars and idlers to work.* It is a type of location of bodies in space, of distribution of individuals in relation to one another, of hierarchical organization, of disposition of centres and channels of power, of definition of the instruments and modes of intervention of power, which

> can be implemented in hospitals, workshops, schools, prisons. When one is dealing with a multiplicity of individuals on whom a task or a particular form of behaviour must be imposed, the panoptic schema may be used. It is—necessary modifications apart—applicable "to all establishments whatsoever, in which, within a space not too large to be covered over or commanded by buildings, a number of persons are meant to be kept under inspection."[14]

The second phase of this constellation, the fulfillment of the means/end logic of panopticism in the production of "useful and docile bodies" and thus the systematization and universalization of biopolitics, is articulated by Foucault in the chapter of *Surveiller et punir* aptly entitled "Docile Bodies":

> The historical moment of the disciplines was the moment when an art of the human body was born, which was directed not only at the growth of its skills, nor at the intensification of its subjection. But at the formation of a relation that in the mechanism itself makes it more obedient as it becomes more useful, and conversely. What was then being formed was a policy of coercions that act upon the body, a calculated manipulation of its elements, its gestures, its behaviour. The human body was entering a machinery of power that explores it, breaks it down, and rearranges it. A "political anatomy," which was also a "mechanics of power," was being born; it defined how one may have a hold over others' bodies, not only so that they may do what one wishes, but so that they may operate as one wishes, with the techniques, the speed, and the efficiency that one determines. Thus discipline produces subjected and practiced bodies, "docile" bodies. Discipline increases the forces of the body (in economic terms of utility) and diminishes these same forces (in political terms of obedience). In short, it dissociates power from the body; on the one hand, it turns it into an "aptitude," a "capacity," which it seeks to increase; on the other hand, it reverses the course of the energy, the power that might result from it, and turns it into a relation of strict subjection. If economic exploitation separates the forces and the product of labour, let us say that disciplinary coercion establishes in the body the constricting link between increased aptitude and an increased domination. (*DP*, 137–138)

The critique of the metaphysical thinking—and its means/end logic—of the humanist Enlightenment era and the disclosure that this universal panoptic mode of knowledge production is not, as it was claimed by its bourgeois proponents, politically liberating (knowledge frees), but deceptively coercive (disciplinary, an apparatus of capture);

that its "political anatomy," or biopolitics, in producing subjected subjects—"useful and docile bodies"—is systematically dehumanizing; that the vocation this panopticism inscribes in its subjects is to slavishly serve the "higher cause" of bourgeois capitalism: all these, I submit, recall Heidegger and Arendt and also anticipate the post-poststructuralists, particularly, as we shall see, Giorgio Agamben. They also, by implication—supported by Foucault's late turn to the "care of the [human] self"—point to the post-poststructuralists' positive valorization of the worldly—radically secular or profane—realm, the realm of the not-at-home and the transient in-between time of the now; and, I submit, to the indirect (Bartlebyan) mode of violently passive resistance that, in refusing to be answerable to the call of the interpellative discourse of those who determine what counts and who counts, calls the "hierarchy by its right name" or, in Agamben's language, revokes—renders the dehumanizing logic of the vocation "inoperative."

3

The group of left Heideggerian theorists I am calling post-poststructuralists include Giorgio Agamben, Alain Badiou, Slavoj Žižek, Jacques Rancière, and Judith Butler, among others. They constitute, admittedly, a somewhat amorphous constellation, but what they have in common—which has hitherto largely been overlooked—is more important: above all, the polyvalent effort to world the ontological decentering of Being; to think resistance to a world structured in domination by taking its directives from the nobodies—"bare life" (Agamben), "the uncounted" or "inexistent" (Alain Badiou);[15] the "part of no part" (Jacques Rancière); the "ungrievable" (Judith Butler), among other such synonyms of the same phenomenon—to which the vast majority of singular humans have been reduced by the dominant capitalist/parliamentarian minority that decides who "counts"; and to imagine a coming polity "founded" in this radically universal (common) singularity of these unaccountable uncounted. For the sake of economy, I will, in what follows, focus primarily on Agamben and Badiou.

Agamben, perhaps more than any of the others in this constellation, epitomizes the legacy that begins with Heidegger and culminates with the post-poststructuralists. Like Hannah Arendt, a student of Heidegger both in the literal and metaphorical senses, Agamben takes his onto-political point of departure from his mentor's ontological de-struction of the metaphysical thinking of the Western ontotheological tradition. Like Heidegger's, Agamben's destruction of Western metaphysical thinking has as its fundamental critical purpose to demonstrate that metaphysics necessarily represents being as teleological (Being): informed by a principle of presence that reduces the temporality of being to a linear/circular beginning-middle-end *structure*. To thematize the optical metaphor that informs thinking *meta ta physica*, its panoptic eye *views* the be-*ing* of being, which is to say, spatializes or structures its singular and unrepresentable dynamics—its nothingness—to render "it" comprehensible, that is, subject to mastery (from the Latin "*prehendere*," to grasp). In other words, like Heidegger's, Agamben's de-structive hermeneutics is intended to reveal that Western metaphysical thinking in all its historical manifestations (Greco-Roman, Christian, and Enlightenment) is informed by the will to power over the phenomena represented by the second term of the teleological binary formula constituting the essence of metaphysical thinking: Identity (Presence) is the condition for the possible of difference (radical temporality, the nothing) and not the other way around. What is different from Heidegger in Agamben's initial critical gesture is his conscious affirmation of the indissoluble relationality of the ontological and the worldly sites on the continuum of being—being and politics—and his sustained effort to think both the critical and positive implications of this affiliation between ontology and worldliness.

According to Agamben, this Western teleological/structuring interpretation of the being of being, particularly in its modern—anthropological—phase, assigns, as an inscribed imperative, the human species its mode of moral comportment toward being's polyvalent sites. It precipitates a binarist means/end logic *vis-á-vis* being in which the means—as in the case of time, the nothing, difference, the question in the metaphysical schema—is subordinated to the End. In Agamben's preferred formulation, this teleological/structuring interpretation of being renders potentiality dependent on the Act.[16] Following and radicalizating Heidegger's critical diagnosis of the "calculative" means/end logic of technological revealing (*Ge-stell:* the Enframing that "challenges forth") and particularly Hannah Arendt's critique of the means/end logic of *homo faber* (man the maker),[17] the presiding figure of man in Enlightenment modernity, Agamben reads this (teleo)logic as imposing a "vocational" ethics on humanity. By "vocation" he means (not too distant from Louis Althusser's "interpellation"—or the Wall Street lawyers' calling of Bartleby in Melville's fiction) a hailing from above that demands the postponement of existential encounters with transient temporality—the "time of the now," to anticipate—in favor of slavishly serving a Higher Cause, that, in providing the human subject with the illusion of being the master of the phenomena of being (a subject), is reduced to "disposable reserve" (Heidegger); "subjected subject" (Althusser); "useful and docile body" (Foucault):

> The fact that must constitute the point of departure for any discourse on ethics is that there is no essence, no historical or spiritual vocation, no biological destiny that humans must enact or realize. This is the only reason why something like ethics can exist, because it is clear that if humans were or had to be this or that substance, this or that destiny, no ethical experience would be possible—there would be only tasks to be done.
>
> This does not mean, however, that humans are not, and do not have to be something, that they are simply consigned to nothingness and therefore can freely decide whether to be or not to be, to adopt or not adopt this or that destiny (nihilism and decisionism coincide at this point). There is in effect something that humans are and have to be, but this something is not an essence nor properly a thing. It is the simple fact of one's own existence as possibility or potentiality.[18]

It is, I suggest, this vocational means/end logic—this calculative mode of knowledge production Heidegger calls the "enframing" that "challenges forth"; or, in Arendt's Marxian formulation, the "socialization" in modernity of the private sphere ("man's metabolism with nature," which is intrinsic to the "worldlessness" of the *oikos* of *animal laborans*)—that Agamben radicalizes in *Homo Sacer*.[19] Taking his directives from Foucault's diagnosis of modern society as a disciplinary society that reduces human life to "useful and docile bodies," or, more precisely, a biopolitical society, in which biopolitics is practiced right down to the capillaries of the body politic, Agamben radicalizes Arendt's account of the re-emergence in late modernity of the totally "unworldly" (i.e., apolitical) *animal laborans* by way, ironically, of the fulfillment of *homo faber*'s means/end logic (his decisive privileging of the Act over potentiality that produces the consumer society). He reads the dehumanizing consequence of the increasing biopoliticization of life in modernity not simply as the reproduction of "*animal laborans*" as such ("man's metabolism with nature") or as "useful and docile body," but as *animal laborans* in its most extreme form—"bare life" (*vida nuda*): life that can be killed without the act being called murder—and the concentration camp, the zone of indistinction between exclusion and inclusion in which bare life is caught, as the paradigmatic liminal space of modernity—totalitarian and democratic—in which the dehumanizing logic of biopolitics becomes thanatopolitics:

> Along with the emergence of biopolitics, we can observe a displacement and gradual expansion beyond the limits of the decision on bare life, in which sovereignty consisted. If there is a line in every modern state marking the point at which the decision on life becomes a decision on death, and biopolitics can turn into thanatopolitics, this line no longer appears today as a stable border dividing two clearly distinct zones. This line is now in motion and gradually moving into areas other than that of political life, areas in which the sovereign is entering into an ever more intimate symbiosis not only with the jurist but also with the doctor, the scientist, the expert and the priest. In the pages that follow, we shall try to show that certain events that are fundamental for the political history of modernity (such as the declaration of rights), as well as others that seem instead to represent an incomprehensible intrusion of biologico-scientific principles into the political order (such as National Socialist eugenics and its elimination of "life that is unworthy of being lived," or the contemporary debate on the normative determination of death criteria), acquire their true sense only if they are brought back to the common biopolitical (or thanatopolitical) context to which they belong. From this perspective, the camp—as the pure, absolute, and impassable biopolitical space (insofar as it is founded solely on the state of exception)—will appear as the hidden paradigm of the political space of modernity, whose metamorphoses and disguises we will have to learn to recognize. (*HS*, 122–123)

If Agamben's first major departure from Heidegger is his radicalization of the latter's disclosure that the vocational means/end logic of modern technology eventually reduces the human species to disposable reserve, the second related departure is his identification of the state of exception as the foundational principle of the accelerating momentum that is reducing human life to bare life and displacing the *polis* by the concentration camp as the hidden paradigm of the modern "democratic" age. In modernity, according to Agamben, the state of exception, as in the case of Nazi Germany or the United States of the George W. Bush presidency, has become the rule. Under its aegis, the primary goal of political decision making has become national security—the preservation of the (national) body politic (the "homeland"). At this paradoxical liminal point in the pursuit of its logic of belonging, the "law"—the human right to be—has been obliterated in the name of saving it. And the binarist Friend/foe logic, which, as Agamben, reading Carl Schmitt against himself, shows, is intrinsic to the exceptionalist sovereign *Logos* of metaphysical thinking, has become not simply biopolitics—the systematic reduction of human life to bare life—but thanatopolitics, a politics in which life can be killed with impunity in the name of the higher exceptionalist cause.[20]

Thus far, I have all too briefly summarized the major critical imperatives of Agamben's radicalization of Heidegger's, Arendt's, and Foucault's de-struction of the anthropological phase of the ontotheological tradition. Equally important are the indissolubly related positive possibilities concerning resistance against the biopolitical democratic/capitalist world order and beyond that the coming *polis*. Following Heidegger's retrieval of temporality—the be-*ing* of being—as an ontological phenomenon, particularly Walter Benjamin's "time of the now" (*Jetztzeit*)—from the oblivion to which the spatializing imperatives of metaphysics have relegated it, Agamben, like Hannah Arendt (and remarkably like Edward Said) reads the post–World War II world as an interregnum or, more precisely, the liminal point in the development of the logic of nation-state belonging that has precipitated for positive thought the nothing (*das Nichts*) that the modern world will, at all costs, have nothing to do with all across the continuum of being from the ontologico-subjective to the more patently socio-political sites. The consequence of this liberation of the polyvalent nothing and its now time precipitated by the evental self-de-struction of the teleological/spatialized time of anthropological modernity and its means/end logic is that potentiality as such has been liberated from its bondage to the Act (the "higher cause"). In this new dispensation the ethical imperative—the human vocation—becomes the "revocation of every vocation." That is, the retrieval of the in-between time of the now renders the sovereign Law—its promise/fulfillment structure; its binary logic of belonging that re-presents the be-*ing* of being as nothing, the uncounted, the superfluous, the ungrievable, the part of no part; and the operations of the vocational ethos—"inoperative" (*inoperosita*). Taking his point of departure from the Jew/Greek (Gentile) opposition that is at the heart of his radically revisionary reading of the Apostle Paul's account of his evental messianic "calling" in "Letter to the Romans," Agamben writes:

> According to the apostle, this movement [of the calling (*klesis*)] is, above all, a nullification: "Circumcision [the Jews] is nothing, and the foreskin [the Greeks or Gentile] is nothing." That which, according to the law, made one man a Jew and the other a *goy*, one a slave and another a free

> man is now annulled by the vocation. What remains in this nothing? Once again, *meneto* (remaining) does not convey indifference. It signifies the immobile anaphoric gesture of the messianic calling, its being essentially and foremost *a calling of the calling.* For this reason, it may apply to any condition; but for this same reason, it *revokes* a condition and radically puts it into question *in the very act of adhering to it.*[21]

The vocation intrinsic to the metaphysical tradition, as we have seen, alienates humans from the time of the now (*ho nyn kairos*), the *inter esse* of its occasion, that generates engaged interest or care (the difference that makes a difference in the world); it orients the human toward a future *Telos* and in so doing reduces its polyvalent potentiality to a fixed identity, its relation to the phenomena it encounters in terms of the binary Friend/foe logic (Jew versus Greek in the above passage), and its practice to undeviating servitude to the higher cause. The evental vocation Agamben derives from Paul, on the other hand, entails "the revocation of every vocation." In taking its directives from the time of the now, it does not obliterate the Law; it renders it *katargein* (in-operative). That is, the Law's promise/fulfillment structure, its means/end economy, and its binary Friend/foe moral logic remain intact, but they no longer work in the invisible and polyvalent deadly way they did under the aegis of the sovereign Law. In this new dispensation, in short, the "Jew" becomes a "non-Jewish Jew" and the "Greek" (or "Gentile") becomes a "non-Greek Greek" (or "non-Gentile Gentile"): exilic figures, who, as such outsider/insiders of the homeland, have no longer any reason to be answerable to the inexorable imperatives of the logic of belonging of the dominant culture, and thus can, to recall Edward Said's gloss on Adorno's Bartlebyan insight into the new anti-identitarian mode of resistance precipitated by the self-destruction of the nation-state/imperial project, "call the hierarchy directly by its name."

It is, in fact, this new "Bartlebyan" mode of resistance, the possibility precipitated by the emergence of the unhomed émigré (Said) or refugee (Arendt) as the presiding figure of the post–World War II global interregnum, that Agamben, though his example is the contemporary capitalist/communist Chinese hierarchy, is attempting to think by way of the coming to be of the singular and unnamable "whatever being" in *The Coming Community*. I requote his symptomatic reading of Tiananmen Square at length not only to demonstrate the affiliative relationship between Agamben's "whatever being" and Bartleby's" "I would prefer not to" but also to underscore the remarkable parallel between the new mode of political resistance he envisages as adequate to the conditions of the demographic conditions of the present interregnum and that envisaged by Edward Said in the wake of the self-destruction of the nation-state system and its imperial project:

> What could be the politics of whatever singularity, that is, of a being whose community is mediated not by any condition of belonging (being red, being Italian, being Communist) nor by the simple absence of conditions (a negative community, such as that recently proposed in France by Maurice Blanchot), but by belonging itself? A herald from Beijing carries the elements of a response.
>
> What was most striking about the demonstrations of Chinese May was the relative absence of determinate contents in their demands (democracy and freedom are notions too general and broadly defined to constitute the real object of a conflict, and the only concrete demand, the rehabilitation of Ho Yao-Band, was immediately granted). This makes the violence of the State's reaction seem even more inexplicable. It is likely, however, that the disproportion is only apparent and that the Chinese leaders acted, from their point of view, with greater lucidity than the Western observers who were exclusively concerned with advancing increasingly less plausible arguments about the opposition between democracy and communism.
>
> *The novelty of the coming politics is that it will no longer be a struggle for the conquest or control of the State, but a struggle between the State and the non-State (humanity), an insurmountable disjunction between whatever singularity and the State organization.* This has nothing to do with the simple affirmation of the social opposition to the State that has often found expression in the protest movements of recent years. Whatever singularities cannot form a societas because they do not possess any identity to vindicate nor any bond of belonging for which to seek recognition. In the final instance the State can recognize any claim for identity—even that of a State identity within the State (the recent history of relations between the State and terrorism is an eloquent confirmation of this fact). What the State cannot tolerate in any way, however, is that the singularities form a community without affirming an identity, that humans co-belong without any representable condition of belonging (even in the form of a simple presupposition). The State, as Alain Badiou has shown, is not founded on a social bond, of which it would be the expression, but rather on the dissolution, the unbinding it prohibits. For the State, therefore, what is important is never the singularity as such, but only its inclusion in some identity, whatever identity (but the possibility of the whatever itself being taken up without an identity is a threat the State cannot come to terms with).

> A being radically devoid of a representable identity would be absolutely irrelevant to the State. This is what, in our culture, the hypocritical dogma of the sacredness of human life and the vacuous declaration of human rights are meant to hide. *Sacred* here can only mean what the term meant in Roman law: *Sacer* was one who had been excluded from the human world and who, even though she or he could not be sacrificed, could be killed without committing homicide (*neque fas est eum immolari, sed occidit parricidio non damnatur*). (It is significant from this perspective that the extermination of the Jews was not conceived as homicide, neither by the executioners nor by the judges; rather, the judges presented it as a crime against humanity. The victorious powers tried to compensate for the lack of identity with the concession of a State identity, which itself became the source of new massacres.)
>
> Whatever singularity, which wants to appropriate belonging itself, its own being-in-language, and thus rejects all identity and every condition of belonging, is the principle enemy of the State. Wherever these singularities peacefully demonstrate their being in common there will be a Tiananmen, and, sooner or later, the tanks will appear. (CC, 85–87; emphasis in original)[22]

In *Culture and Imperialism*, it will be recalled, Edward Said, having borne witness to the implosion of the Western imperial project and its logic of belonging, perceived its multitudinous living victims as constituting the basis of a new mode of resistance adequate to the de-centered global conditions of the interregnum: "It is no exaggeration to say that liberation as an intellectual mission, born in the resistance and opposition to the confinements and ravages of imperialism, has now shifted from the settled, established, and domesticated dynamic of culture to its unhoused, *decentered*, and exilic energies, energies whose incarnation today is the migrant and whose consciousness is the intellectual and artist in exile, the political figure between domains, between forms, between homes, and between languages." In a remarkably similar way, Agamben, too, recognizes that resistance in the deracinated global era can no longer take the form demanded by the identitarian logic intrinsic to the nation-state. Seen from this alienated perspective, his "whatever-beings"—the identityless identities to whom the interregnum has returned the "linguistic being" they were denied by the spectacular identity logic of belonging of "nations of the earth"[23]—become paradoxically, precisely as the expressive uncounted and inarticulate, like Said's unhomed Bartlebyan émigrés, the "principal enemy of the State."

But Agamben's insight into the revolutionary implications of the interregnum—the self-destruction of the logic of nation-state belonging and the precipitation of the refugee as its defining figure—is not limited to this novel mode of Bartlebyan resistance against a world structured in domination. It also entails, again like Said's insight into the political potential inhering in the émigré, the envisioning of an alternative *polis*. In the passage from *Culture and Imperialism* quoted at the beginning of this chapter, Said, it will be recalled, asserts that the alienated exilic perspective of the interregnum not only announces a radically new form of resistance, but also—and no doubt with the question of Palestine in mind—a radically new idea of the human community using the language of music as his model: "From this [exilic or in-between] perspective also, one can see 'the complete consort dancing together' contrapuntally." I have addressed elsewhere and at length the question of the political meaning of this resonantly enigmatic phrase, which takes the form of a *discordia concors*, a yoking by violence of a line from T.S. Eliot's *Four Quartets*, an ostensibly Christian poem modeled on the tonality of the sonata form, with a word from the domain of musical counterpoint that is seemingly antithetical. Here, therefore, I will, for the sake of convenient brevity, quote a summary statement of that argument:

> What would be the character of a polity envisaged as "'the complete consort dancing together' contrapuntally"? Taking one's directive from what has been disclosed by Said's account of the intellectual and artist in exile . . . one is enabled to say at the outset that such a polity or world would be radically different from the world fabricated according to the logic of the modern Western nation-state system. The world of the latter, as the exilic consciousness bears witness, is a world whose inclusive/exclusive, biopolitical logic of belonging is intended to render nativity, territory, and citizenship an identical and harmonious unity (a complete consort, as it were) that derives its power from drawing borders with its others—"Us and them," in Said's ubiquitous phrase, or "Friend and foe"—in which the powerless latter are necessarily dehumanized, rendered non-beings, and their space a no-place (*terra nullius*) begging occupation and "improvement." The polity implied by Said's musical metaphor, on the other hand, would emerge from that radically unhomed and de-familiarized—de-*structured*—world, from, more specifically, the rubble of the de-nationalized world of the Western nation-state—in which everything and everyone is therefore singular: "counter, original, spare, strange." This is not to say that such a new and estranged space would annul the cultural identities of those who inhabit it. As opposed to their ontological Origin under the aegis of

> the nation-state, it would, rather, render them *conscious* of their historical origins: their constructedness as opposed to the "naturalness" attributed to them by the nation-state system. To return to the specific case of Palestine, the Palestinians would remain Palestinians and the Jews would remain Jews. But like the Jew who becomes a non-Jewish Jew and a Palestinian who becomes a non-Palestinian Palestinian in the in-between of pariahdom or exile, the murderous binary, stripped of its essentialist ontological (or sacred) ground, would, to use the resonantly appropriate term from Giorgio Agamben I invoked earlier, not only become inoperative (*inoperosita*), but also unendingly creative: an *open-ended* dialectic, means without end, i.e., a beginning—that always already mutually deepens both sides—or more precisely for my purpose, the "voices"—of the binary.[24]

The coming community Agamben envisages, both its ontological origins and its practical operations, is strikingly similar to Edward Said's. Like Said, he takes his directives from the figure of the refugee, though it is by way of Hannah Arendt's neglected war-time essay "We Refugees" (1943), in which, it will be recalled, she identifies the refugee as the symptom of the disintegration of the nation-state system and proleptically announces the paradoxical notion that these stateless figures, "driven from country to country are the vanguard of their people":

> One ought to reflect on the meaning of [Arendt's proclamation that with the advent of the conscious pariah "History is no longer a closed book to them (refugees) and politics is no longer the privilege of Gentiles"], which after fifty years has lost none of its relevance. It is not only the case that the problem presents itself inside and outside of Europe with just as much urgency as then. It is also the case that, given the by now unstoppable decline of the nation-state and the general corrosion of traditional political-juridical categories [by way of the establishment of the state of exception as the norm], *the refugee is perhaps the only thinkable figure for the people of our time and the only category in which one may see today—at least until the process of dissolution of the nation-state and of its sovereignty has achieved full completion—the forms and limits of a coming political community*. It is even possible that, if we want to be equal to the absolutely new task ahead, we will have to abandon decidedly, without reservation, the fundamental concepts through which we have so far represented the subjects of the political (Man, the Citizen and its rights, but also the sovereign people, the worker, and so forth) and build our political philosophy anew starting from the one and only figure of the refugee.[25] (my emphasis)

Having established the stateless refugee as the paradigmatic precipitate of the self-de-struction of the nation-state system, Agamben then, following Arendt's devastating critique of the latter and its "hypocritical" doctrine of human rights in *The Origins of Totalitarianism* (Part II), goes on to show that, in producing the refugee—the "superfluous," the "stateless person," the "outlaw" in Arendt's alternative terms—as the paradigmatic figure of the post–World War II age, this biopolitical logic of belonging of the nation-state (embodied in the trinity "State-Nation-Territory") also paradoxically produces the specter that, like Said's Bartlebyan émigré, haunts the very structure of its regime of Truth:

> If the refugee represents such a disquieting element in the order of the nation-state, this is primarily because, by breaking the identity between the human and the citizen and that between nativity and nationality, it brings the originary fiction of sovereignty to a crisis. . . . What is new in our time is that growing sections of human kind are no longer representable inside the nation-state—and this novelty threatens the very foundations of the latter. Inasmuch as the refugee, an apparently marginal figure, unhinges the old trinity of state-nation-territory [this locution derives from Hannah Arendt (OT, 232)], it deserves instead to be regarded as the central figure of our political history. (MWE, 21–22)

It is at this point, after showing that the hitherto disavowed refugee has become a spectral presence that, precisely in its recalcitrant unnameability, menaces the very structure of the nation-state, that Agamben goes beyond the question of resistance to meditate on the coming community. His example, like Arendt's and Said's, is the globally fraught space of "Jerusalem," the epitome of the problem of the contemporary Western *polis*. In opposition to the Zionist state, the apartheid policy of which, like that of the Nazis *vis-á-vis* the German Jews, has rendered the Palestinian people a population of stateless refugees, Agamben, like them, calls for a binational state, in which Jerusalem would "become—simultaneously and without any partition—the capital of two different states." It is this "paradoxical condition of reciprocal extraterritoriality (or better yet, aterritoriality)," oriented by the stateless figure of the refugee, that will characterize the space of the new *polis*, and, as such, bears a remarkable similarity to the *polis* Said envisages on the resonant model of musical counterpoint (MWE, 24):

> Instead of two national states separated by uncertain and threatening boundaries, it might be possible to imagine two political communities insisting on the same region and in a condition of exodus from each other—communities that would articulate each other via a series of reciprocal extraterritorialities in which the guiding concept would no

> longer be the *ius* (right) of the citizen but rather the *refugium* (refuge) of the singular. In an analogous way, we could conceive of Europe not as an impossible "Europe of the nations," whose catastrophe one can already foresee in the short run, but rather as an aterritorial or extraterritorial space in which all the citizen and noncitizen residents of the European states would be in a position of exodus or refuge; the status of European would then mean the being-in-exodus of the citizens (a condition that obviously could also be one of immobility). European space would thus mark an irreducible difference between birth [*nascita*] and nation in which the old concept of people (which, as is well known, is always a minority) could again find a political meaning, thus decidedly opposing itself to the concept of nation (which has so far unduly usurped it). (*MWE*, 24–25)

This paradoxical space, according to Agamben, "would coincide neither with any of the homogeneous national territories nor with their *topographical* sum" (*MWE*, 25). Invoking a metaphor that, in its structureless structure in which boundaries are put under erasure, is absolutely analogous to the two (or more)-in-one voices of Said's "counterpoint," he goes on to say that, on the contrary, "it would . . . act on them by articulating and perforating them *topologically* as in the Klein bottle or in the Möbius strip, *where exterior and interior in-determine each other*. In this new space, European cities would rediscover their ancient vocation of cities of the world by entering into a relation of reciprocal extraterritoriality" (*MWE*, 25; the last emphasis is mine). In the profane time of the now of this "unhomed homeland," the binarist identitarian logic of belonging and the borders it produces would remain. The Jew, for example, would remain a Jew and the Palestinian, a Palestinian. In the process, however, as in the case of the Klein bottle or Möbius strip, in which "exterior and interior in-determine each other," the Jew would become a non-Jewish Jew and the Palestinian a non-Palestinian Palestinian. And the deadly vocational operations of their original binarist configuration in the nation-state—the war to the end between Native and foreigner, Filiation and non-filiation, Friend and foe, Citizen and refugee, Belonging and not belonging, in which the second term (the voiceless voice) doesn't stand a chance—would be rendered inoperative. Instead, these dehumanizing and life-destroying binaries—these oppositions that produce bare life and the thanatopolitics of the concentration camp—would metamorphose, as they do in Said's contrapuntal *polis*, into an open-ended playful or loving strife—a *discordia concors*—in which both agonic voices, released from the vocational servitude to a "higher cause"—which is to say, from the banalizing univocal determinism of the means/end logic endemic to the nation-state—always deepen and enrich each other's humanity.

4

> A political truth is a series of consequences, organized on the condition of an Idea, a massive popular event, in which intensification, contraction, and localization replace an identitarian object, and the separating names bound up with it, with a real presentation of the generic power of the multiple.
>
> —Alain Badiou, *The Rebirth of History*

Of all those I have included in this constellation of post-poststructuralist theorists, Alain Badiou is, perhaps, the most difficult to justify. After all, he has overtly expressed serious reservations about certain key aspects of the thought of Hannah Arendt and Giorgio Agamben, not least their alleged commitment to "debate" and "communicability" as opposed to "decision" and "action"—what he calls the "truth procedure"—which is to say, their sympathy with a parliamentarian democracy that distances the participant from the site of *praxis*. Thus, for example, in an essay criticizing Arendt's lectures on Kant's political philosophy (and the exegetical commentary of her editor, Myriam Revault D'Allonnes) he writes:

> Long before being Arendtian or Kantian, the theme of the irreducible opposition of truth and opinion is Platonic [metaphysical]; as is, equally the idea of a philosophical monopoly of truth—an idea surrounded by the connection between truth and the "philosophical life." . . . But what is *not* Platonic is the idea that politics (the "political life") is forever devoted to opinion, forever disjoined from all truth. We know what this amounts to: sophistry. And it certainly seems to be the case that what Arendt and Revault d'Allonnes mean by "politics" . . . is sophistry in the modern sense of the word, that is to say, a sophistry dedicated to the promotion of an entirely particular politics. In other words: parliamentary politics.
>
> In fact, what we have here is an orientation of thought whose tradition has been established ever since the Greeks, and which disqualifies, in matters of politics, the theme of truth as univocal and tyrannical. Everyone knows that there is a precious "freedom of opinion," whereas

> the "freedom of truth" remains in doubt. In the lengthy succession of banalities pronounced on the "dogmatic," "abstract" and "constrained" character of the idea of truth—banalities forever invested in defense of political regimes whose (general economic) authority to exercise power is concealed behind the "freedom of opinion"—Arendt declares that "every truth unequivocally demands recognition and refuses debate to the extent that debate constitutes the very essence of political life."[26]

There is, admittedly, a tendency in Arendt's political thinking that renders her espousal of communicability (saying, debate) as the *sine qua non* of a polity susceptible to Badiou's charge that it recuperates the spectatorial sophistry of liberal democracy. But I think it is a tendency countered by another, more revolutionary one that understands human speech and action—"saying and doing," as she invariably puts it in *The Human Condition*—not as antitheses, but as belonging together. This is testified by her decisive privileging of the *vita activa* over the mere "metabolism with nature" of *animal laborans* and the utilitarian and vocational means/end making of *homo faber*, the logics of which end in the reduction of life to bare life and politics to biopolitics. In other words, in overdetermining the theme of "opinion" in her political discourse, Badiou is not addressing the Arendt whose being as "conscious pariah" was formed by her historical/existential exilic condition, and whose intellectual origins resided in Nietzsche's and Heidegger's revolutionary "destruction" of the metaphysical logic of belonging that reduced her to that statelessness. Rather, I suggest, he is criticizing the "communitarian" Arendt produced in the 1970s and 1980s by the Habermasian school of political philosophy, whose *raison d'être* was to salvage some form of democracy in the wake of its self-destruction.[27] Understood in this context, it would be more accurate to say that Badiou is radicalizing Arendt, not necessarily putting her in a binary opposition with his work.

Be that as it may, the fact remains that Badiou's prolific oeuvre, from its articulation of the "event," through the critique of the world structured in domination by the capitalist/parliamentary system and its ethics of "human rights," to the radical communism it anticipates, constitutes a radicalization of the Heideggerian destruction of the onto-theological tradition and a remarkably productive dialogue with the constellation of contemporary theorists who, because they insist on the indissoluble relationality between ontology and politics, I have been calling post-poststructuralists.

From Badiou's alienated perspective on the contemporary global occasion, the inaugural "event" is a radicalization of Nietzsche's and Heidegger's "anti-philosophy." (I am thinking here particularly of the latter's declaration that philosophy came to its end—fulfillment and demise—in modernity when its spatializing logic rendered being a total "world picture," in which every time and thing took its proper place in the large panoptic whole.) Indeed, in his subversive reading of Saint Paul's epistles, Badiou says that "Paul provides an anticipatory critique of what Heidegger calls onto-theology, wherein God is thought as supreme being, and hence as the measure for what being as such is capable of" (*SP*, 47). The event, it will be recalled, discloses the "void" "around which is organized the complacent plenitude established by the rule" of the dominant (capitalist/parliamentarian) culture, which has its *raison d'être* in an interpretation of being that is teleological, an interpretation, in other words, that produces a discourse of mastery (and servitude), a mode of knowledge production that represents the singularity of being *meta ta physica*, from after or above things they are, and a morality of duty (to a higher cause) and guilt and reduces the truth of the event (the universality of the singularity) into a Truth. Thus, for Badiou, the event constitutes not only a critique of "philosophy" that discloses the will to power intrinsic to the identitarian imperatives of its teleological perspective, but also, as a consequence of this decisive disclosure, the "gift of grace" (*kharis*) that categorically annuls guilt and affirms the time of the now.[28] In this sense, as we shall see, Badiou, like Said, Arendt, and Agamben, understands the alienating interregnum, the in-betweenness of the contemporary evental occasion, as a situation that calls for the revocation of the vocational calling imposed on humanity by the ontotheological tradition, particularly in its most imperial last—anthropological—phase (the rejection of works in favor of faith or fidelity to the event).

From this in-between time of the now of the evental perspective, Badiou, like Said, Arendt, and Agamben, is enabled not only to perceive—contrapuntally, as it were—the polyvalent operations of the dehumanizing will to power that is intrinsic to the "complacent plentitude established by the rule of those who possess capital," but also to avow the abjected victims that its binary logic of belonging always disavows. Put in the language he employs to identify the militant Saint Paul as "our contemporary," the event announces the "resurrection"—the "uprising," the "becoming someone"—of those whom the dominant culture has reduced to nobodies.

Analogous to the diagnoses of global modernity under the aegis of parliamentary capitalism undertaken by Arendt, Foucault, Said, Agamben, Žižek, Rancière, and Butler, Badiou's first critical gesture shows that capitalist democracy is, in fact, structured in domination. Far from freeing humanity from the tyranny of fascist and communist totalitarianisms, it insidiously reduces the "existence" of its vast majority to "non-existents" who serve the dominant minority culture or, when that service is no longer productive, become disposable. Arendt, Foucault, Said, Agamben, Žižek, Rancière, and Butler identify these included excluded entities, respectively, as the "superfluous," "useful and docile bodies," "the émigré," "bare life," "the part of no part," "the ungrievable." Badiou names them the "uncounted" in a "*configured*" (spatialized) system in which what counts is determined by those who count:

> *Our [capitalist democratic] world is in no way as "complex" as those who wish to ensure* its operation. It is even, in its broad outline, perfectly simple. On the one hand, there is an extension of the automatisms of capital, fulfilling one of Marx's inspired predictions: the world finally *configured*, but as a market, as a world market. This configuration imposes the rule of an abstract homogenization. Everything that circulates falls under the unity of the count, while inversely, only what lets itself be counted in this way can circulate. Moreover, this is the norm that illuminates a paradox few have pointed out: in the hour of generalized circulation and the phantasm of instantaneous cultural communication, laws and regulations forbidding the circulation of persons are being multiplied everywhere. So it is that in France, never have fewer foreigners settled than in the recent period! Free circulation of what lets itself be counted, yes, and above all of capital, which is the count of the count. Free circulation of that uncountable infinity constituted by a singular human life, never! For capitalist monetary abstraction is certainly a singularity, but a singularity as indifferent to the persistent infinity of existence as it is to the evental becoming of truths.
>
> On the other side, there is a process of fragmentation into closed identities, and the culturalist and relativist ideology that accompanies this fragmentation. (*SP*, 10)

Put alternatively, the event enables those whom it seizes to perceive that the capitalist democratic state employs an identitarian logic of belonging that at once fictionalizes a national identity (and the duties it entails) that must be adhered to and gives "*separating names*" to those who do not conform to this national "identitarian object," names that "justify" dehumanizing repression ranging from relegation to pariahdom to the biopoliticization of the body:

> The state can virtually be defined as an institution with the means for imposing norms on a whole population that prescribe what pertains to this state, the duties it imposes and the rights it confers. In the context of this definition, the state fictionalizes an *identitarian object* (for example, the "French person") that individuals and groups have a duty to resemble as closely as possible, if they are to merit positive attention from the state. Anyone declared unduly dissimilar from the identitarian object will also be entitled to attention from the state, but in a negative sense (suspicion, police checks, internment, expulsion, and so on).
>
> A *separating name* refers to *a particular way of not resembling the fictive identitarian object.* It enables the state to separate certain groups from the collectivity, who therefore call for particular repressive measures. These can range from "immigrant," "Islamist," "Muslim" and "Roma" to "youth from the *banlieues*." Let us note that "poor" and "mentally ill" are in the process of being constructed before our very eyes as separating names.[29]

As in the case of the other theorists in the post-poststructuralist constellation, however, the eventality of the event—the now time that remains after the (self) destruction of the teleologic of anthropological time—enables Badiou to perceive that this very condition of abjection—its "un(a)countability"—to which the multitude, or, more precisely, the "universality of the singular," has been reduced by the dominant minority culture becomes, like the unnamable "refugee" for Arendt, the "émigré" for Said, and the dissidents in Tiananmen Square for Agamben, the paradoxical spectral agent of resistance against its "complacent plenitude." I am referring to the Bartlebyan figure who, in refusing to be answerable to the call of the naming Subject, "can call the hierarchy directly by its name."

In Badiou, this violently passive resistance begins with a transvaluation of (hegemonic) values he calls "the transversal of difference" (*SP*, 98), which is remarkably similar to Agamben's "revocation of every vocation": the gesture, activated by the de-centering of the *Anthropologos* (and the retrieval of the "nothing," the "time of the now," the "universal singular"), that renders the death-oriented operations of the binarist identitarian logic of belonging of the Jews and Greeks, Law and Philosophy, inoperative. As in the case of Agamben, Badiou takes the point of departure of his paradoxical revolutionary political gesture from Saint Paul's "Epistle to the Corinthians" (I. 1.177–229), where the latter retrieves the polyvalent phenomena that have been reduced to "nought" by the Law: "For consider your call, brethren; not many of you were wise according to worldly standards, not many were powerful, not many were of noble birth, but God chose the foolish things of the world to confound the wise, and God chose the weak things of the world to confound the strong; God chose what is base and despised in the world, and even things that are not, to bring to nought things that are, so that no one might glorify himself in his presence." Pursuing the implications of this retrieval of the nought from the Law, Badiou writes:

> At the very moment in which he sets out to depose the law and elucidate its relation to unconscious avidity [the sinful and life-destroying desire produced by the Law], Paul points out that "the law is holy, and the commandment is holy and just and good [*he entole hagaia kai dikaia kai agathe*]" (Rom. 7.12). What is more, apparently overturning at a stroke all the foregoing dialectic, he asserts that "the law is spiritual [*ho nomos pneumatikos*]" (Rom. 7.14)
>
> Thus, it seems necessary to distinguish between a legalizing subjectivation [interpellation by the Law], which is a power of [subjective] death, and a law raised up by faith, which belongs to the spirit and to [subjective] life.
>
> *Our task consists in thinking the apparent contradictions between two statements:*
>
> 1. "Christ is the end of the law [*telos nomou Khristos*]" (Rom. 10.40).
>
> 2. "Love is the fulfillment of the law [*pleroma nomou he agape*]" (Rom. 13.10).
>
> Under the condition of faith, *of a declared conviction* [incumbent on the event], love names a nonliteral law, one that gives to the faithful subject his consistence, and effectuates the postevental truth in the world. (*SP*, 87; my emphasis)

Analogous to Agamben's interpretation of Paul's calling, the deadly binarist and identitarian logic of the Law—work toward an End it demands—is rendered inoperative. The Law and the binary identities it produces remain but in the wake of the evental call, they undergo a "transversal." History becomes historicity (transience); the *Telos* becomes the "time of the now"; the vocational (interpellated) self—the named subject who has been subjected by the hailing of the telic Law—becomes an unsubjected subject; and the binary logic of the truth regime of the Law (Friend/foe) becomes agonic love.

To put this "transversal of difference" enacted by Badiou alternatively, it could be said that through Saint Paul's rendering of the

Law—Jewish identity (prophecy) and Greek identity (philosophy)—inoperative, Badiou radicalizes the poststructuralist reversal of the determinative principle of Western metaphysical knowledge production: that Identity (the One) is the condition for the possibility of difference (the many). In the wake of this radicalized reversal, this "transversal of difference," the retrieved difference, which under the aegis of the Law is given a *particular* identity (name) and subordinated (subjected) to a larger autonomous and sovereign whole, *becomes* the universal, or, as Badiou puts it, the "All" refers not to an identitarian Totality but to an infinite singularity. Commenting on the principle of Pauline principles, which privileges faith (fidelity to the event) and grace (*kharis*), not the Law and Works (the vocational ethic)—"For we hold that a man is justified by faith apart from works. Or is God the God of the Jews only? Is he not the God of Gentiles also? Yes, of Gentiles also, since God is one; and he will justify the circumcised on the grounds of their faith and the uncircumcised through their faith" (Rom. 3, 27–30)—Badiou writes:

> *The fundamental question is that of knowing precisely what it means for there to be a single God. What does the "mono" in monotheism mean? Here Paul confronts—but also renews the terms of—the formidable question of the One. His genuinely revolutionary conviction is that the sign of the One is the "for all," or the "without exception."* That there is a single God must be understood not as a philosophical speculation concerning substance or the supreme being, but on the basis of a structure of address. The One is that which inscribes no difference in the subjects to which it addresses itself. The One is only insofar as it is for all: such is the maxim of universality when it has its root in the event. *Monotheism can be understood only by taking into consideration the whole of humanity.* Unless addressed to all, the One crumbles and disappears. . . .
>
> *What can measure up to the universality of an address? Not legality, in any case. The law is always predicative, particular, and partial. Paul is perfectly aware of the law's unfailing* "statist" character. By "statist" I mean that which enumerates, names, and controls the part of a situation. If a truth is to surge forth eventally, it must be nondenumerable, impredictable, uncontrollable. This is precisely what Paul calls grace: that which occurs without being couched in any predicate, that which is translegal, that which happens to everyone without an assignable reason. Grace is the opposite of law insofar as it is what comes without being due. (SP, 76–77; second and third emphases are mine)

This paradoxical "all," which Badiou claims to be at the core of Paul's militant revolutionary saying, is also at the core of Badiou's anti-philosophical communism. Earlier in *Saint Paul*, as if to signal its import for what is to follow, he writes:

> *Paul's general procedure is the following: if there has been an event, and if truth consists in declaring it and then in being faithful to this declaration, two consequences ensue. First, since truth is evental, or of the order of what occurs, it is singular. It is neither structural, nor axiomatic, nor legal. No available generality can account for it, nor structure the subject who claims to follow in its wake. Consequently, there cannot be a* law of truth. Second, truth being inscribed on the basis of a declaration that is in essence subjective, no preconstituted subset can support it; nothing communitarian or historically established can lend its substance to the process of truth. Truth is diagonal relative to every communitarian subset; it neither claims authority from, *nor (this is obviously the delicate point) constitutes any identity. It is offered to all, or addressed to everyone, without a condition of belonging being able to limit this offer, or this address.* (*SP*, 14; my emphasis)

What, for the purpose of this intervention, is remarkable about Badiou's paradoxical way of putting this universalization of the singular is its similarity to the "transversal of difference" Edward Said enacts in *Culture and Imperialism*,[30] when, in opposition to the neo-colonial politics of identity, he proffers the communal vision of Aimé Césaire:

> *et aucune race*
> *ne possède le monopole de la beauté, de l'intelligence, de la force*
> *et il est place pour tous au rendez-vous de la conquête*
>
> [and no race
> possesses the monopoly of beauty, of intelligence, of force,
> and there is a place for all at the rendezvous of victory]

As I have observed, Arendt, Said, and Agamben, each in their own way, bear decisive witness in the interregnum to the bankruptcy of the dominant nation-state culture and to the urgent need for a radically new mode of resistance to its depredations that does not rely on the structural alternatives permitted by its identitarian logic of belonging. Like them, Badiou, by way of rendering the Law inoperative, finds the point of departure of this new mode of resistance precisely in the "void" or, in Paul's language, the spectral "nought," which the sovereign Law (particularly in its modern neoliberal avatar) will have nothing to do with and therefore will, at all costs, impose "separating names" on all its manifestations. Agamben, for example, as we have seen, invokes Bartleby, the unnamable figure who, in "prefer[ring] not to" answer the call of Wall Street, "revokes every vocation," to symbolize such unidentifiable contemporary multitudes as that which manifested its revolutionary power in Tiananmen Square. Similarly, Badiou, following the directives of Saint Paul's rendering of the Law's statist will to "enumerate, name, and control the parts of a situation" inoperative, invokes the "uncounted"—precisely the condition of the "nondenumerable, unpredictable, uncontrollable" nonentities produced by those who determine what counts—as the agents of resistance and of the evental truth procedure.

Badiou's contemporary historical example of this paradoxical transvaluation of rebellious praxis is the Arab Spring of 2011, which, not incidentally, as the title of his analysis, *The Rebirth of History*, suggests, he understands as an interregnum precipitated by the fulfillment of the logic of Western capitalist parliamentarianism,[31] or, in his language, an "intervallic period," in which the reactionary remnants are still able, "precisely because the revolutionary road is feint," to derail the evental truth and to reaffirm the viability of the old dispensation (*RH*, 38). By the "Arab Spring," then, Badiou means, on the one hand, an uprising that, as opposed to "immediate riots" and "latent riots," constitutes an "historical riot," a riot, that is, whose "location ceases to be limited, but grounds in the occupied space the promise of a new, long term temporality;" whose "*composition stops being uniform, but gradually outlines a unified representation in mosaic form of all the people*"; and, finally, in which "the negative growling of pure rebellion is succeeded by the assertion of a shared demand, whose satisfaction confers an initial meaning on the word 'victory'" (*RH*, 35; my emphasis). On the other hand, Badiou also means a riotous situation that in its amorphousness can be interpreted by the Western political class—the Obamas, the Sarkozys, the Camerons, the Merkels—and its sycophantic media as "*a desire for the West*. A desire to 'enjoy' everything that we, the drowsy, satisfied inhabitants of the affluent countries, already 'enjoy.' A desire finally to be included in the 'civilized world' which Westerners, incorrigible descendants of racist colonists, are so certain of representing that they set up international courts to judge anyone who asserts different values. . . . In so doing, Westerners wrapped in the flag of Right forget that their alleged power to state the Good is nothing but the modernized name of Imperial intervention" (*RH*, 48–49).

Far from an expression of "desire for the West," Tahrir Square, according to Badiou, is symptomatic of a decisive rejection of the Western neo-colonial system, and, not least, of the traditional—"domesticated," in Said's term—identity-oriented reformist categories—class, race, gender, age, and so on—permitted by its "democratic" state. Taking his directives, like Arendt, Said, and Agamben, from the "nought" to which the vast majority of humanity has been reduced by capitalist parliamentarianism, Badiou interprets the Arab Spring as an uprising—a resurrection—of the unnamable—"universal singularity"—of humanity that the dominant neocapitalist minority and its ventriloquized satellite regimes have reduced to "non-existents":

> In a world structured by exploitation and oppression masses of people have, strictly speaking, no existence. They count for nothing. . . . Let us call these people, who are present in the world but absent from its meaning and decisions about its future, the inexistent of the world. We shall then say that a change of world is real when an inexistent of the world starts to exist in this same world with maximum intensity. This is exactly what people in the popular rallies in Egypt were saying and are still saying: we used not to exist, but now we exist, and we can determine the history of the country. This subjective fact is endowed with an extraordinary power. *The inexistent has arisen*. That is why we refer to *uprising*: people were lying down, submissive; they are getting up, picking themselves up, rising up. This rising is the rising of existence itself: the poor have not become rich; people who were unarmed are not now armed, and so forth. Basically, nothing has changed. What has occurred is restitution of the existence of the inexistent, conditional upon what I call an *event*. (*RH*, 56)

Indeed, this unnamable or, in Badiou's vocabulary, "unpredicable" character of the Arab Spring uprising is fundamental to the evental truth procedure. "When an emancipatory event [such as the French Revolution, which announced that Jews and Protestants were citizens of France like the others] is, in fact, rooted in an historical riot," Badiou writes, "we straightway observe the disappearance of, or at least a considerable reduction in separating names" that hitherto justified the extermination of the humanity of those they thus named. What emerges from this rendering inoperative of the identitarian logic of belonging of the state is, as it did at the time of the Paris Commune (1871), the *generic Idea of the people*: "whoever proves by their actions that they are concerned with the human race must be treated in egalitarian fashion as one of us" (*RH*, 89). It is to this emergence of the "generic" from the separating names of the state that the "historical riots" of the Arab Spring bear witness. "The great rallies in Egypt," he writes, "have forcefully reminded us of this principle and revitalized it for our times. They have occurred publicly without any identitarian selection. We have seen Muslims and Copts, men and women, veiled women and 'bareheaded' women, intellectuals, and workers, young and old, and so on, side by side. All identities were in a sense absorbed by the movement, but the movement itself was not reducible to any one of them."[32] What is remarkable about Badiou's retrieval of the generic Idea of the people by way of his transversal of the identitarian logic of the state—this universalization of human singularity that collapses the deadly distinction between "Muslims" and "Copts," "men" and "women," "intellectuals" and "workers," and so on—is how closely it resembles Agamben's retrieval of the human in the figure of the Bartlebyan—and communal—"coming whatever being":

> *The Whatever in question here relates to singularity not in its indifference with respect to a common property (to a concept, for example, being red, being French, being Muslim), but only in its being* such as it is. *Singularity is thus free from the false dilemma that obliges knowledge to choose between the ineffability of the individual and the intelligibility of the universal. The intelligible, according to a beautiful expression of Levi ben Gershon (Gersonides), is neither a universal nor an individual included in a* series, but rather "singularity insofar as it is whatever singularity." In this conception, such-and-such being is reclaimed from its having this or that property, which identifies it as belonging to this or that set, to this or that class (red, the French, the Muslims)—and it is reclaimed not for another class . . . (CC, 1–2; my emphasis)[33]

This retrieval of the generic, not incidentally, clearly demonstrates that the post-poststructuralists are not anti-humanist, as it has been claimed by their traditionalist humanist opponents, but opposed to the traditional representation of humanism as an identitarian category; that is, they are committed to retrieving a more authentic, non-foundational understanding of the human.

What is different about Badiou's analysis of the riotous occasion he announces as "the rebirth of history" from Agamben's is his urgent insistence on the need for the "organization" of the masses—the initiative of a cadre of militants that, in enabling and sustaining the "intensification, contraction, and localization" of "a massive popular event" can alone replace "an identitarian object, and the separating names bound up with it with a real presentation of the generic power of the multiple" (*RH*, 85). But this, it is important to underscore, is a difference not of kind but of degree. Badiou, in fact, categorically rejects the "party-form" of political organization (*RH*, 80)—the form that, as in the unfortunate cases of Lenin and Mao, came to privilege a group that represented an *identifiable part of* the generic whole—the working class—and thus betrayed the very genericity their respective revolutionary events disclosed for positive thought, that is, reduced "the communist movement" to "state communism" (*RH*, 80).[34] Though for Badiou, as for Saint Paul, identities are tolerable, indeed productive—insofar as they are understood to be historically constructed—what matters, for him, as for Agamben—indeed, for Arendt, Said, Butler, Žižek, and Rancière—is the ultimately "nondenumerable, unpredictable, uncontrollable" whole of humanity—humanity understood as a universal singularity—that is ontologically prior to the historical names the state has given it. For in this new dispensation of the generic, in which the naming system has been rendered inoperative, this new humanity is not only enabled, like the Bartleby figure, to refuse to be answerable to the separating names of the identitarian state—or, rather, to turn their negativity (their invisible existence) into a spectral force—and in so doing to call the life-damaging (dehumanizing) hierarchical structure of the capitalist parliamentary state by its right name. It also enables this new humanity to articulate a radically communal *polis*, in which identities, having been rendered inoperative and subordinated to the ontologically prior universal singularity of generic humanity, no longer manifest themselves in the Hobbesian war to the end:

> When there is a massive popular event, it tends by its very nature to *destroy the identitarian object and the separating names bound up with it.* What arrives in the square is a real *presentation*, the affirmation that what exists—what unconditionally, dictatorially proclaims what exists and must exist—is the people who are there and are acting together, *whatever the name given them by the state.* In this sense the historical riot *deposes names.* It is in the latent state of this deposition that a political organization is going to develop the consequences of a new existence, the existence of what used not to exist: the existence of the anonymous, the purely popular political existence of the people.
>
> Finally, it will be said of all these people, who are nameless for the state, that they represent the whole of humanity, for what drives them in their intense localized rallying possesses a universal significance. And that is something everyone realizes. Why? Because they have constructed a site where, *the fictive identitarian object being inoperative, or even abolished, it is no longer identity that counts*, but non-identity: the universal value of the Idea, its generic virtue—that is what concerns, what enthuses, humanity in general. (*RH*, 93–94; first and third emphases are mine)[35]

Indeed, if we recall Badiou's commentary on Saint Paul's indifference to the names "Jew" and "Greek,"[36] we might say, with Agamben, that the deadly opposition manifests itself as a communal space in which the identities "in-determine each other" as the inside and outside do in the Möbius strip or Klein bottle, or, with Said, that these hitherto warring identities become "'the complete consort dancing together' contrapuntally."

5

In this chapter, I have shown that the contemporary occasion constitutes an interregnum characterized by the waning of the nation-state system (its logic of belonging and its vocational ethics) incumbent on the self-destruction of its imperial project and the emergence of a predatory capitalist global initiative that would secure the entire planet for the neoliberal "free market." (The U.S. government's unending War on Terror and its normalization of the state of exception in the aftermath of 9/11 epitomize this disastrous global initiative.) I have also shown that this predatory dominant minority culture has inadvertently revolutionized the demographics of the earth by way of precipitating a vast global population of refugees variously characterized as "the stateless," "the superfluous," "the displaced," "migrants," "the uncounted," "bare life," "the part of no part," "the countless," "the inexistent," and "the ungrievable"—all *worldly allotropes* of the ontological "nothing" (*das Nichts*) that, according to Heidegger, modern knowledge production (empirical science) will, at all costs, have nothing to do with, and resonating with its spectral meaning. As a result of this revelatory precipitation of the hitherto marginalized figure of the "refugee" to center stage of the contemporary global occasion, not only the "liberal"—nation-state—mode of ameliorating injustice has been rendered obsolete, as Edward Said observed in 1993. Equally, if not more important, the spectral exilic figure has rendered both poststructuralism and the more radical post-colonial forms of resistance it has influenced inadequate to the conditions of the volatile demography of the interregnum insofar as the former remains tethered to textual—worldless—indeterminacy or to the vocational imperatives of a transcendental Other (Levinas, Derrida), and the latter to the vocational imperatives of the waning nation-state. As I have argued, the representatives of the post-poststructuralist constellation I have invoked, on the other hand, perceive the present global occasion as an interregnum—an "in-between" or "now time," a time of beginnings (not of a Beginning)—in which the ethos of this vocational system has been rendered inoperative. Thus, as I have also argued, they take the point of departure of both their revocation of the vocational imperatives of the nation-state and the neoliberal global free market system that would replace it and their projection of the "stateless" coming *polis* from their awareness of the spectral condition of the refugee in this volatile interregnum. It is, I submit, precisely their thematization of this paradoxical (self-de-structive) consequence (*telos*) of the logic of belonging and vocational ethics of capitalist parliamentary democracy—this *onto-political* rising to center stage (irreparable haunting visibility) of the refugee's former marginality (invisibility)—that renders the post-poststructuralist thought of Giorgio Agamben, Alain Badiou, Slavoj Žižek, Jacques Rancière, Judith Butler, among others, more adequate than the available alternatives for resisting the catastrophic predations of neocapitalism and for thinking the positive onto-political potentialities opened up by the closure of the nation-state, which is to say, of the interregnum that constitutes the contemporary global occasion.

6

Edward W. Said and World Literature

Thinking the Worldly Imperatives of the Interregnum

But within that old territory, a new object of study: instead of concrete, individual works, a trio of artificial constructs—graphs, maps, and trees—in which the reality of the text undergoes a process of deliberate reduction and abstraction. "Distant reading," I have once called this type of approach; where distance is however not an obstacle, but *a specific form of knowledge*: few elements, hence a sharper sense of their overall interconnection. Shapes, relations, structures, forms, models.

—Franco Moretti, *Graphs, Maps, Trees: Abstract Models for Literary History*

Editors of *Herodote*: The point that needs to be emphasized here is that certain spatial metaphors are equally geographic and strategic, which is only natural since geography grew up in the shadow of the military. A circulation of notions can be observed between geographical and strategic discourses. The region (from *regere*, to command), a province is a conquered territory (from *vincere*). Field evokes the battlefield.

Michel Foucault: People have often reproached me for these spatial obsessions, which have indeed been obsessions for me. But I think through them I did come to what I had basically been looking for: the relations that are possible between power and knowledge. Once knowledge can be analyzed in terms of a region, domain, implantation, displacement, transposition, one is able to capture the process by which knowledge functions as a form of power and disseminates the effects of power. There is an administration of knowledge, a politics of knowledge, relations of power which pass

> via knowledge and which, if one tries to transcribe them, lead one to consider forms of domination designated by such notions as field, region and territory. And the politico-strategic term is an indication of how the military and the administration actually come to inscribe themselves both on a material soil and within forms of discourse.
>
> —"Questions of Geography: Interview between Michel Foucault and the editors of *Herodote*"

One of the late Edward W. Said's insistent directives to contemporary Western (particularly American) intellectuals of the Left was to break the insidious hold that the nation-state system, particularly in its larger centripetal imperial (Eurocentric) avatar, had on literary/critical production in favor of a wider, more global or transnational perspective. Following the potentially revolutionary comparativist initiative of Goethe and, more immediately, Erich Auerbach, his purpose, in so doing, to put it provisionally and all too simply, was not only to underscore the violence of the nation-state logic of belonging ("Us against them," as he tirelessly put this binarist nationalist/imperial imperative), and to produce an open-ended cultural discourse that would enable "them"—the dispossessed colonized peoples that had hitherto been spoken for by "Us," the nation-state/imperial West—to "speak" for themselves. Equally, if not more important, his purpose in calling the binarist logic of the Western nation-state/imperial system into question was to enable the possibility of a world community to come that was not infected by the life-damaging Us and them/identitarian nationalist virus, or, as he put this future positively at the end of his magisterial *Culture and Imperialism*, a polity in which "'the complete consort danc[es] together' *contrapuntally*."[1] I will return to this enigmatic, indeed, paradoxical, but resonant formulation later. Here, in keeping with these inaugural remarks, I want to announce the thesis of this chapter on Said's legacy. The recent and burgeoning "World Literature" movement that Said's (among others') call instigated in the last decade of the twentieth century is, despite its liberating expansion of the nation-state frame to incorporate the global context, ironically, accomplishing the antithesis of what he intended by his call: the "unworlding" of the world of world literature. However diverse and inchoate, this "World Literature" movement, to put it provisionally, has one defining element in common: it privileges, in Franco Moretti's exemplary term (to which I will return) "distanced reading."[2] Which is to say, it recuperates the spatializing panoptic eye (the "center elsewhere," in Jacques Derrida's equally appropriate language).[3] I mean, more precisely, the privileged metaphysical perspective concerning knowledge production of the Western (onto-theo-logical) tradition (thinking *meta ta physica*: from after or above things as they are: the differences time always already disseminates) that the poststructuralist revolution of the 1970s and 1980s unconcealed—brought down into the finite arena of free-play—and thus ostensibly delegitimized.

Said proffered his anti- or post-nationalist call for a *Weltliteratur* most urgently in the early 1990s with the publication of *Culture and Imperialism*, in response to the criticism that *Orientalism* said little about the historical cultural and political actualities of the Orient that the Orientalists, amateurs and scholars, represented from their Eurocentric perspective. This was the post–Cold War occasion when the disclosive effects of the fulfillment of the binarist logic of the nation-state/imperial project in the immediate aftermath of World War II had fully manifested themselves at the liminal point of its unerring ravaging progress. Since that time nothing radical has changed in the historical conditions of the global context Said diagnosed in that book—nothing, that is, that would warrant the total abandonment of the question of the nation-state and its imperial imperatives. If anything, these fraught conditions have been exacerbated by the United States' declaration of its unending unilateral (exceptionalist) global War on Terror in the wake of *al Qaeda*'s bombing of the World Trade Center and the Pentagon, or, in the exceptionalist language of the American political class, the outrageous invasion of the American homeland on September 11, 2001. Given this patent historical reality and its remarkable invisibility in the discourse of the new "World Literature" movement, it becomes an urgent historical imperative to undertake a repetition in Heidegger's language (*Wiederholung*): a return to Said's call for a postnationalist *Weltliteratur* in *Culture and Imperialism* with the intent of retrieving its original and proleptic meaning.

Said announced the general itinerary for World Literature early in *Culture and Imperialism* in the chapter entitled "Connecting Empire to Secular Criticism," in which he invokes Goethe's inaugural—and Eric Auerbach's later, more geographically inclusive, but essentially similar—idea of *Weltliteratur*, both to initiate an urgent cultural project as well as to dismiss their versions as inadequate to the "present" global occasion. "To us, a century later," Said observes of those early twentieth-century exponents of world systems that the literary community was drawing from, "the coincidence or similarity between one vision of a world system and the other, between geography and literary history [in the work of

George Chisholm and Lucien Febvre, among others], seems interesting but problematic. What should we do with this similarity?" In response to this interesting question he invokes the contemporary post-colonial global historical occasion:

> First of all, I believe, it needs *articulation* and *activation*, which can only come about if we take serious account of the *present, and notably of the dismantling of the classical empires and the new independence of dozens of formerly colonized peoples and territories*. We need to see that the contemporary global setting—*overlapping territories, intertwined histories*—was already prefigured and inscribed in the coincidences and convergences among geography, culture, and history that were so important to the pioneers of comparative literature. Then we can grasp in a new and more dynamic way *both the idealist historicism which fueled the comparatist "world literature" scheme and the concretely imperial world map of the same moment*. (CI, 48; my emphasis, except for the first)

However, this potentializing estrangement of the *idealist* historicism of comparative literature and the *concrete* imperial world map, Said goes on, emphasizing the necessity of engaging with the *present* historical occasion, "cannot be done without accepting that what is common to both is an elaboration of power." And, he observes, it is this indifference to the operations of power that is common to both—the operations of power that have become manifest in the wake of the self-destruction of the nation-state/imperial project in the post–World War II era—that characterizes the concept of *Weltliteratur* inherited from Goethe. Indeed, it is what renders this mode of World Literature, despite its liberating intent *vis-á-vis* the coerciveness of the logic of belonging of the nation-state, complicitous with empire:

> The genuinely profound scholarship of the people who believed in and practiced *Weltliteratur* implied *the extraordinary privilege of an observer located in the West who could actually survey the world literary output with a kind of sovereign detachment*. Orientalists and other specialists about the non-European world—anthropologists, historians, philologists—had that power, and . . . it often went hand in glove with a consciously undertaken imperial enterprise. We must articulate these various sovereign dispositions and see their common methodology. (CI, 48)

Though he does not overtly say so, Said, that is, understands this Goethian view of *Weltliteratur* as the cultural manifestation of the modern West's defining Eurocentrism: its exceptionalist self-interpretation *vis-á-vis* its "Others." More specifically, as the reiterated key Foucauldian word "survey" clearly suggests, he understands it as the logical extension in the domain of cultural production of metaphysics, the defining ontological mode of knowledge production of the West. I mean that thinking *meta ta physica*, that, in privileging the distancing—panoptic—eye (of the "objective observer"), enables its "dis-interested" practitioner to impose his (imperial) will to power over the relay of recalcitrant differential objects it oversees (supervises): over, that is, the continuum (however historically uneven) of be-*ing*, from the "sites" of ontology and epistemology (the knowledge producing self) through the "sites" of the ecos, economy, race, and gender, to the site of the political (the nation-state and the international). Said, in other words, understands the Goethian initiative, despite its anti-nationalist potential, as essentially a *systematization* or, more pointedly, a *spatialization* or *structuration* of temporality. Or, to invoke the fundamental metaphor of the contemporary proponents of World Literature, he is underscoring the *mapping*—the *cartographing*—of the historical differences that time disseminates in order to accommodate them, as the European explorers of the "New World" did by way of the displacement of the older immediate *periplus* by the distancing Eurocentric technology of Mercutor's Projections,[4] to its imperial metropolitan *Logos* (the Greenwich meridian), that is, to colonize their errant and unproductive energies.

It is true, of course, that Said adapts Antonio Gramsci's anti-Hegelian/Marxist "*imaginative geographical*" orientation, which has its origins in Giambattista Vico, to the question of Western imperial power over what he refers to as the "temporal" perspective he identifies with Georg Lukács and the Hegelian/Marxist tradition. And, I think, it is this simplified binarist version of the complex opposition between space and time that the recent exponents of World Literature have by and large unwittingly adopted as their hermeneutic model. But such an interpretation of Said's understanding of Gramsci's "imaginative geography," which puts space and time in a binary opposition, is not, in my view, what Said meant in invoking Gramsci's and Vico's spatial language. On the contrary. As the oxymoron "imaginative geography" suggests in pointing to the *fiction* of geographical space, Said, in choosing the latter over the dominant Hegelian/Marxist tradition, was pointing to the strategic/ideological uses to which geography was put at its origins. More specifically, he was attempting, like Foucault and the geographers of *Herodote* in my second epigraph, to retrieve the *temporal history* or, more precisely, the radical historicity, that the Hegelian dialectical/teleological view of history (History with a capital H—i.e., a secularized theology), like the historicity of the Western ontotheological tradition at large, including orthodox Marxism, *structured* into a larger identical and spatial—territorialized and colonized—Whole: a global map seen from an Archimedean perspective.[5]

Since I have argued this complex, but crucial, point, which relates time and space, history and geography, in an indissoluble belonging (History with a capital H), elsewhere and at length, it will suffice here to quote my summary of the ideological issues at stake:

> The overdetermination of temporality in the discourse of the Hegelian [and orthodox Marxist] tradition conceals *its fundamentally spatializing/territorializing function*—that it is the (metaphysical) Hegelian view of being that has represented time and the differences that time disseminates (history) in the imaginary geographical terms in which modernity perceives it. To put this alternatively, Gramsci's overdetermination of spatial terms (geography) was intended to use this Hegelian "imagined geography," as Gramsci did with Cuvier's "little bones" against itself; that is, it was intended to expose the will to power over singularity (the "heterogeneous, discontinuous, nonidentiarian, and *unequal* geographies of human habitation and effort") that is endemic to this metaphysical view of being.[6]

In short, Said's purpose in appropriating Gramsci's "imaginary geography" against the Hegelian/Marxist teleological temporal perspective to address the issue of World Literature was *to retrieve historicity from the spatializing Hegelian perspective (History)* and to put "it" back into open-ended dialectical play with structuration, the local with the global, the historical occasion with the spatializing/territorializing map. To put this in Said's language, his purpose was to re-world the world that a totalizing mapping paradoxically unworlded in order to territorialize and colonize "its" recalcitrant errancy.

This general project for World Literature announced by Said at the theoretical beginning of *Culture and Imperialism* is, in fact, repeated at the end, but now in a more historically specific—and unequivocal—way, after he has elaborated the history of the Western cultural/imperial project that self-de-structed in the post–World War II era. I mean the history that bore witness at this liminal point to the implosion of the imperial West's binarist spatializing logic—epitomized by the de-centering emigration of formerly colonized peoples that Said, playing on the perennial Western binary between Visitor and visited, Se(e)r and seen, refers to as "the voyage in": the visitation, the coming to concrete presence—*in the imperial metropolis* of the empire's spectral nomadic others (the visited) who, as in Jane Austen's *Mansfield Park*, hitherto had only haunted that imperial center from a long distance. This disclosive moment—we can call it "evental" (*évenémentiel*) in Alain Badiou's sense of the word—Said is careful to say, does not, as the World Literature initiative by and large appears to assume it does, announce the demise of the nation-state and its imperial project, thus releasing the oppositional critical consciousness, which hitherto focused on the depredations of the nation-state (the local), to overdetermine the global. On the contrary, it bears witness to the emergence of a *historical interregnum*—an in-between occasion characterized by the dying *but by no means dead* nation-state (and its imperial project) and a new, post-colonial—globally oriented—world struggling to be born. Here is how Said puts this evental post-colonial global occasion, this de-centering and nomadizing in-between time: the time of the now, in Walter Benjamin's language, which is the remainder of the self-destruction of the spatializing/colonizing teleological time of the Western metaphysical tradition:

> We can perceive this truth [the resistance to institutionalization inherent in the nomadic consciousness Gilles Deleuze and Félix Guattari, building on Paul Virilio, posit in *A Thousand Plateaus*] on *the political map of the contemporary world*. For surely it is one of the unhappiest characteristics of the age to have produced more refugees, migrants, displaced persons, and exiles than ever before in history, most of them as an accompaniment to and, ironically enough, as afterthoughts of great post-colonial and imperial conflicts. As the struggle for independence produced new states and new boundaries, it also produced homeless wanderers, nomads, and vagrants, unassimilated to the emerging structures of institutional power, rejected by the established order for their intransigence and obdurate rebelliousness. And insofar as these people *exist between the old and the new, between the old empire and the new state, their condition articulates the tensions, irresolutions, and contradictions in the overlapping territories shown on the cultural map of imperialism.*

But Said's diagnosis of the contemporary occasion, it is important to add, is pointedly not limited to the emergence of a post-colonial "demography" that is characterized by its in-between status. It also underscores the emergence of the intrinsic oppositional intellectual imperative of this interregnum: the *exilic consciousness*—the in-between figure—who is *simultaneously* at-home and not-at-home in his or her homeland, inside and outside, local and global, a part of and apart from the nation:

> There is a great difference, however, between the optimistic mobility, the intellectual liveliness, and "the logic of daring" described by the various theoreticians on whose work I have drawn, and the massive dislocations, waste, misery, and horrors endured in our century's migrations and mutilated lives. Yet it is no exaggeration to say that liberation as an intellectual mission, born in the resistance and opposition to the confinements and ravages of imperialism, has now shifted from the settled, established, and domesticated dynamics of culture to its unhoused, decentered, and exilic energies, energies whose incarnation today is the migrant, and whose consciousness is that of the intellectual and artist in exile, *the political figure between domains, between forms, between homes, and between languages*. From this perspective then all things are indeed counter, original, spare, strange. From this perspective also, one can see "the complete consort dancing together" contrapuntally. (*CI*, 332–333)

To be sure, Said diagnosed the global occasion in terms of an interregnum twenty years ago, immediately after the end of Cold War and the emergence of the postcolonial occasion. But, as I have noted, the in-between conditions he singled out then as its essence have not changed. Indeed, as Said pointed out in the aftermath of 9/11 in an address to the Modern Language Association,[7] they have been exacerbated, as the United States' unending "war on terror" in the name of its exceptionalist (nation-state) ethos and *Pax Americana* bears depressing witness. Despite the often-noted waning of the nation-state system and the resistance of post-colonial peoples to its imperial practice, the world as it exists in the present post-9/11 age remains separated and related, nation-state oriented and global, an interregnum under the aegis of the United States and the state of exception it has normalized. Despite its apparent submission to the globalizing imperatives of the free market since the Reagan administration, the United States, in fact, has harnessed the neoliberal strategy—the "free" global market—for its national/neocolonial purposes. In short, to return to Said's initial formulation of what I have been calling the interregnum, for Said: (1) the local and the global *belong together*, are "overlapped or intertwined" in strife; and thus (2) precipitate the exilic consciousness—the figure "between domains, between forms, between homes, between languages"—as the essential intellectual imperative of this historical interregnum.[8]

2

It is precisely this persuasive, radically worldly, Saidian diagnosis of the contemporary "post-colonial" global occasion as an interregnum that, despite its intensification in the post-9/11 era, is more or less absent in the globalist perspective of the prominent exponents of World Literature and thus renders it inadequate to the urgent task of resistance; indeed, is inadvertently in complicity with the globalizing—neoliberal—turn of the nation-state accompanying the United States' initiation of its unending global War on Terror. It is, of course, impossible in this limited space to do justice to this paradigm-changing World Literature movement, especially because it is so various, contradictory, and inchoate—a consequence, no doubt, of the intrinsically human impossibility to *see* the whole of literary production, both spatially and temporally, globally and historically, simultaneously: in Heidegger's language, a "world picture" (*Weltbild*). I will, therefore, restrict my critical commentary to what I take to be from its own rhetoric the most foundational and determining tenet of its otherwise apparently various framing perspective—its *global*, as opposed to *local*, transnational, as opposed to national, perspective—and to a few evident and hopefully inescapable generalizations indissolubly related to this grounding distancing perspective about this movement inferred from a reading of several prominent examples from its rapidly growing archive.

The underlying essence of the World Literature movement, as I noted in the inaugural epigraph of this chapter, is its commitment to what Franco Moretti (and most of the proponents of World Literature) has privileged as "*distanced reading*" against what it takes (erroneously) to be the traditional "close" or "local" analysis of literature:

> The title of this short book deserves a few words of explanation. To begin with, this is an essay on literary history: literature, the old territory (more or less) unlike the drift towards other discourses so typical of recent years. But within that old territory, *a new object instead:* instead of concrete, individual works, a trio of artificial constructs—graphs, maps, and trees—in which the reality of the text undergoes a process of deliberate reduction and abstraction. "Distant reading," I have once called this type of approach; where distance is however not an obstacle, but a specific form of knowledge: fewer elements, hence a sharper sense of the overall interconnection. *Shapes*, *relations*, *structures*. *Forms*. *Models*. (*GMT*, 1; my emphasis)

I mean by this World Literature, more specifically, the modern global perspective on literary production that has its origins in the application of Fernand Braudel and Immanuel Wallerstein and the "world system" school of sociology they founded to the Goethean call, sponsored in modernity by Said, for a *Weltliteratur*. My reservations with this "distanced reading" initiative of the World Literature movement does not lie in its will to break from the hold of the "local"/canonical that has in modernity tethered literary production and the discourse about it to the nation-state. On the contrary, this will to emancipate literature from the nationalist bonds of the nation-state in favor of a more global or transnational perspective is a welcomed initiative. What, taking my directives from Edward Said's diagnosis of the post-imperial occasion, is disabling about the employment of "distance reading" by the proponents of World Literature—Moretti, Pascale Casanova, David Damrosch, Wai Chee Dimock, Lawrence Buell, and Paul Giles, among others—is its tendency to extremist practice: to separate—and reject—the local/national from the global, to abandon attention to the nation-state altogether in favor of the planetary, a tendency that flies in the face of contemporary historical reality—the interregnum. Indeed, this extreme "distanced reading" (and the "shapes, relations, structures, forms, models," it enables) espoused and practiced by Moretti and all too many of the proponents of World Literature—and this is the point I would add to Said's diagnosis of the post-colonial occasion—constitutes, not something "new," as Moretti surprisingly puts it inaugurally in *Graphs, Maps, Trees*, but a paradoxical recuperation of the Western teleological perspective that was delegitimized by the poststructuralist revolution of the post–Algerian/Vietnam War era. I mean generally the Western metaphysical perspective that, in privileging the panoptic eye—the eye distanced from the contingencies of *physis*—effaced the (differential) historicity of being. More immediately, I mean that modern, anthropological, moment of the Western metaphysical tradition, whose panoptic perspective, as the period of "exploration" bears compelling witness, reduced the ineffable historicity of history to a totalized static or, more precisely, determined map whose longitudes and latitudes were not only crucial to the enclosure movement that produced the modern nation-state system but also facilitated the "exceptionalist" West conquest of "the New World," and the colonization of its indigenous peoples.

As I have shown, the post-structuralist revolution (including Said's) decisively interrogated this presiding distanced panoptic or global perspective—its essential reliance on cartography for its polyvalent imperial purposes (recall the second epigraph of this chapter)—and retrieved (de-colonized) history (the "worldliness" of literature in Said's language). Understood in this historical way, it comes as something of a surprise that the metaphor of mapping has recently (from the time of Braudel's and Wallerstein's "world systems" and Fredric Jameson's Marxist call for "cognitive mapping"[9] to the present) been recuperated (without the effort to justify it) as the presiding, indeed, "new" and essential, means of characterizing the "world" of World Literature, a movement ostensibly committed to the liberation of a singular humanity from the constraints of the logic of belonging of the nation-state and its (later) imperialist/colonialist imperative. I am not only referring to Moretti's *systemic* representation of Western literary history as visual diagrams and maps (as in the case of *Graphs, Maps, Trees*), a procedure that apparently in the name of progressive history in fact obliterates the fraught particular history it is representing, as, for example, in the case of his "distant reading" of Mary Mitford's *Our Village* (five volumes, 1824–1892): the devastating enclosure movement that, as Robert Marzec, following Foucault and Deleuze and Guattari, has shown, was fundamental in the establishment of the British modern nation-state and its horrific imperial project.[10] This history-reducing global initiative is also essentially that of the highly visible scholarship of exponents of World Literature such as Pascale Casanova (*The Republic of Letters* [2004])[11] and David Damrosch (*What Is World Literature?* [2003]), who, though they may not explicitly invoke the map structure as such to represent the historicity of World Literature, nevertheless undertake their re-presentations of the history of World Literature from a highly overdetermined global/panoptic—unworldly—"distanced" perspective. For example, despite Casanova's remarkably erudite command of world literary history, not least the tensions between Western literary metropolises and the literatures of the peripheral "weak spaces," her fundamental reliance on the metaphor of the "Greenwich Meridian," the determining cartographic center of her version of the World Literature of modernity, is exemplary of this cartographical perspective and the inadvertent (exceptionalist) Eurocentrism it perpetuates. More generally, this distanced reductive spatial point of view seems endemic to the prominent websites inaugurated by Robert Talley and Rob Wilson entitled "Geo-criticism" and "Rethinking World Literature," respectively, both of which, like Moretti's signature practice, overdetermine, despite occasional avowals to the contrary, the cartographic image over the fraught historical actuality in their representations of literature and its world. Not least, as I have shown elsewhere,[12] this recuperated and disabling suggestion has, unfortunately, come to dominate New Americanist studies inaugurated by the post-Myth and Symbol School American critics such as Sacvan Bercovitch, Richard Slotkin, and Richard Drinnon,[13] and rendered a powerful counter-mnemonic critical instrument of American exceptionalism by John Carlos Rowe, Amy Kaplan, Russ Castronovo, and, above all, Donald E. Pease. As the conflicting *belongingness* of the local and the global implicit in the terms "post-nationalist" or "trans-nationalist" that the latter use to proselytize for a more global perspective suggests, the exilic consciousness—the in-between, inside-outside mind that alone is capable of perceiving contrapuntally the history to which the inside (local/national) mind is necessarily blind—prevails. In this "new" New Americanist dispensation, on the other hand, the exilic consciousness, like that of the World Literature movement, has distanced itself entirely from the immediate historical occasion. To appropriate W.B. Yeats's famous phrase from "The Second Coming" for my subversive purpose, its practitioners can no longer "hear the falconer": "things fall apart, the center will not hold." In the justifiable effort to rise above the Origin/Local/National in the name of liberation from its constraints, current Americanists, paradoxically, arrive at a transcendent—panoptic—perspective, an at-homeness, as it were, that, like their metaphysical opponents at the other end of the gyre, obliterates the historicity of history: specifically, the interregnum entirely dominated by an exceptionalist United States unerringly committed to "regime change"—which is to say, the transformation of what it represents as "rogue states" into ventriloquized client nation-states.[14]

This colonization of the New Americanist initiative by the World Literature movement is borne witness to by such prominent Americanists as Wei Chee Dimock, Lawrence Buell, Brian Edwards and Dilip Parameshwar Gaonkar, and Paul Giles.[15] Its most disturbing symptom, given the historical immediacy of the world that Said, in the name of instigating *Weltliteratur*, diagnoses in *Culture and Imperialism* as a world "between the old and the new, between the old empire and the new state," and I, as "an interregnum," is its remarkable silence about the fundamental reality of the present precarious historical occasion: the United States' destabilizing, unending global War on (Islamist) Terror undertaken in the name of American exceptionalism, that is, of the local, the nation-state. I am referring, more specifically, to the United States' unerring commitment to the life-destroying doctrines of "preemptive war," "regime change" (the reduction of "rogue states" to client states), and the tactics of the spectacle (the "shock and awe" that strikes the historical spectator dumb, i.e. bereaves him or her of speech). That is to say, its exceptionalist global normalization of the state of exception ends, as I have noted, in Giorgio Agamben's inescapable formulation, in the reduction of *bios* to *zoé*, *human* life to *bare life* (*nuda vida*), life that can be killed without the act being called homicide.

To put this spatializing/distancing perspective that tacitly obliterates the local/historical present in the name of the global alternatively—in terms of the related temporal category David Damrosch uses to justify his totally globalized perspective—the proponents of World Literature resist the post-colonial will to "modernize the canon"—that is, its tendency to commit itself to "*presentism*":

> All too often, students of imperialism, colonialism, nationalism, and globalization do indeed define their topics in such a way as to restrict their investigations to just the last five hundred years of human history, or the last hundred years, or even the last few years. If we do, however, we reproduce one of the least appealing characteristics of modern American—and global commercial—culture: the insistent *presentism* that erases the past as a serious factor, leaving at best a few nostalgic postmodern references, the historical equivalent of the "local color" tipped in to distinguish the lobby of the Jakarta Hilton from that of its Cancun counterpart.
>
> Not only does this presentism deprive us of the ability to learn from a much wider range of empires, colonies, politics, and migrations; it also leaves out of account the dramatic ways in which the canons of the earlier periods themselves are being reshaped through new attention to all sorts of long-neglected but utterly fascinating texts.[16]

Despite the judicious warning against discounting the past, this all too easy—and incredibly reductive—critique of "presentism" by a prestigious member of the World Literature movement is, in fact, a tacit critique of Edward Said's overdetermination of the in-between time, what I have been calling, after Walter Benjamin and Giorgio Agamben (and Saint Paul), the time of the now (*ho nyn kairos*) that remains after the evental self-destruction of Western teleological time between the implosion of the Western imperialist project and the United States' declaration of its unending War on Terror. This existential adherence to the time of the now does not, as Damrosch and the proponents of World Literature assume, mean indifference to the historical past or the future and the global context. On the contrary, it means engaging both the temporal past and/or future and the spatial global from the *ontic-ontological* perspective of the present—the irreparable time in which we live as human beings. In keeping with Edward Said's long-time commitment to "beginnings," this affirmation of the in-between time of the now is not meant simply as a political statement. It is also intended as an ontological imperative addressed to the hubris of the humanist proponents of World Literature, who continue to assume, despite the decisive witness of history—and the poststructuralist revolution—the sacredness of the secular West and the transcendence of Man.

Understood in the context of this ontological dimension of the poststructuralist revolution, my criticism of the anti-presentism of the exponents of World Literature is not limited to its disablement of an adequate resistance to the depredations of the neoliberal state that would recuperate the nation-state's waning authority on a global scale. Tethered as it is to radical historicity—the in-betweenness of human finitude (the ontic-ontological and its exilic condition), its thrownness in the world—its de-structive hermeneutics projects a coming community that is faithful to the finite human condition—by which I mean Said's radical "non-humanist humanism."[17] More specifically, this coming community is fundamentally different from the utopian vision of the proponents of World Literature. Here, in what Heidegger once called the ontological "rift" (*das Riss*)[18] and later poststructuralist theorists called "the time of the now" (Agamben) or "beginnings" (Said), where difference is the ontological condition for the possibility of identity, the "identities" that human history has produced—gender, race, ethnicity, even nations—remain, but the old binarist—Friend/foe—metaphysical nation-state logic of belonging, as in the case of the radical humanism of Said's non-humanist humanism, is rendered inoperative. Under the decentering and disoperating imperatives of the unhoming of Man, the life-damaging ravages of this old Friend/foe dispensation of the nation-state give way to an intimate—loving—strife, in which the question takes priority over the answer, difference over identity, temporality over space, potentiality as such over the act, and thus, in which this loving strife enhances—deepens and broadens—the irreparable finite life of the different participants of the human *polis*. At the end of *Culture and Imperialism*, Said, it will be recalled, not only offered us in the post-imperial world a new viable mode of "distilling," "articulating," and resisting "the predicaments that disfigure modernity—mass deportation, imprisonment, population transfer, collective dispossession, and forced immigrations" (*CI*, 333)—by way of attuning his readers to the exilic consciousness of the in-between time of the now—to the interregnum. More important, however muted, he also anticipates the possibility of such a non-humanist humanist *polis* by way of invoking the metaphor of counterpoint, which articulates in the medium of atonal music not only the rendering inoperative of the old binary logic of belonging, but also the life-enhancing loving strife that supersedes its deadly violence:

> From this [exilic perspective of the in-between time] all things are indeed counter, original, spare, strange [potential]. From this perspective also one can see "'the complete consort dancing together' contrapuntally." (*CI*, 333)

This courageous non-humanist humanist *polis*, in which "'the complete consort dances together' *contrapuntally*" (my emphasis), I submit, is Edward Said's primary legacy to the fraught in-between world—the rift—we precariously inhabit. It is also the coming community that affiliates Said—*pace* many of Said's followers—with those recent post-poststructuralist thinkers who, as I have shown in chapter 5, would contribute to the retrieval and restoration of the speech—and the polity—of the multitude—the dehumanized "bare life" (Agamben), the "nonidentities" (Badiou), the "ungrievable" (Butler), "the part of no part" (Rancière), in their language—who have been bereft of them by the binary logic of belonging of the spectacle-oriented modern parliamentary capitalist nation-state.

Notes

Chapter 1. Posthumanism in the Age of Globalization: Rethinking *The End of Education*

1. I am referring to "the American jeremiad," that national ritual inaugurated by the founding Puritans, that, by way of instilling anxiety—the threat of the "frontier" or "enemy"—precluded recidivism—the backsliding of the covenantal people into the decadent conditions of the Old World from which they were escaping. See Sacvan Bercovitch, *American Jeremiad* (Madison: University of Wisconsin Press, 1978), p. 23. See also its latest avatar, Samuel P. Huntington's post-9/11 book *Who Are We?: Challenges to America's National Identity* (hereafter *WAW*; New York: Simon and Schuster, 2004), which focuses on the period between the end of the Cold War and the George W. Bush administration's announcement of its War on Terror in the aftermath of *al Qaeda*'s bombing of the World Trade Center and the Pentagon. As in the American past, Huntington reads the end of conflict with an enemy, in this case, the end of the Cold War with the Soviet Union, as a threat to the exceptionalism that, allegedly, has always distinguished America from the Old World:

> Democracy was left without a significant secular ideological rival, and the United States was left without a peer competitor. Among American foreign policy elites, the result was euphoria, pride, arrogance—and uncertainty. The absence of an ideological threat produced an absence of purpose. "Nations need enemies," Charles Krauthammer [a prestigious neo-conservative pundit] commented as the Cold War ends. "Take away one, and they find another." The ideal enemy for America would be hostile, racially and culturally different, and militarily strong enough to pose a credible threat to American security. The foreign policy debates of the1990s were already over who might be such an enemy. (*WAW*, 262)

Following the spectacularizing imperatives of the American jeremiad, Huntington continues (the rhetoric of relief should not be overlooked):

> The cultural gap between Islam and America's Christianity and Anglo-Protestantism reinforces Islam's enemy qualifications. And on September 11, 2001, Osama bin Laden ended America's search. The attacks on New York and Washington followed by the wars with Afghanistan and Iraq and the more diffuse "war on terrorism" make militant Islam America's first enemy of the twenty-first century. (*WAW*, 264–265)

2. See the chapter entitled "The Devastation of Language under the Dictatorship of the Public Realm: Reading Global American with Hannah Arendt," in William V. Spanos, *Exiles in the City: Hannah Arendt and Edward W. Said in Counterpoint* (Columbus: Ohio State University Press, 2012), pp. 5–48.

3. See my chapter entitled "The Apollonian Investment of Modern Humanist Educational Theory: The Examples of Matthew Arnold, Irving Babbitt, and I. A. Richards," in *The End of Education* (Minneapolis: University of Minnesota Press, 1993), 65–117.

4. Jacques Derrida, "Structure, Sign, and Play in the Discourse of the Human Sciences," in *Writing and Difference*, trans. Alan Bass (Chicago: University of Chicago Press), pp. 279–280.

5. Martin Heidegger, *Being and Time*, trans. John Macquarrie and Edward Robinson (New York: Harper and Row, 1962):

> The Necessity for Explicitly Restating the Question of Being
>
> This question has today been forgotten. Even though in our time we deem it progressive to give our approval to "metaphysics" again, it is held that we have been exempted from the exertions of a newly rekindled *gigantomachia peri tis ousias*. Yet the question we are touching upon is not just any question. It is one which provided a stimulus for the researches of Plato and Aristotle, only to subside from then on *as a theme for actual investigation*. What these two men achieved was to persist through many alterations and "retouchings" down to the "logic" of Hegel. And what they wrested with the utmost intellectual effort from the phenomena, fragmentary and incipient though it was, has long since become trivialized. (p. 2)

6. Martin Heidegger, "Letter on Humanism," trans. J. Glenn Gray and Frank A. Capuzzi, in *Basic Writings*, revised edition, ed. David Farrell Krell (New York: Harper and Row, 1993), pp. 224–225. See also Heidegger, *Parmenides*, trans. André Schuwer and Richard Rojcewicz (Bloomington: Indiana University Press, 1992), pp. 58–61.

7. Martin Heidegger, "The Question Concerning Technology," trans. William Lovitt. *Basic Writings*, p. 298. Further references will be abbreviated to QT and placed in parentheses.

8. Michel Foucault, *Discipline and Punish: The Birth of the Prison*, trans. Alan Sheridan (New York: Vintage Books, 1977), p. 148.

9. Louis Althusser, "Ideology and Ideological State Apparatuses (Note Towards an Investigation)," in *Lenin and Philosophy and Other Essays* (New York: *Monthly Review*, 1971), p. 181.

10. See especially Edward W. Said, "Reflections on American 'Left' Criticism," in *The World, the Text, and the Critic* (Cambridge, MA: Harvard University Press, 1983), pp. 158–177.

11. William V. Spanos, *The Legacy of Edward W. Said* (Urbana: University of Illinois Press, 2009).

12. Bill Readings, *The University in Ruins* (Cambridge, MA: Harvard University Press, 1996).

13. Arif Dirlik, "Transnationalization and the University: The Perspective of Global Modernity." *boundary 2*, vol. 39, no. 3 (Fall 2012), pp. 54–55.

14. See William V. Spanos, "The Devastation of Language under the Dictatorship of the Public Realm: Rethinking Global American with Hannah Arendt," in *Exiles in the City*, pp. 5–48.

15. Giorgio Agamben. *Homo Sacer: Sovereign Power and Bare Life*, trans. Daniel Heller Roazen (Stanford, CA: Stanford University Press, 1998), p. 83.

16. Hannah Arendt, *Eichmann in Jerusalem*: "The trouble with Eichmann was precisely that so many were like him, and that the many were neither perverted nor sadistic, that they were, *and still are*, terribly and terrifyingly normal. From the viewpoint of our legal institutions and of our moral standards of judgment, this normality was much more terrifying than all the atrocities put together, for it implied . . . that this new type of criminal who is in actual fact *hostis generis humani*, commits his crimes under circumstances that make it well-nigh impossible for him to know or to feel that he is doing wrong" (p. 276).

17. "occasion": immediately from the Latin *occasus*, "the setting of the sun," and ultimately from the ablative form of *cadere*: "to fall," "to die," "to perish." I use the word to evoke other related words that have been colonized by the first term of the metaphysical binary Identity/difference, such as "case" (as in "being-in-the-world is our case"), "accidental," and "incidental." Not least, I use the word to call attention to its relation to "Occident," from *occidere*, "to go down," "to set."

18. Giorgio Agamben, *The Time That Remains: A Commentary on the Letter to the Romans*, trans. Patricia Dailey, (Stanford, CA: Stanford University Press, 2005) p. 29; the last emphasis is mine. See also Alain Badiou, *Saint Paul: The Foundation of Universalism*, trans. Ray Brassier (Stanford, CA: Stanford University Press, 2003), p. 87.

19. Spanos, *Exiles in the City*, p. 89.

20. Following Hannah Arendt's critique of the means/end logic that constitutes the essence of *homo faber*, Agamben writes: "If producing is a means in view of an end and praxis is an end without means, the gesture then breaks with the false alternatives between ends and means that paralyzes morality and presents instead means that, *as such*, evade the orbit of mediality without becoming, for this reason, ends." *Means without End: Notes on Politics*, trans. Vincenzo Binetti and Cesare Casarino (Minneapolis: University of Minnesota Press, p. 57.

21. See Spanos, *Exiles in the City*, pp. 97–103.

22. Edward W. Said, *Humanism and Democratic Criticism* (New York: Columbia University Press, 2004), pp. 76–77; my emphasis. Said also invokes Deutscher's concept of the non-Jewish Jew in his *Freud and the Non-European* (London: Verso, 2003), pp. 52–55.

23. Spanos, *The Legacy of Edward W. Said*: The failure of the poststructuralists to explicitly realize the symptomatic worldliness of their theory, I argue, "resulted from their quite justifiable early and inaugural emphasis on the inordinate difficulty of breaking free from the constraints of a discourse of knowledge production and its justifications—schools, the media, the culture industry, and so on—that pervasively represented themselves as disinterested, humane, and democratic and, as Foucault observed, saturated the Western body politic, right down to its capillaries" (p. 164).

24. Jacques Rancière, *Disagreement: Politics and Philosophy*, trans. Julie Rose (Minneapolis: University of Minnesota Press, 1998); Judith Butler, *Frames of War: When Is Life Grievable?* (London: Verso, 2009); Alain Brossat, "*L'inarticulable*," in *Lignes* 8, *Vainqueurs/Vaincus: Un monde en guerre* (May 2002); Alain Badiou, *Ethics: An Essay on the Understanding of Evil* (London: Verso 2001).

25. The inaugural issue of *American Political Thought*, published by the University of Chicago Press and edited by Michael Zuckert, which features a symposium entitled *American Exceptionalism: Is it Real; Is it Good?*, bears telling witness to this unfortunate disciplinary divide between the social sciences and the humanities. In the five substantial essays on the question of American exceptionalism written by prestigious political scientists, there is no reference to the massive scholarship on the subject published in the last decade or more by the so-called New Americanist literary and cultural critics such as Donald E. Pease, John Carlos Rowe, Amy Kaplan, Russ Castronovo, among many others, which is deeply critical of the American exceptionalist ethos for its disavowal of the violence that they show decisively to be intrinsic to its logic. This symposium include the following: James W. Ceaser, "The Origins and Character of American Exceptionalism"; Patrick J. Deneen, "Cities of Man on a Hill"; Hilde Eliassen Restad, "Old Paradigms in History Die Hard in Political Science: US Foreign Policy and American Exceptionalism"; Peter S. Onuf, "American Exceptionalism and National Identity"; Rogers M. Smith, "'Our Republican Example': American Experiments in Government in the Twenty-First Century."

26. See, for example, Winfried Fluck, Donald E. Pease, and John Carlos Rowe, eds. *Reframing the Transnational Turn in American Studies* (Hanover, NH: University Press of New England, 2011); Russ Castronovo and Susan Gilman, eds. *States of Emergency: The Object of American Studies* (Chapel Hill: University of North Carolina Press, 2009); Wai Chee Dimock and Lawrence Buell, eds. *Shades of the Planet: American Literature as World Literature* (Princeton, NJ: Princeton University Press 2007); Paul Giles, *Global Remapping of American Literature* (Princeton, NJ: Princeton University Press, 2010). All the essays in

these volumes call productively for the transnationalization of American studies. However, some, in overdetermining the global, marginalize the local, thus betraying the contrapuntal imperatives of the interregnum. Paul Giles's *Global Remapping of American Literature* is symptomatic of this excess. For an amplification of this critique, see chapter 6, "Edward Said and World Literature: Thinking the Imperatives of the Interregnum."

Chapter 2. Speaking the Lie of the Truth to Power: A Meditation on the Truth of Modernity by an Incorrigible Caviler

1. Michel Foucault, *Discipline and Punish: The Birth of the Prison*, trans. Alan Sheridan (New York: Pantheon, 1977), pp. 137–138.

2. Edward W. Said. *Orientalism* (New York: Vintage, 1979), pp. 92–93.

3. For amplified accounts of my revision of Foucault's and Said's genealogy of Western modernity, see especially Spanos "Heidegger and Foucault: The Politics of the Commanding Gaze," in *Heidegger and Criticism: Retrieving the Cultural Politics of Destruction* (Minneapolis: University of Minnesota Press, 1993), pp. 132–180; and "Heidegger, Foucault, and the Empire of the Gaze: Thinking the Territorialization of Knowledge" in Spanos, *The Legacy of Edward W. Said*, pp. 26–69.

4. See Edward W. Said, "Reflections on American 'Left' Literary Criticism," in *The World, the Text, and the Critic* (Cambridge, MA: Harvard University Press), 158–178; originally published in *boundary 2*, vol. 28, 12 (Fall 1979).

5. Alain Badiou, *Ethics: An Essay on the Understanding of Evil* (London: Verso, 2001), p. 69.

6. Martin Heidegger, "The End of Philosophy and the Task of Thinking," in *Basic Writings*, pp. 427–449.

7. Martin Heidegger, "The Age of the World Picture," in *The Question Concerning Technology and Other Essays*, trans. and ed. William Lovitt (New York: Harper and Row, 1977), pp. 115–154.

8. Martin Heidegger, "What Is Metaphysics?" in *Basic Writings*: "The nothing—what else can it be for science but an outrage and a phantasm? If science is right, then only one thing is sure: science wishes to know nothing of the nothing. Ultimately this is the scientifically rigorous conception of the nothing. We know it, the nothing, in that we wish to know nothing about it" (p. 96); further references will be abbreviated to *WM* and placed in parentheses.

9. See especially Heidegger's pervasive etymological analyses of the language of knowledge production and of everyday language, which demonstrate the truth to be a matter of reducing the be-ing of being to seeing/grasping.

10. Jacques Derrida, "Structure, Sign and Play in the Discourse of the Human Sciences," in *Writing and Difference*, trans. Alan Bass (Chicago: University of Chicago Press, 1978), p. 279.

11. Carl Schmitt, *Political Theology: Four Chapters on the Concept of Sovereignty*, trans. George Schwab, with a foreword by Tracy Strong (Chicago: University of Chicago Press, 2004).

12. See Spanos, *The Legacy of Edward W. Said*; and Spanos, *Exiles in the City*.

13. See "Edward W. Said and the Poststructuralists," in *The Legacy of Edward W. Said*, pp. 1–25.

14. Martin Heidegger, "Letter on Humanism," in *Basic Writings*, pp. 224–225.

15. Éliane Escoubas, "Heidegger la question romaine, la question impériale: Autour du 'tourant,'" in *Heidegger: Questions ouvertes*, ed. Éliane Escoubas (Paris: Éditions Osiris, 1988), 163–188.

16. Martin Heidegger, *Parmenides*, trans. André Schuwer and Richard Rojcewicz (Bloomington: Indiana University Press, 1992), pp. 58–61; translation modified.

17. Jacques Derrida, "Structure, Sign, and Play in the Discourse of the Human Sciences," p. 279.

18. Jacques Derrida, *Specters of Marx: The State of the Debt, the Work of Mourning, and the New International*, trans. Peggy Kamuf (New York: Routledge, 1994).

19. Jean François Lyotard, *The Postmodern Condition: A Report on Knowledge*, trans. Geoff Bennington and Brian Massumi, with a foreword by Fredric Jameson (Minneapolis: University of Minnesota Press, 1984); and *Differend: Phrases in Dispute*, trans. Georges Van Den Abbeele (Minneapolis: University of Minnesota Press, 1988).

20. Philippe Lacoue-Labarthe, *Heidegger, Art, and Politics: The Fiction of the Political*, trans. Chris Turner (London: Blackwell, 1990).

21. Jean-Luc Nancy, *The Inoperative Community*, trans. Peter Connor, Lisa Garbus, Michael Holland, and Simona Sawhney, with a foreword by Christopher Fynsk (Minneapolis: University of Minnesota Press, 1991).

22. See especially Louis Althusser, "Ideology and Ideological State Apparatuses," trans. Ben Brewster, pp. 127–186; and "From *Capital* to Marx's Philosophy," in Louis Althusser and Etienne Balibar, *Reading Capital*, trans. Ben Brewster (London: Verso, 1970), pp. 11–70.

23. No one has put this onto-politics of the dominating (lie of the) Western Truth more succinctly and forcefully than the Indian Subaltern Studies scholar Dipesh Chakrabarty in *History and Difference* (Princeton, NJ: Princeton University Press, 2000).

24. See "We Refugees," in Hannah Arendt, *The Jewish Writings*, ed. Jerome Kohn and Ron Feldman (New York: Schocken Books, 2007), 264–274; and, above all, Hannah Arendt, "The Decline of the Nation-State and the End of the Rights of Man," in *The Origins of Totalitarianism, Part Two: Imperialism* (New York; Harcourt, 1976), pp. 267–304.

25. Edward W. Said, *Culture and Imperialism* (New York: Vintage, 1994), p. 332.

26. Giorgio Agamben, *Homo Sacer*, pp. 183–184.

27. Giorgio Agamben, *The Coming Community*, trans. Michael Hardt (Minneapolis: University of Minnesota Press, 1993), pp. 1–2.

28. Jacques Rancière, "The Beginning of Politics," in *Dis-agreement: Politics and Philosophy*, trans. Julie Rose (Minneapolis: University of Minnesota Press, 1999), pp. 1–21.

29. Alain Badiou, *The Rebirth of History: Times of Riot and Uprisings*, trans. Gregory Eliot (London: Verso 2012), p. 56. Elsewhere in this book, Badiou, echoing Rancière, refers to this "inexistent" more precisely in terms of its difference ("separating name") from the "*identitarian object*" privileged by the nation-state:

> [T]he state fictionalizes an *identitarian object* (for example, the French person) that individuals and groups have a duty to resemble as closely as possible, if they are to merit positive attention from the state. Anyone declared unduly dissimilar from the identitarian object will also be entitled to the attention of the state, but in a negative sense (suspicion, police checks, internment, expulsion, and so on).
>
> A separating name refers to a particular way of not resembling the fictive identitarian object. It enables the state to separate certain groups from the collectivity, who therefore call for particular repressive measures. These can range from "immigrant," "Islamist," "Muslim," and "Roma" to "youth from the banlieues." (p. 92)

30. Judith Butler, *Frames of War: When Is Life Grievable?* (London: Verso, 2009): "If the Islamic populations destroyed in recent and current wars are considered less than human, or outside the cultural conditions for the emergence of the human, then they belong either to a time of cultural infancy or to a time that is outside time as we know it. In both cases, they are regarded as not yet having arrived at the idea of the rational human. It follows from such a viewpoint that the destruction of such populations, their infrastructures, their housing, and their religious and community institutions, constitutes the destruction of what threatens the human, but not the human itself. It is also precisely this particular conceit of a progressive history that positions 'the West' as articulating the paradigmatic principles of the human—of the humans who are worth valuing, whose lives are worth safeguarding, whose lives are precarious, and, when lost, are worth public grieving" (p. 125).

31. Maurice Blanchot, *The Writing of Disaster*, trans. Ann Smock (Lincoln: University of Nebraska Press, 1986), pp. 17ff, 145; Gilles Deleuze, "Bartleby; or, the Formula," in *Essays Critical and Clinical*, trans. Daniel W. Smith and Michael A. Greco (Minneapolis: University of Minnesota Press, 1997); Michael Hardt and Antonio Negri, *Empire* (Cambridge, MA: Harvard University Press, 2000), pp. 203–204; Slavoj Žižek, "The Violence of Subtraction," in *In Defense of Lost Causes* (London: Verso, 2009), p. 409.

32. Giorgio Agamben, *The Coming Community*, pp. 34–37; and "Bartleby, or On Contingency," in *Potentialities: Collected Essays in Philosophy*, trans. Daniel Heller-Roazen (Stanford, CA: Stanford University Press, 1999), pp. 243–273. Edward Said, not incidentally, though his source is the Theodor Adorno of *Minima Moralia*, not Bartleby, makes the same fundamental point in *Culture and Imperialism* about resistance in the interregnum as the post-poststructuralists do:

> "The past life of émigrés, is, as we know, annulled," says Adorno in *Minima Moralia*, subtitled *Reflections from a Damaged Life* . . . . Why? "Because anything that is not reified, cannot be counted and measured, ceases to exist," or, as he says later, is "consigned to mere background." Although the disabling aspects of this fate are manifest, its virtues or possibilities are worth exploring. Thus the émigré consciousness . . . discovers in its marginality that a "gaze averted from the beaten track, hatred of brutality, a search for fresh concepts not yet encompassed by the general pattern, is the last hope for thought." Adorno's general pattern is what in another place he calls the "administered world" or, insofar as the irresistible dominants in culture are concerned, "the consciousness industry." "There is then not just the negative advantage of refuge in the émigré's eccentricity; there is also the positive benefit of challenging the system, describing in language unavailable to those it has already subdued":
>
> In an intellectual hierarchy which constantly makes everyone answerable unanswerability alone can call the hierarchy directly by its name. . . . He who offers for sale something unique that no one wants to buy, represents, even against his will, freedom from exchange. (p. 333; my emphasis)

That Said may have had Melville as well as Adorno in mind at this climatic point in *Culture and Imperialism* is borne witness to by the following strikingly analogous passage from *After the Last Sky: Palestinian Lives* (New York: Columbia University Press, 1999):

> To the Israelis, whose incomparable military and political power dominates us, we are at the periphery, the image that will not go away. Every assertion of our non-existence, every attempt to spirit us away, every new effort to prove that we were never really there, simply raises the question of why so much denial of, and such energy expended on, what was not there? Could it be that even as alien outsiders we dog their military might with our obdurate moral claim, our insistence (like that of Bartleby the scrivener) that 'we would prefer not to," not to leave, not to abandon Palestine forever?" (pp. 41–42)

For an amplified version of my reading of Bartleby, see William V. Spanos, " 'Benito Cereno' and 'Bartleby, the Scrivener': Reflections on the American Calling," in *Herman Melville and the American Calling: The Fiction after* Moby-Dick, *1851–1857* (Albany, NY: State University of New York Press, 2008), pp. 105–160.

33. Giorgio Agamben, *The Coming Community*, pp. 84–87.

34. Giorgio Agamben, *The Time That Remains*, pp. 143–145.

35. See Giorgio Agamben, "In Praise of Profanation," in *Profanations*, trans. Jeff Ford (New York: Zone, 2007), pp. 73–92.

36. Agamben derives this term immediately from George Bataille and Jean-Luc Nancy (*Communauté désoeuvrée*, "Inoperative Community"), but his primary source is Saint Paul's *katergein*: "*Katargeō* is a compound of *argeō*, which in turn derives from the adjective *argos*, meaning 'inoperative, not-at-work (*a-ergos*), inactive.' The compound therefore comes to mean: 'I make inoperative, I deactivate, I suspend the efficacy.'" *The Time That Remains*, pp. 95–99.

37. My interpolation and emphasis.

38. Hannah Arendt, "We Refugees," p. 274.

39. Giorgio Agamben, "Beyond Human Rights," in *Means without End*, trans. Vincenzo Binetti and Cesar Casarino (Minneapolis: University of Minnesota Press, 2000), pp. 23–25.

40. Agamben, *The Time That Remains*, pp. 23–24.

Chapter 3. American Exceptionalism and the State of Exception: A Genealogy of the Contemporary Security State

1. Martin Heidegger, "The Question Concerning Technology," in *Basic Writings*, pp. 322–324.

2. Hannah Arendt, "The Decline of the Nation-State and the End of the Rights of Man," in *The Origins of Totalitarianism, Part Two: Imperialism* (New York: Harcourt, 1976), pp. 267–302.

3. Michel Foucault, *The Birth of Biopolitics: Lectures at the College de France, 1978–1979*, eds. François Ewald and Alessandro Fontana; trans. Graham Burchell (New York: Palgrave Macmillan, 2008).

4. Giorgio Agamben, *Homo Sacer*. Further citations will be abbreviated to *HS* and placed in parentheses.

5. John Winthrop, "A Model of Christian Charity," in Perry Miller, ed. *The American Puritans: Their Prose and Poetry* (New York: Columbia University Press, 1982), pp. 79–84.

6. See Peter Hulme, *Colonial Encounters: Europe and the Native Caribbean, 1492–1797* (London: Routledge, 1986), pp. 157–158: "[I]n 1629 in New England John Winthrop assimilated [Samuel] Purchas's point to the legal argument of *vacuum domicilium* by which the Indian had 'natural' but not 'civil' rights over the land because they had not 'subdued' it" (p. 158).

7. Raymond Williams, *Marxism and Literature* (Oxford: Oxford University Press, 1977), pp. 109–110.

8. John L. O'Sullivan, "The Great Nation of Futurity," *The United States Democratic Review*, vol. 6, no. 21 (November 1839), p. 427.

9. John O'Sullivan, "Annexation (1845)" in *Democratic Review 17*, no. 1 (July–August 1845), pp. 5–10. Further citations will be abbreviated to A and placed in parentheses.

10. Quentin Youngberg, "Morphology of Manifest Destiny: The Justified Violence of John O'Sullivan, Hank Morgan, and George W. Bush," in *Canadian Review of American Studies*, vol. 35, no. 3 (2005), 315–333. Further citations will be abbreviated to MMD and placed in parentheses. Only at the end does Youngberg come close to indicating the relation between the theological and the secular in O'Sullivan's text: "The primary characteristics of Manifest Destiny, which emerged under that name midway through the nineteenth century as the legacy of the Puritanical rhetoric of the colonial founders of the American nation, are a supreme self-righteousness and a keen sense of national exceptionalism. Both of these characteristics tend to naturalize the impulse to extend American institutions beyond the nation's political borders and then to naturalize the extension of its borders to match the reach of those institutions" (MMD, 322–323).

11. The quotations from John Cotton derive from his "God's Promise to His Plantation," London, 1634.

12. See, for example Exodus 16:2–3: "And the whole congregation of the children of Israel murmured against Moses and Aaron in the wilderness. And the children said unto them, would to God we had died by the hand of the Lord in the land of Egypt, when we sat by the fleshpots and when we did eat bread to the full; for ye have brought us forth into this wilderness to kill this whole assembly with hunger."

13. For example, the terms "settlement," "betterment," and "improvement," put always in opposition to the native's "vagabondage," saturate James Fenimore Cooper's Leather-Stocking novels.

14. Sacvan Bercovitch, *American Jeremiad* (Madison: University of Wisconsin Press, 1978), p. 11. Further citations will be abbreviated to *AJ* and placed in parentheses.

15. For an extended analysis of the Puritan calling, see William. V. Spanos, "American Exceptionalism and the Calling: A Genealogy of the Vocational Ethic," in *Redeemer Nation in the Interregnum: An Untimely Meditation on the American Calling* (New York: Fordham University Press, 2015).

16. John Milton, "Areopagitica": http://www.dartmouth.edu/~milton/reading_room/areopagitica/text.html (my emphasis).

17. William V. Spanos, *American Exceptionalism in the Age of Globalization: The Specter of Vietnam* (Albany, NY: State University of New York Press, 2008), pp. 191–198. Further citations will be abbreviated to *AE* and placed in parentheses.

18. In invoking the metaphorics of monumentalizing, I am referring to Foucault's devastating Nietzschean critique of monumental history—and to Guy Debord's critique of the "the society of spectacle." See the chapter entitled "The Nothingness of Being and the Spectacle: The American Sublime Revisited,"

in Spanos, *Redeemer Nation in the Interregnum: An Untimely Meditation on the American Calling*.

19. See, for example, Ernest Lee Tuveson's Cold War cultural history, *Redeemer Nation: The Idea of America's Millennial Role* (Chicago: University of Chicago Press, 1966).

20. Edward Said, *Orientalism* (New York: Vintage, 1979): "It may appear strange to speak about something or someone holding a *textual* attitude, but a student of literature will understand the phrase more easily if he will recall the kind of view attacked by Voltaire in *Candide*, or even the attitude to reality satirized by Cervantes in *Don Quixote*. What seems unexceptionable good sense to these writers is that it is as fallacy to assume that the swarming, unpredictable, and problematic mess in which human beings live can be understood on the basis of what books—texts—say; to apply what one learns out of a book literally to reality is to risk folly or ruin. One would no more think of using *Amadis of Gaul* to understand sixteenth-century (or present-day) Spain than one would use the Bible to understand, say, the House of Commons" (pp. 92–93).

21. Richard Slotkin, *Regeneration through Violence: The Mythology of the American Frontier, 1600–1860* (Norman: University of Oklahoma Press, 2000; originally published by Wesleyan University Press, 1973), p. 5; my emphasis. See also Slotkin, *The Fatal Environment: The Myth of the Frontier in the Age of Industrialization, 1800–1890* (Middleton, CT: Wesleyan University Press, 1985); and *Gunslinger Nation: The Myth of the Frontier in Twentieth-Century America* (New York: Atheneum, 1992).

22. Francis Parkman, *The Oregon Trail* and *The Conspiracy of Pontiac* (New York: Library of America, 1991), p. 347; my emphasis. Originally published in 1851.

23. For an extended critical study of Twain's novel that focuses on its jeremiadic function, see William V. Spanos, *Shock and Awe: American Exceptionalism and the Imperatives of the Spectacle in Mark Twain's* A Connecticut Yankee in King Arthur's Court (Hanover, NH: Dartmouth College Press, 2013).

24. Frederick Jackson Turner, "The Significance of the Frontier in American History," in *The Frontier in American History* (New York: Henry Holt, 1953), p. 138.

25. In responding to Greene's novel, Lederer and Burdick, in part, proffer a radically different version of the American from Greene's "Quiet American," the American exceptionalist Alden Pyle (modeled on the legendary Colonel Edward Lansdale), who, in the name of his textual attitude—his reading of the Cold War historian York Harding—leaves blood wherever he steps in Vietnam. Modeled on the same Colonel Lansdale, their equivalent to Pyle is the young American soldier, Edwin Hillandale, whom they represent as the epitome of the mythical Natty Bumppo figure of the frontier era. See William V. Spanos "Who Killed Alden Pyle? The Oversight of Oversight in Graham Greene's *The Quiet American*," in *American Exceptionalism in the Age of Globalization*, pp. 57–97.

26. John F Kennedy, "Address Accepting the Democratic Party Nomination for the Presidency of the United States," July 15, 1960: http://presidency.ucsb.edu/ws/?pis—25966. It is worth observing in this context that, in keeping with the jeremiadic themes, Kennedy established the Special Forces (better known as the Green Berets, which, modeled on the frontier figure, were intended to engage in a kind of warfare that was adequate to the conditions of the wilderness of Vietnam) and the Peace Corps.

27. Michael Herr, *Dispatches* (New York: Vintage, 1991), p. 71.

28. Francis Fukuyama, *The End of History and the Last Man* (New York: Free Press, 1994).

29. See PNAC, "Rebuilding America's Defenses: Strategy, Force, Resources for a New Century," Sept. 2000.

30. For a celebratory summary account of these periodic "Great Awakenings," see Samuel P. Huntington, *Who Are We? Challenges to America's National Identity* (New York: Simon and Schuster, 2004), pp. 226–227.

31. George W. Bush, "9/11 Address to the Nation," September 12, 2001: http://www.americanrhetoric.com/speeches/gwbush911addresstothenation.htm. Further citations will be abbreviated to AN and placed in parentheses.

32. Samuel P. Huntington, *The Clash of Civilizations and the Remaking of World Order* (New York: Simon and Schuster, 1996). As Edward Said has shown, the phrase, which is invariably identified with Huntington, was, in fact, coined by the Orientalist (and Zionist) scholar Bernard Lewis. See Said, "The Clash of Definitions," in *Reflections on Exile and Other Essays* (Cambridge, MA: Harvard University Press, 2000), pp. 571–572.

33. William V. Spanos, *American Exceptionalism in the Age of Globalization: The Specter of Vietnam*, pp. 217–236.

34. Typical of the liminal nature of his jeremiad, Huntington, it is important to notice, in quoting Sacvan Bercovitch, does not indicate that the latter's meticulous cultural history of the Massachusetts Bay Puritans is ideologically antithetical to his.

35. William V. Spanos, *The Exceptionalist State and the State of Exception: Herman Melville's* Billy Budd, Sailor (Baltimore: The Johns Hopkins University Press, 2012).

Chapter 4. The Human in Modernity: A Genealogy of Bare Life

1. Martin Heidegger, "The Question Concerning Technology," p. 325; trans. modified.

2. Martin Heidegger, "Letter on Humanism," in *Basic Writings*, p. 221. Further citations will be abbreviated to LH and placed in parentheses.

3. This notorious passage derives from an unpublished text made prominent by Philippe Lacoue-Labarthe in *La Fiction du politique*, p. 58. Labarthe's

source is a citation from Wolfgang Schirmacher, *Technic und Gelassenheit* (Freiberg: Karl Alber, 1984). For examples of the outrage this passage has provoked among traditional humanists, see Richard Wolin, "The French Heidegger Debate," *New German Critique*, vol. 45 (Fall 1988), pp. 158–159; *The Politics of Being* (New York: Columbia University Press, 2016), pp. 168–169; "Introduction," *The Heidegger Controversy* (Boston: MIT Press, 1992), p. 15; David H. Hirsch, *The Deconstruction of Literature*, pp. 18–19; and Tom Rockmore, *On Heidegger's Nazism and Philosophy*, pp. 241–242.

4. The exception is Dana Villa, *Heidegger and Arendt: The Fate of the Political* (Princeton, NJ: Princeton University Press, 1996).

5. Hannah Arendt, *The Human Condition* (Chicago: University of Chicago Press, 1958), p. 99. Further references will be abbreviated to HC and placed in parentheses.

6. See especially Hannah Arendt, "The Decline of the Nation-State and the End of the Rights of Man," in *The Origins of Totalitarianism* (New York: Harcourt, 1968), pp. 267–302.

7. See Theodor Adorno and Max Horkheimer, *Dialectic of the Enlightenment*, trans. Edmund Jephcott (London: New Left Books, 1974); and Walter Benjamin, "Theses on the Philosophy of History," in *Illuminations*, ed. Hannah Arendt (New York: Schocken, 1969).

8. Hannah Arendt, *Eichmann in Jerusalem: A Report on the Banality of Evil*. Rev. Ed. (New York: Penguin, 1965), p. 276.

9. This ostracism continues to this day. See Mark Lilla's November 21, 2013, review of the film *Hannah Arendt* (2013) by the German director Margarette von Trotta in *The New York Review of Books*: http://www.nybooks.com/articles/2013/11/21/arendt-eichmann-new-truth/

10. Hannah Arendt, *The Life of the Mind* (New York: Harcourt Brace, 1978), pp. 3–4.

11. William V. Spanos "Heidegger and Foucault: The Politics of the Commanding Gaze," in *Heidegger and Criticism: Retrieving the Cultural Politics of Destruction* (Minneapolis: University of Minnesota Press, 1993), pp. 132–180.

12. Michel Foucault, *History of Sexuality, Vol. I: An Introduction*, trans. Robert Hurley (New York: Pantheon, 1978), p. 10.

13. Michel Foucault, *Discipline and Punish: The Birth of the Prison*, trans. Alan Sheridan (New York: Pantheon, 1977), p. 138; my emphasis. Further citations will be abbreviated to DP and placed in parentheses.

14. Giorgio Agamben, *Homo Sacer*, p. 83 (emphasis in the original).

15. Martin Heidegger, "What Is Metaphysics?" in *Basic Writings*: "The nothing—what else can it be for science but an outrage and a phantasm? If science is right, then only one thing is sure: science wishes to know nothing of the nothing. Ultimately this is the scientifically rigorous conception of the nothing. We know it, the nothing, in that we wish to know nothing about it" (p. 96). Further citations will be abbreviated to WIM and placed in parentheses.

16. Judith Butler, *Frames of War: When Is Life Grievable?* (London: Verso, 2009), p. 31.

17. Alain Badiou, *Ethics*.

18. What distinguishes Badiou's reading of the revolutionary potential of Tahrir Square from Agamben's reading of Tiananmen Square is his insistence on what he calls "contraction": "The historical situation contracts around an active, thinking minority whose provenance is multifaceted. It produces a sort of presentation of itself, which is simultaneously pure, complete and very limited, a sample of the generic being of a people." *The Rebirth of History: Times of Riots and Uprisings*, trans. Gregory Elliott (London: Verso, 2012), p. 91. But, it should be emphasized that this "contracted" voice, as the conclusion of the passage makes clear, should not be interpreted as an identifiable "party" in the old Stalinist sense: "What arrives in the square is a real *presentation*, the affirmation that what exists and must exist—is the people who are there and are acting together, whatever the name given them by the State. In this sense the historical riot *deposes names*. It is in the latent state of this deposition that a political organization is going to develop the consequences of a new existence, the existence of what used not to exist, the existence of the anonymous, the purely popular political existence of the people" (p. 93). See also Slavoj Žižek, *In Defense of Lost Causes*.

19. Alain Badiou, *The Rebirth of History*, pp. 92–93; emphasis in the original.

20. Jacques Rancière, *Dis-agreement: Politics and Philosophy*, trans. Julie Rose (Minneapolis: University of Minnesota Press, 1999), p. 11.

21. Hannah Arendt, "The Jew as Pariah: A Hidden Tradition," in *The Jew as Pariah: Jewish Identity and Politics in the Modern Age*, ed. Ron H. Feldman (New York: Grove Press, 1978).

22. Hannah Arendt, "We Refugees," in Arendt, *The Jew as Pariah*, pp. 65–66.

23. Said, *Culture and Imperialism*, p. 332.

24. Maurice Blanchot, *The Writing of Disaster*, trans. Ann Smock (Lincoln: University of Nebraska Press, 1993), pp. 33–36; Gilles Deleuze, "Bartleby or the Formula," in *Essays Critical and Clinical*, trans. Daniel W. Smith and Michael Greco (Minneapolis: University of Minnesota Press, 1997); Antonio Negri and Michael Hardt, *Empire* (Cambridge, MA: Harvard University Press, 2000), pp. 203–204; Giorgio Agamben, "Bartleby, or Contingency," in *Potentialities: Collected Essays in Philosophy*, trans. Daniel Heller-Roazen (Stanford, CA: Stanford University Press, 1999), pp. 243–271; Slavoj Žižek, *In Defense of Lost Causes*, pp. 353, 409.

25. For an amplified analysis of Melville's "Bartleby," see William V. Spanos, "'Benito Cereno' and 'Bartleby, The Scrivener': Reflections on the American Calling," in *Herman Melville and the American Calling: The Fiction after* Moby-Dick, *1851–1857*, pp. 105–165.

26. Giorgio Agamben, *The Coming Community*, trans. Michael Hardt (Minneapolis: University of Minnesota Press, 1999), pp. 85–87).

27. "*Katargeö* is a compound of *argeō*, which in turn derives from the adjective *argos*, meaning 'inoperative, not-at-work (*a-ergos*), inactive.' The compound comes to mean 'I make inoperative, I deactivate, I suspend the efficacy. . . .'" Giorgio Agamben, *The Time That Remains: A Commentary on the Letter to the Romans*, trans. Patricia Dailey (Stanford, CA: Stanford University Press, 2005), p. 95. Further citations will be abbreviated to *TR* and placed in parentheses. See also Alain Badiou, *Saint Paul: The Foundation of Universalism in the Present*.

28. Giorgio Agamben "Beyond Human Rights," in *Means without End*, p. 25; emphasis in the original. See also Edward Said's remarkably analogous metaphor for the coming community—"'the complete consort dancing together' contrapuntally"—in *Culture and Imperialism*, p. 332. For an amplified reading of the relationship between Agamben's Klein bottle/Möbius strip metaphor and Said's counterpoint metaphor, see Spanos, *Exiles in the City*, pp. 188–204.

Chapter 5. Revoking the Vocational Imperative: Post-poststructuralist Theory and the Interrogation of the Interpellative Call

1. Badiou, *Ethics*, p. 69.

2. Edward W. Said, *Beginnings: Intention and Method* (New York: Basic Books, 1975): "*The state of mind that is concerned with origins is . . . theological. By contrast, and this is the shift [in Giambattista Vico's thinking], beginnings are eminently secular, or gentile*, continuing activities. Another difference must be noted briefly here, since in my discussions of Freud and of modern texts I have already examined one aspect of this difference in detail: a beginning intends meaning. But the continuities and methods developing from it are generally *orders of dispersion*, of *adjacency*, and of *complementarity*. A different way of putting this is to say that whereas an origin *centrally* dominates what derives from it, the beginning (especially the modern beginning) encourages nonlinear development, a logic giving rise to the sort of multileveled coherence of dispersion we find in Freud's text, in the texts of modern writers, or in Foucault's archeological investigations" (pp. 372–373); the first emphasis is mine.

3. Said, *Culture and Imperialism*, p. 333; my emphasis.

4. Martin Heidegger, "Letter on Humanism," in *Basic Writings*, pp. 222–223.

5. Martin Heidegger, "The Question Concerning Technology," p. 17.

6. It was in part to retrieve the importance of Arendt's Jewish writings from the oblivion to which they were relegated by the combined Habermasian emphasis and the Jewish community's outrage at her *Eichmann in Jerusalem* that Ron Feldman edited *Hannah Arendt, The Jew as Pariah: Jewish Identity and Politics in the Modern Age* (New York: Grove Press, 1978). See especially, "The Jewish

Pariah: A Hidden Tradition," in *Hannah Arendt: The Jewish Writings*, ed. Jerome Kohn and Ron Feldman (New York: Schocken, 2007), pp. 275–297.

7. I derive this resonant phrase from Edward Said, who, following the imperatives of the exilic condition concerning identity, invokes Isaac Deutscher's book of essays *The Non-Jewish Jew*, in which the latter offers "an account of how great Jewish thinkers—Spinoza chief among them as well as Freud, Heine, and Deutscher himself—were in, and at the same time renounced, their tradition, preserving the original tie but submitting it to the corrosive questioning that took them well beyond it, sometimes banishing them from the community in the process."

8. Hannah Arendt, *The Life of the Mind* (New York: Harcourt Brace, 1977), p. 188.

9. See Edward W. Said, *Beginnings* (New York: Basic Books, 1975).

10. Hannah Arendt, *The Human Condition* (Chicago: University of Chicago Press, 1958), pp. 140–141; further references will be abbreviated to HC and placed in parentheses.

11. Louis Althusser, "Ideology and Ideological State Apparatuses (Notes towards an Investigation)," pp. 181–183.

12. Hannah Arendt, "We Refugees," in *Hannah Arendt: The Jew as Pariah*, ed. Ron H. Feldman, pp. 65–66.

13. Giorgio Agamben, "Beyond Human Rights," in *Means without End*, pp. 20–21. Agamben, not incidentally, derives this trinity from Arendt. See *Origins of Totalitarianism*, p. 232.

14. Michel Foucault, *Discipline and Punish*, pp. 205–206, my emphasis.

15. Alain Badiou puts this resonantly by way of his radical rereading of Paul's first epistle to the Corinthians (I.17–29):

> Paul prescribes an anticipatory critique of what Heidegger calls onto-theology, wherein God is thought as supreme being, and hence as the measure for what being as such is capable of.
>
> The most radical statement in the text we are commenting on is in effect the following: "God has chosen the things that are not [*ta me onta*] in order to bring to nought those that are [*to onta*]." That the Christ-event causes nonbeing rather than beings to arise as attesting to God; that it consists in the abolition of what all previous discourses [Old Testament scripture and "Greek" philosophy] held as existing, or being, gives a measure of the ontological subversion to which Paul's anti-philosophy invites the declarant or militant.

Saint Paul: The Foundations of Universalism, trans. Ray Brassiere (Stanford, CA: Stanford University Press, 2003), pp. 46–47. Further citation will be abbreviated to *SP* and placed in parentheses.

16. Giorgio Agamben, *Homo Sacer*: "Aristotle always takes great care to affirm the autonomous existence of potentiality—the fact that the kithara player

keeps his ability [*potenzas*] to play even when he does not play. . . . What Aristotle undertakes to consider in Book Theta of the *Metaphysics* is, in other words, not potentiality as a merely logical possibility but rather the effective mode of potentiality's existence. This is why, if potentiality is to have its own consistency and not always disappear immediately into actuality, it is necessary that potentiality be able *not* to pass over into actuality, that potentiality constitutively be the *potentiality not to* (do or be), or as Aristotle says, that potentiality be also im-potentiality (*adynamia*)" (pp. 44–45).

17. Hannah Arendt, *The Human Condition*: "The actual work of fabrication is performed under the guidance of a model in accordance with which the object is constructed. This mode can be an image beheld by the eye of the mind or a blueprint in which the image has already found a tentative materialization through work. In either case, what guides the work of fabrication is outside the fabricator and precedes the actual work process in much the same way as the urgencies of the life process within the laborer precedes the actual labor process. . . . The process of making is itself entirely determined by the categories of means and end. The fabricated thing is an end product in the twofold sense that the production process comes to an end in it ("the process disappears in the product," as Marx said) and that it is only a means to produce this end" (pp. 140–141, 143).

18. Giorgio Agamben, *The Coming Community*, trans. Michael Hardt (Minneapolis: University of Minnesota Press, 1993), pp. 42, 4–5. Further references will be abbreviated to CC and placed in parentheses.

19. Agamben's title, I suggest, is intended to recall Arendt's *homo faber* but now in its most extreme avatar, *animal laborans* reduced to *bare life*.

20. See Giorgio Agamben, *The State of Exception*, trans. Kevin Attell (Chicago: University of Chicago Press, 2005).

21. Giorgio Agamben, *The Time That Remains: A Commentary on the Letter to the Romans*, trans. Patricia Daily (Stanford, CA: Stanford University Press, 2005), p. 23; the last two emphases are mine.

22. See also the section of *The Coming Community* entitled "Bartleby" and his essay "Bartleby and Contingency" in *Potentialities: Collected Essays in Philosophy*, trans. Daniel Heller-Roazen (Stanford, CA: Stanford University Press, 1999), pp. 253–256.

23. In the section preceding "Tiananmen," Agamben, following Hannah Arendt's decisive Heideggerian identification of speech ("saying and doing") with the *polis* invokes the liminal (or in his language, "threshold") moment in the development of the logic of belonging of the nation-state:

> Even more than economic necessity and technological development, what drives the nations of the earth toward a single common destiny is the alienation from linguistic being, the uprooting of all peoples from their vital dwelling in language.

But, he goes on,

> For this very reason . . . the era in which we live is also that in which for the first time it is possible for humans to experience their own linguistic being—not this or that content of language, but language *itself*, not this or that proposition, but the very fact that one speaks. Contemporary politics is this devastating *experimentum linguae* that all over the planet unhinges and empties traditions and beliefs, ideologies and religions, identities and communities.
>
> Only those who succeed in carrying it to completion—without allowing what reveals to remain veiled in the nothingness that reveals, but bringing language itself to language—will be the first citizens of a community with neither presupposition nor a State, where the nullifying and determining power of what is common will be pacified and where the Shekinah will have stopped sucking the evil milk of its own separation. (CC, 823.3)

24. Spanos, *Exiles in the City*, p. 193.

25. Giorgio Agamben, "Beyond Human Rights," in *Means without End*, p. 16.

26. Alain Badiou, "Against Political Philosophy," in *Metapolitics*, trans. Jason Barker (London: Verso, 2012), pp. 13–14. See also Badiou, *The Rebirth of History: Times of Riots and Uprisings*, trans. Gregory Elliot (London: Verso, 2012), p. 86.

27. For an amplified discussion of this distinction between these two representations of Arendt, see Spanos, *Exiles in the City*, 141–147. See also Dana Villa, *Heidegger and Arendt: The Fate of the Political* (Princeton, NJ: Princeton University Press, 1996).

28. See Badiou, *Saint Paul*: "What can measure up to the universality of an address? Not legality, in any case. The law is always predicative, particular, and partial. Paul is perfectly aware of the law's unfailingly 'statist' character. By 'statist' I mean that which enumerates, names, and controls the parts of a situation. If a truth is to surge forth eventally, it must be nondenumerable, impredicable, uncontrollable. This is precisely what Paul calls grace: that which occurs without being couched in any predicate, that which is translegal, that which happens to everyone without an assignable reason. Grace is the opposite of law insofar as it is what comes *without being due*" (pp. 76–77). For a similar critique of what I am calling the vocational ethic, see Judith Butler's analysis of Walter Benjamin's essay "Critique of Violence."

29. Alain Badiou, *The Rebirth of History: Times of Riots and Uprisings*, pp. 92–93.

30. See also Said, *Humanism and Democratic Criticism* (New York: Columbia University Press, 2004).

31. Alain Badiou, *The Rebirth of History: Times of Riots and Uprisings*, trans. Elliot Gregory (London: Verso, 2012). Further references will be abbreviated to *RH* and placed in parentheses.

32. For an analysis of the Arab Spring that is remarkably similar to Badiou's, see my essay "Arab Spring, 2012: A Symptomatic Reading of the Revolution," *Symplokē*, vol. 20, pp. 1–2.

33. Giorgio Agamben, *The Coming Community*, trans. Michael Hardt (Minneapolis: University of Minnesota Press, 1993).

34. Badiou makes it clear that Lenin and Mao were backed into this disabling "party-form of political organization" that betrayed the generic by way of recuperating the statist identitarian logic of belonging:

> Let us take the word "proletariat." It was the name of the power of the generic. Under the name "proletariat" Marx thought possible the emancipation of the whole of humanity. However, in a certain "objective" Marxism, and under the name of "working class," that word, because it designated a component of social analysis as leadership of the revolutionary movement (the communist party as "party of the working class"), also represented the possibility of an identitarian instrumentalization. The great revolutionaries [Lenin and Mao] were always careful to block any identitarian drift in the word. . . .
>
> However, Lenin and Mao intervened in the framework of the party-form. But if the party-form is obsolete, what is an organized process that lives off a kind of rectitude and genuine fidelity to the struggle of the politically generic—whose norm is equality—against state identity, which separates and suppresses? This is the main problem bequeathed to us by the state communism of the last century. (*RH*, 79–80)

For an amplification of this issue as it pertains to the Chinese Communist Revolution, see Badiou, *The Communist Hypothesis*, trans. David Macey and Steve Corcoran (London: Verso, 2010), pp. 41–100.

35. Taking my directive from his philosophical roots, I read Badiou's use of the world "destroy" in the first sentence of this quotation, not as meaning "to annihilate," but, rather, as an invocation of Heidegger's destructive hermeneutics (*Destruktion*): the de-structuration of the structure imposed by metaphysical thinking on temporality, or, as Badiou puts it later in the quoted passage, the rendering of the spatializing or reifying logic of thinking things as they are from above (*meta*) inoperative.

36. See especially the chapter entitled "University and the Traversal of Difference." Commenting on Paul's Corinthians 1.9.19–22, in which the apostle identifies himself with both the Jews and the Greeks ("I have become all things to all men"), Badiou writes: "This is not an opportunist text, but an instance of what Chinese communists will call 'the mass line,' pushed to its ultimate expression in 'serving the people.' It consists in supposing that, whatever people's opinions and customs, once gripped by a truth's postevental work, their thought becomes capable of traversing and transcending those opinions and customs *without having to give up the differences that allow them to recognize themselves in the world*" (p. 99).

Chapter 6. Edward W. Said and World Literature: Thinking the Worldly Imperatives of the Interregnum

1. Said, *Culture and Imperialism*, p. 332; my emphasis. Further references will be abbreviated to *CI* and placed in parentheses.

2. Franco Moretti, *Graphs, Maps, Trees: Abstract Models for Literary History* (London: Verso, 2005), 1. Further references will be abbreviated to *GMT* and placed in parentheses.

3. Jacques Derrida, "Structure, Sign, and Play in the Discourse of the Human Sciences," in *Writing and Difference*, trans. Alan Bass (Chicago: University of Chicago Press, 1978): "It has always been thought that the center, which is by definition unique, constituted that very thing within a structure which while governing the structure, escapes structurality. This is why classical thought concerning structure could say that the center is, paradoxically, *within* the structure and *outside it*. The center is the center of the totality, and yet, since the center does not belong to the totality (is not part of the totality), the totality *has its center elsewhere*. The center is not the center. The concept of centered structure—although it represents coherence itself, the condition of the *episteme* as philosophy or science—is contradictorily coherent. And as always, coherence in contradiction expresses the force of desire. The concept of centered structure is in fact the concept of a play based on a fundamental ground, a play constituted on the basis of a fundamental immobility and a reassuring certitude which itself is beyond the reach of play. And on the basis of this certitude anxiety can be mastered" (p. 279).

4. Ezra Pound, as far as I know, was the first (post) modern to point to this distinction between an earlier mapmaking that existentially engaged the mapmaker, on the one hand, and, on the other, the later distancing mapmaking that enabled the colonization of the "New World": "periplus, not as land looks on a map / but as sea bord seen by men sailing," Canto LIX of *The Cantos*. See also Charles Olson's "On First Looking out through Juan de la Cosa's Eyes," in *The Maximus Poems*. (Behaim made his famous map of the world from the distance of Europe; de la Cosa made his onboard Columbus's flag ship):

> Behaim—and nothing
> insular Azores to
> Cipangu . . .
>
> But before de la Cosa, nobody
> could have
> a mappemunde

5. For an extended commentary on this distinction, see William V. Spanos, "Charles Olson and Negative Capability: A De-structive Interpreta-

tion," in *Repetitions: The Postmodern Occasion in Literature and Culture* (Baton Rouge: Louisiana State University Press, 1987), pp. 122–130. For a version of Said's Gramscian geography that points symptomatically to the temporality it would release from Hegelian/Marxist structuration, see the interview conducted by Joseph Buttigieg and Paul Bové with Said in *boundary 2*, vol. 20, no. 1 (Spring 1993). See also my commentary on this interview in *The Legacy of Edward W. Said*, pp. 91–97.

6. Spanos, *The Legacy of Edward W. Said*, p. 96.

7. Edward W. Said, "Globalizing Literary Study," *PMLA*, vol. 116, no. 1 (January 2001).

8. Said is not alone in this. As I have shown in *Exiles in the City: Hannah Arendt and Edward W. Said in Counterpoint*, Hannah Arendt precedes Said, and Giorgio Agamben follows him, in asserting the "exilic consciousness"—her term is "conscious pariah"—is the essential intellectual perspective of the interregnum.

9. Fredric Jameson, *Postmodernism or the Cultural Logic of Late Capitalism* (Durham, NC: Duke University Press, 1991), pp. 50–54.

10. Robert P. Marzec, *An Ecological and Postcolonial Study of Literature: From Daniel Defoe to Salman Rushdie* (New York: Palgrave Macmillan, 2007). See also, Marzec, *Militarizing the Environment: Climate Change and the Security State* (Minneapolis: University of Minnesota Press, 2016).

11. Pascale Casanova, *The World Republic of Letters*, trans. M.B. DeBevoise (Cambridge, MA: Harvard University Press, 2004; originally published by Editions du Seuil, Paris, 1999). Ironically, Said accepted Casanova's book in the series "Convergences" that he edited for Harvard University Press.

12. William V. Spanos, "The Center Will Not Hold: The Widening Gyre in the New Americanist Studies," in *Redeemer Nation in the Interregnum: An Untimely Meditation on the American Calling* (New York: Fordham University Press, 2015).

13. Sacvan Bercovitch, *The American Jeremiad* (Madison: University of Wisconsin Press, 1978); Richard Slotkin, *Rejuvenation through Violence: The Mythology of the Frontier, 1800–1860* (1973); *The Fatal Environment: The Myth of the Frontier in the Age of Industrialization, 1800–1890* (1985); *Gun Slinger Nation: The Myth of the Frontier in Twentieth Century America* (1992); and Richard Drinnon, *Facing West: The Metaphysics of Indian-Hating and Empire-Building* (Minneapolis: University of Minnesota Press, 1980).

14. See especially Brian Edwards and Dilip Parameshwar Gaonkar, "Introduction: Globalizing American Studies," in *Globalizing American Studies* (Chicago: University of Chicago Press, 2010), pp. 1–44.

15. David Damrosch, *What Is World Literature?* (Princeton, NJ: Princeton University Press, 2003); Wei Chee Dimock and Lawrence Buell, eds., *Shades of the Plant: American Literature as World Literature* (Princeton, NJ: Princeton University Press, 2007); Brian Edwards and Dilip Parameshwar Gaonkar, eds.

Globalizing American Studies (Chicago: University of Chicago Press, 2010); Paul Giles, *The Global Remapping of American Literature* (Princeton, NJ: Princeton University Press, 2011); and Russ Castronovo and Susan Gilman, eds., *States of Emergency: The Object of American Studies* (Chapel Hill: University of North Carolina Press, 2009). Emily Apter's *Against World Literature: On the Politics of Untranslatability* (London: Verso, 2013) is an important exception to this rule. But it is the untranslatability of texts rather than the historical interregnum that is determinative of its perspective on World Literature.

16. Damrosch, *What Is World Literature?*, p. 17.

17. In his posthumously published *Humanism and Democratic Criticism* (New York: Columbia University Press, 2004), Said returns again to the issue of humanism and his exilic consciousness, now by way of invoking Isaac Deutscher's "insufficiently known book of essays, *The Non-Jewish Jew*," in which Deutscher offers "an account of how great Jewish thinkers—Spinoza chief among them as well as Freud, Heine, and Deutscher himself—were in, and at the same time renounced, their tradition, preserving the original tie by submitting it to the corrosive questioning that took them well beyond it, sometimes banishing them from the community in the process." After emphasizing its significance for the exilic consciousness, he adds: "Not many of us can or would want to aspire to such a dialectically fraught, sensitively located class of individuals, but it is illuminating to see in such a destiny the crystallized role of the American humanist, the *non-humanist humanist, as it were*" (p. 77). This importance of the paradoxical formulation, in which the original binarist terms become inoperative, is underscored by Said's repeating it in his reading of Freud's intellectual identity in *Freud and the Non-European* (London: Verso, 2007), pp. 52–55.

18. See Martin Heidegger, "The Origins of the Work of Art," in *Basic Writings*, ed. David Farrell Krell (New York: Harper and Row, 1977):

> The setting up of a world [*Welt*] and the setting forth of earth [*Erde*] are two essential features in the work-being of the work [of art, for example, Van Gogh's "Peasant Shoes"]. This is the unity we seek when we ponder the self-subsistence of the work and try to tell of this closed, unitary repose of self-support. . . .
>
> The world is the self-opening openness of the broad paths of the simple and essential decisions in the destiny of a historical people. The earth is the spontaneous forthcoming of that which is continually self-secluding and to that extent sheltering and concealing. *World and earth are essentially different from one another and yet are never separated. The world grounds itself on the earth, and the earth juts through the world. But the relation between world and earth does not wither away into the empty unity of opposites unconcerned with one another.* The world, in resting upon the earth, strives to surmount it. As self-opening it cannot endure anything closed. The earth, however, as sheltering and concealing, tends always to draw the world into itself and keep it there.
>
> The opposition of world and earth is strife. But we would surely all too easily falsify its essence if we were to confound strife with discord and dispute, and

thus see it only as disorder and destruction. In essential strife, rather, opponents raise each other into the self-assertion of their essential natures. Self-assertion of essence, however, is never a rigid insistence upon some contingent state, but surrender to the concealed originality of the provenance of one's own Being. In strife, each opponent carries the other beyond itself. Thus the strife becomes ever more intense as striving, and more properly what it is. The more strife overdoes itself on its own part, the more inflexibly do the opponents let themselves go into the intimacy of simple belonging to one another. The earth cannot dispense with the open region of the world if it itself is to appear as earth in the liberated surge of its self-seclusion. The world in turn cannot soar out of the earth's sight if, as the governing breadth and path of an essential destiny, it is to ground itself on a resolute foundation.

In setting up a world and setting forth the earth, the work is an instigating of this strife. This does not happen so that the work should at the same time settle and put an end to the conflict in an insipid agreement, but so that the strife may remain strife. Setting up a world and setting forth the earth, the work accomplishes this strife. The work-being of the work consists in the instigation of strife between world and earth. It is because the strife arrives at its high point in the simplicity of intimacy that the unity of the work comes about in the instigation of strife. The latter is the continually self-overreaching gathering of the work's agitation. The repose of the work that rests in itself thus has its essence in the intimacy of strife. (pp. 172–173)

Index